# PUNISHMENT

This book explores the concept of punishment: its meaning and significance, not least to those subject to it; its social, political and emotional contexts; its role in the criminal justice system; and the difficulties of bringing punishment to an end. It explores how levels of criminal punishment could and should be reduced, without compromising moral standards, public safety or the rights of victims of crime.

Core contents include:

- Why punishment matters, the salience of emotions in its various discourses and the role of culture.
- The politicisation of punishment and legitimacy.
- The penal system, the prominence of the prison in research on punishment and the role of community sanctions.
- The aims of punishment, its limits and the role of power.
- The ethics of punishment and human rights.
- Punishment and social order.

This book is essential reading for all criminologists, as well as students taking courses on punishment, penology, prisons and the criminal justice system.

**Rob Canton** is Professor in Community and Criminal Justice at De Montfort University, Leicester, UK.

# KEY IDEAS IN CRIMINOLOGY

*Key Ideas in Criminology* explores the major concepts, issues, debates and controversies in criminology. The series aims to provide authoritative essays on central topics within the broader area of criminology. Each book adopts a strong individual 'line', constituting original essays rather than literature surveys, and offer lively and agenda setting treatments of their subject matter.

These books will appeal to students, teachers and researchers in criminology, sociology, social policy, cultural studies, law and political science.

## Series Editor

Tim Newburn is Professor of Criminology and Social Policy, Director of the Mannheim Centre for Criminology, London School of Economics and President of the British Society of Criminology. He has written and researched widely on issues of crime and justice.

Other titles in the series:

John Pratt: *Penal Populism*
Tony Ward and Shadd Maruna: *Rehabilitation*
Lucia Zedner: *Security*
Benjamin Goold: *Surveillance*
Claire Renzetti: *Feminist Criminology*
Ian Loader and Richard Sparks: *Public Criminology?*
Michael Kempa and Clifford Shearing: *Policing*
Alex Alvarez: *Genocidal Crimes*
Walter S. DeKeseredy: *Contemporary Critical Criminology*
Katja Franko: *The Crimmigrant Other*
David Churchill, Henry Yeomans and Iain Channing: *Historical Criminology*

# PUNISHMENT

*Rob Canton*

Routledge
Taylor & Francis Group

LONDON AND NEW YORK

Cover image: timsa / Getty Images

First published 2022
by Routledge
4 Park Square, Milton Park, Abingdon, Oxon OX14 4RN

and by Routledge
605 Third Avenue, New York, NY 10158

*Routledge is an imprint of the Taylor & Francis Group, an informa business*

*British Library Cataloguing-in-Publication Data*
A catalogue record for this book is available from the British Library

*Library of Congress Cataloging-in-Publication Data*
A catalog record has been requested for this book

ISBN: 978-0-367-15228-4 (hbk)
ISBN: 978-0-367-15230-7 (pbk)
ISBN: 978-0-429-05582-9 (ebk)

DOI: 10.4324/9780429055829

Typeset in Bembo
by Taylor & Francis Books

To Liz, instead of a ruby

# CONTENTS

# FOREWORD AND ACKNOWLEDGEMENTS

I have many people to thank for advice, encouragement and support. This is my second attempt to write about punishment and, while this book is altogether different, those acknowledged in my earlier effort (2017) are asked to consider themselves thanked here again. In some cases, I have been exchanging thoughts with you for so long that it is hard for me to disentangle my own ideas from yours. You know who you are.

Mike Nellis and Anne Burrell were among those who gave me some good ideas about what I should be reading. Sarah Nixon, David Hayes and Jane Dominey each read a chapter, while Andrew Henley and Anne Worrall both went through two chapters, giving generously of their time. Their feedback was invaluable and I'm sure this would have been a better book had I taken their advice more often.

Series editor Tim Newburn suggested I should write this book and has been a mentor throughout. At Routledge, Tom Sutton and Jessica Phillips have been encouraging, patient and supportive. I have bothered friends and family with my reflections, and above all Liz has endured my confusions and anxieties with love and good humour. To all of these wonderful folk, I offer my warmest thanks.

Two short reflections. First, my account rests heavily on my famil-iarity with modern practice in England and Wales. I know much less than I should about practices at other times and in other places, and readers should be on the lookout for over-generalisation. I suspect that some arguments here do have a wider relevance, but no doubt some ideas travel better than others. Second, almost all of the book was written during the time of the Covid-19 global pandemic. Although locked down and often worried, I have tried not to lose sight of the privileges that have sustained me and which have been unavailable to so many. The book says nothing about the pandemic, which seems remiss and an evasion, although its longer-term effects on the institutions and practices of punishment are so difficult to gauge. What can be said is that the miseries of the pandemic have tracked the usual gradients of power and disadvantage, with some of the worst miseries heaped upon the most deprived and vulnerable people, including those inside the penal system and especially in prisons. Whatever changes now occur in penal practices, this must not be forgotten, serving as a reminder of the pains of punishment, which often go far beyond what they are imagined to be, and of our collective responsibility to do much better.

Rob Canton
Keyworth, Nottinghamshire
August 2021

# INTRODUCTION

## White Bear

She wakes up in bed, groggy and confused, head aching. She sees bandages on her wrists, pills and their bottles scattered on the floor. Her memory is a blank: she looks in the mirror but doesn't recognise herself. She spots a photograph of herself on the mantelpiece with a man and a little girl. This picture triggers some elusive but troubling flash-backs. A family photo? Her daughter maybe?

So begins *White Bear*, a story in Charlie Brooker's remarkable *Black Mirror* television series. The woman ventures outdoors and sees people filming her on their phones from neighbouring houses. She calls out to some bystanders who say nothing, they too taking pictures on their phones. Now a man in a bizarre mask arrives, armed with a shotgun, and starts to chase her. Her pleas to the bystanders meet with silence as they continue to film. She seems at last to have found some help from a couple who come to her rescue. They explain that people have been mesmerised through their TV screens and phones: they must reach and destroy the White Bear transmitter that sends out these signals. The mention of White Bear sparks another painful but splintered memory. A nightmarish pursuit takes place as they try to escape grotesquely masked, armed hunters. Coming to a wood, they find scenes of pain and death and now one of her allies reveals himself as a hunter, tethers her to a tree

DOI: 10.4324/9780429055829-1

and threatens her with torture. More filming onlookers arrive. Escaping, she and her rescuer reach the transmitter, but before they can destroy it they are attacked by hunters. Snatching a gun from one of them she shoots in terror: from the barrel come showers of tinsel.

Doors open behind and she finds herself centre stage before an enthusiastically cheering audience. While hunters and allies alike take their bow, she is seated and manacled. She is informed of her identity by the master of ceremonies, Baxter (the rescuer turned hunter), and made to watch a film which discloses her identity as Victoria Skillane. The girl in the photograph is Jemima Sykes, abducted and murdered by Victoria and her fiancé. The only clue to the child's whereabouts had come from the finding of her white teddy bear, which became a symbol of the search for her. Victoria had filmed their deception of Jemima, her distress and terror, and it was from this film that they had been identified.[1] After their arrest, her fiancé killed himself, while Victoria was sentenced to undergo the torments she has just gone through, in the area known as the 'White Bear Justice Park'. What has been happening has been her *punishment*, which the trial judge had declared to be 'proportionate and considered'. The defence that she had been coerced into her participation by her vicious and controlling boyfriend had been rejected. All these disclosures bring tears and distress, which look like manifestations of shame and remorse, but are derisively rejected by Baxter as bogus and self-serving. Even now many in the audience continue to film, Baxter encouraging them to show their feelings of hostility and contempt towards her.

Weeping and exhausted, Victoria is next paraded in a slow-moving vehicle, fully visible through tough, see-through screens. A large crowd has assembled and is encouraged to scream abuse and to pelt her. For all its violence and absence of decorum, this parade has the qualities of a procession – *charivari*, a ceremonial and communal ritual of mockery and denunciation (Thompson 1993). Back at the original residence, she pleads for death, but is made to watch the film she had taken of Jemima in her final sufferings. Victoria meanwhile has electrodes fastened to her head which will wipe her memory in an agonising process, so that the entire experience can be repeated the following day when she will wake up with an aching head, groggy and confused. And the next day, and the next …

The story ends with the day's visitors being welcomed to the White Bear Justice Park and briefed about their role in the events ahead. They are warned this is a dangerous woman and although their safety is assured, they need to hold this in mind and keep their distance. Above all, Baxter insists, they are to *enjoy themselves*. In the very last scenes, we are shown some shots of the audience reliving and relishing the day through the films they have been taking.

## *Reflections on* White Bear

*White Bear* raises many questions that will occupy us in this book. For the first half of the film, all our sympathies rest with Victoria, who seems to be persecuted and tormented for no reason. Once it is explained that she is being punished and why, she (and we) come to understand these dreadful events in quite another way and our sympathies are destabilised as we learn more about her appalling crime. Even so, to her fear and horror are now added humiliation, shame, remorse and despair – emotions that invite compassion. We do not have to agree with Baxter that this remorse is sham and in any case worthless. Victoria begs for death, as, Baxter tells her, she always does.

While these psychological cruelties seem extreme, there is a sense in which the punishment all too exactly fits the crime – it is an *exquisite* punishment. Jemima had been tricked and brutalised, had looked for protection and comfort from an adult who should have looked after her, and had found indifference at best and perhaps something much uglier as Victoria filmed her distress, refusing to engage with her in any other way. Victoria's punishment echoes this precisely. It could be said that not only is she punished *for* her crime, but *by* and *through* her crime. That a punishment should match the crime is taken sometimes as a requirement of justice, but this film shows that achieving this makes the punishers troublingly like the offender.

When compassion for offenders is urged, the response is sometimes heard that they showed no such sympathies towards their victims – as if moral standards are to be set by behaviour of the very worst kind. Neither the trial judge, apparently, nor Baxter and his audience will allow the claim that she had been forced into her crime by her boyfriend: even if coerced, the adult Victoria should have found the strength to protect Jemima or at least to refuse to look on and film. Victoria is reduced to and defined by her shocking crime; no other dimension of her life is allowed to emerge. Could we or should we even try to think what it would have been like for her and how she came to be involved or would the mere attempt be corrupting?

The role of the onlookers is of especial interest. Almost all modern penal practices involve delegating the implementation of punishment to authorised professionals, who carry out their tasks away from the public gaze; at White Bear, much of what is done in the public's name is done *by* members of the public. Although passive during the chase, their very passivity contributes actively to Victoria's distress. Later, in the audience and the procession, they film and jeer throughout. Critically, this seems less like the sober satisfaction of witnessing justice being done than enjoyment, exhilaration, the thrill of the theme park.

What sense can be made of this? Many of the conventional explanations and justifications of punishment hardly apply. Punishment may attempt to induce remorse, but any signs of this from Victoria are instantly rejected. No one is interested in her feelings anyway, so long as she is suffering. There is no possibility of reform or rehabilitation: the punishment will persist indefinitely. Perhaps a case could be made for deterrence – others, seeing how Victoria has been treated, will refrain from crimes – although it is worth pondering if Victoria herself could have been deterred or whether her moral sensibilities were so warped (or perhaps her boyfriend's intimidation so oppressive) that prospects of punishment were no part of her thinking. This is retribution at its most stark – without regard to a future and unconstrained by other moral considerations.

As well as provoking troubling thoughts about the nature of this punishment, the story raises many tough questions, some of them off-stage, as it were. The punishers at White Bear have worked their way through a carefully choreographed sequence of events, all designed to maximise Victoria's misery to the satisfaction of the audience. Ordinarily this would be denounced as the cruellest of conduct. Presumably they do this often: how do they understand what they do, what meaning do they find in it? They might see themselves as agents of justice, vindicating the misery inflicted on Jemima, or helping to make society safer, but there may be darker motives at work – perhaps even sadism. Is this mere entertainment? Much of Baxter's behaviour seems gratuitously cruel. And what does it do to the actors' well-being and their own personal relationships, spending their days making someone as terrified and miserable as possible? The victim, Baxter would declare, is honoured in and by this punishment, but we might wonder about Jemima's family: do they feel that making her murder into a theme park experience respects their child's suffering and enables them to grieve? Victoria too may have a family.

How are others punished in this world? What would be a fitting 'White Bear' punishment for a rapist or a drug dealer? Perhaps more familiar punishments are still used, Victoria's crime so exceptional that this torment was devised just for her. Again, what kind of government has introduced punishments of this kind? We may speculate that a government that encourages or could even countenance punishments like this may have political and social policies we would not like: this is not a society in which most of us would choose to live. And what of the wider effects of these punitive practices on how society understands itself and the relationships among its members? Cruel punishments may make for a cruel society; forms of punishment are not only shaped by social and cultural ideas and practices but have their own reciprocal influences – and indeed partly constitute – a society and culture.

The technologies prompt other thoughts. These are technologies of an imagined future, but not, perhaps, an unimaginable one. The use of the phone is already ubiquitous: very many people carry phones which they may use to film exciting (and sometimes horrible) events, sharing them with friends on social media. The technology of memory wiping, at least in this form, does not, to my knowledge, exist, but a time could be envisaged when this might be possible, while it evokes thoughts of the 're-education' practices of totalitarian regimes. There are times when technologies, developed for one purpose – or maybe for no known purpose, but devised *simply because it has been found to be possible* – find and make their own trajectory and lead to unforeseen and disquieting practices. This may be all the more likely when commerce, in its demands for expansion, seeks new markets for its technological innovations.

A final reflection on *White Bear* draws attention to punishment's emotional power. Among the onlookers, emotions of anger, disgust, fear are prominent, but so are thrill, exuberance and celebration. And perhaps these proclaimed emotions are not always what they seem. The staff at White Bear insist that Victoria is dangerous, but to us she is terrified and bewildered, any risk she may pose coming only from weapons that were made available to her. Describing her as dangerous may evoke thrill and fear, but more likely it is anger and disgust masquerading as fear. All these emotions shape – and are shaped by – the way in which these events are to be understood. What was at first meaningless to Victoria and to us becomes disquietingly meaningful as her story is gradually disclosed. But while the story develops and moves towards its end, these meanings shift again as the activities at White Bear are variously constructed by her punishers, by the audience, by Victoria herself and by us watching on our televisions at home.

## Punishment, people and society

Almost all of this book discusses criminal punishment, but our understanding can be made both deeper and more rounded by attention to other forms and conceptions of punishment besides. For now, it will be enough to work with an inclusive concept of punishment that covers *any reprobative response to behaviour that signals that what has been done ought not to have been done*. Punishment is one among a set of reactive attitudes and practices – practices that include reward, revenge, praise, anger, gratitude and resentment. These are a part of the very fabric of human exchange: holding people accountable for what they do is integral to our associations with one another and when people do wrong they will meet with 'resentment' (Strawson 1962). Perhaps, then, a society without punishment *at all* is inconceivable.

Children learn about right and wrong through guidance, commandment, fable and example, but perhaps most plainly through the reaction of others to their behaviour – praise and reward, rebuke and punishment. Punishment plays its part, then, in learning about values, the customary conventions of right and wrong (which mature thinkers reflect upon, criticise and refine). And while later in life, people may come to think that misbehaviour ought to be punished because it is wrong, at an earlier stage they discover that some conduct is wrong because it tends to attract recrimination and punishment. In this way, punishment exposes common values and plays a significant role in transmitting them to the next generation.

How parents and others respond to behaviour seems to be critical to psychological well-being. Children of erratic and punitive parents are thought to grow up with an overdeveloped sense of guilt, anxieties and often resentment that can manifest itself in unpleasant ways in later life (Farrington 2007; Braithwaite 1989: ch. 4). Punishment can cause anxiety and a disturbance in relationships. In a family, the feelings aroused are uncomfortable and usually everyone is anxious to restore things to normal. Often the passing of time is sufficient, but especially for more serious wrongs there may need to be active repair work. Some families remain scarred by the injuries of past exchanges which leave behind them feelings of mistrust and resentment.

Rebuke and punishment can be met with resentment and defiance or by guilt, shame and apology, and often a complex and volatile mixture of all these emotions. Commonly a rebuke leads to a dialogue, as people seek to defend themselves − typically by denying or mini-mising either the seriousness of the wrong or (and / or) their responsi-bility for it. In step with learning about rights and wrongs, then, children come to negotiate and discover the boundaries of personal responsibility − their own and others'. It is plausible to suppose that these early-life experiences construct a template for later understandings of responsibility and desert. The law has its own ways of understanding culpability, but its legitimacy rests on an at least sufficient concordance with general notions of responsibility and desert, as well as right and wrong (Darley 2009). Our sense of agency and responsibility, more-over, is central to a conception of personal identity. Often identity is asserted by affirming membership of a group, but behaviour and char-acter make for an individual's uniqueness within any group: in an important sense, who we are is what we do and our self-esteem and our understanding of our identity is worked out through our conduct and the reactions of other people to it.

Perhaps humans are 'hardwired' with motivations to punish (McCullough 2008). Any such propensities are reinforced and inflected by stories and motifs of punishment, which pervade literature and arts, sacred texts and other religious instruction, moulding views about what are suitable amounts and forms of punishment. Novels, films and television series tell innumerable stories of crime, both fictional and 'true crime' – between which genres boundaries are increasingly blurred (Cusac 2009). The more behaviour is forbidden, the more attractive and seductive it may seem: even if people can repress inclinations to act on these temptations, they may gain a vicarious thrill from watching the bad behaviour of others. Punishment can evoke comparable emotions, of enticement as well as aversion (Duncan 1996). Punishment may become a preoccupation. People entertain fantasies about revenge more than any other imaginings, except probably sex (Pinker 2011). And while attempts have been made to differentiate punishment from revenge (Nozick 1981), their emotional mainsprings are close to one another and probably the same.

Punishment also instructs people about the social order and their place in it. One way of coming to understand authority (and sometimes to see authority unmasked as bare power) is by discovering who is able to punish and who gets punished – and who does not. The influential thesis that some modern societies are *governing through crime* (Simon 2007) holds that ways of thinking about crime, criminal justice and enforcement, as well associated practices, technologies and mentalities, have come to pervade other domains of civil society. Governing through crime encompasses more than governing through punishment. For example, the political deployment of the fear of crime has admitted any number of crime prevention and surveillance mechanisms that people seem prepared to tolerate – especially when it intrudes into the lives of others, but even when it impinges on their personal domain. These are not necessarily meant or felt as punishment. But governing through crime is perhaps especially governing through punishment and borrows much of any legitimacy it enjoys from deep-seated assumptions that punishment is both intrinsically fitting and makes for a safer society.

'Justice systems and the societies in which they operate are richly intertwined.' writes Baz Dreisinger (2016: 21). In that case, it may be possible to 'read back' from the practices and institutions of punishment to deepen understanding of society. In this sense, punishment has been insufficiently put to use in social, cultural and political studies. In moral philosophy too, abstract ideas have an immediate and pointed application when reasoning about punishment (Canton 2017). As Linda

Radzik insists, 'Our moral theories should tell us not just what is right and what is wrong but also how to deal with wrongdoing once it occurs' (Radzik 2009: 3). And while many moral philosophers have pondered the problems of punishment, reflections on responses to wrongs could go much further. Notably, the familiar assumption that punishment, with its ready associations with hard treatment, is the only or best way to 'deal with wrongdoing' needs much more scrutiny.

Punishment matters and its study might provide valuable insights into the specific concerns of other academic disciplines. If the mentalities and technologies of punishment infiltrate systems of governance, politics and economics, its study should have much to say about the values and culture of any society, as well as about the power relations that structure it. Punishment can influence ideas of agency, what is deserved and what we owe to one another – ideas that are fundamental to our identity and our understanding of our relationship with others as well as the wider social order.

## About this book

Chapter 1 addresses the question *what is punishment?*, discussing the difficulties of constructing definitions and trying to mark out the scope of its study. Some practices that do not satisfy all the criteria of formal definitions are nevertheless meant and experienced as punishment. Must respect for a definition rule these out as punishment or exclude them from penological studies? Attention is drawn especially to the communicative and expressive character of punishment – what punishment 'says' and means. Punishment is always reprobative and censuring and the processes of criminal law enforcement and sanctioning diminish (and are typically intended to diminish) the civil and moral standing of offenders.

Chapter 2 considers the influences that shape penal policies and practices. There is no attempt to summarise the accounts of the most influential thinkers on this subject, although reference is made to many of them in the discussion. While the chapter does not advance any theory of its own, there is particular emphasis on the importance of the emotional in understanding the social and political salience of punishment and an attempt to identify some of these emotions more precisely.

Chapter 3 turns to some of the institutions and practices of punishment. At different times and in different places, punishments have taken many forms. This chapter considers the most common punishments in modern Western societies: the prison, community sanctions and financial penalties. The purposes set for these forms of punishment; the extent to which they do (or even could) achieve any such purposes; and their (typically contested) significance and meanings to wider society will be explored.

Chapter 4 explores *what it is like to be punished* – how people subject to punishment regard their experiences and what sense they make of them. There is also discussion of how personnel involved in the implementation of punishment understand their work. These topics are relatively neglected, but of fundamental importance: understanding what punishment 'is' can hardly be confined to the pronouncement of the sentence at court, but must involve attention to how sentences are put into effect. This must include an appreciation of the meanings those subject to punishment find and make of their experiences.

The theme of Chapter 5 is *the ends of punishment* – both the purposes set for it and that point at which punishment may be taken to have been completed. Chapter 1 suggested that punishment involves a diminishment of status; this chapter asks what it might take for this process to be reversed. At what point can the wrongful act be regarded as successfully resolved? The emotions discussed in Chapter 2 may explain not only the will to punish, but also why this end state can be so difficult to achieve.

Chapter 6 tries to draw out some implications from the earlier discussions. One reason why punishment is studied is in the service of penal reform, which involves attention to the feasibility of change (calling for an understanding of the dynamics of development, explored in Chapter 2), but also a normative vision of the direction that change ought to take. It is argued that many discussions of penal ethics (commonly written about under the rubric of *the justification of punishment*) take much too narrow a purview and are flawed by an inadequate appreciation of the nature of this complex social institution (Garland 1990). What should be the place of punishment in a good society?

## Note

1. No British viewer of a certain generation could watch this without thinking of the crimes of Ian Brady and Myra Hindley. They abducted and tortured children, and Hindley used the technology of her day (audio-tape) to record these cruelties. Many felt Hindley had been led by Brady and deserved less of a punishment, although this was vehemently rejected by others. A fuller discussion of this case and of *White Bear* would raise the matter of gender. A cultural expectation of women is that they should be caring and protective of children, and Hindley's and Victoria's crimes are regarded by some as all the worse for betraying that duty.

# 1

# THE MEANINGS OF PUNISHMENT

This chapter begins by discussing the difficulties of defining punishment and the proper scope of its study. It is concluded that definition is elusive; most elements of the conventional definition can be questioned. The chapter goes on to argue that punishment has an abundance of meanings, often contested, and it is debate around meaning more than effectiveness that determines the direction of penal policy. A third section argues that communication of blame is a defining condition of any punishment, which typically has the effect of diminishing status.

## Defining punishment

One approach to *What is …?* questions is to attempt a definition and this is how philosophical accounts of punishment typically begin. The core elements of the most influential definition (Flew 1954) are:

i Punishment involves imposing pain, hardship, deprivation or at least something unwanted ('hard treatment').
ii It must be for an offence.
iii It must be imposed on the offender.
iv It must be imposed by an authority.

Feinberg (1965) pointed to another essential condition that was absent from (or at least under-stated in) the conventional definition – the *communicative* aspect of punishment:

v Punishment is always an act of censure or blaming (von Hirsch 1993). It expresses disapproval and declares the individual responsible for an offence.

All of these elements need further scrutiny and perhaps some qualification (see further Boonin 2008; Brooks 2012).

## *i.* Punishment involves 'hard treatment'

At first sight, hard treatment seems a necessary condition of being a punishment. At various times, people have been punished by death, tortures, mutilations and brandings, by expulsion, exile and transportation; they have been confined in chains, held in dungeons and prisons and enslaved; they have been deprived of civic rights, had property confiscated and made to make financial payments. Yet some sentences of a modern criminal court are better understood as warnings or threats (discharges, suspended sentences) rather than hard treatment in themselves – although perhaps a persistent looming threat is in itself hard treatment (McNeill 2018). Other sanctions (for example, probation supervision) may be meant to be – and are at least sometimes experienced as – supportive and helpful. These sanctions involve imposition and even hardship or pains (Durnescu 2011), but often probation agencies do all they can to mitigate these burdens. And if a response to wrongdoing is not meant as punishment by those who decide upon it or those who carry it out, variably felt as a punishment by those who experience it and not regarded as a punishment at all by others – a common criticism of non-custodial sanctions – it is not easy to see the sense in which it *is* a punishment. One response might be to argue that these sentences are indeed not punishment, but while it is sometimes necessary to distinguish them from the imposition of hard treatment intended as such, any account of punishment must have regard to sanctions of this type.

## *ii.* It must be for an offence *and iii.* It must be imposed on the offender

Punishment, the definition insists, is *for* an offence and *of* an offender. It is possible to speak of the punishment of an innocent person, but if someone was not believed to be guilty or even a pretence of their guilt made, this would be more like oppression or persecution. This, then, seems a necessary condition for punishment. Yet perhaps there are exceptions or at least circumstances in which the relationship between offence and punishment is less clear. Probably more than 3 million people worldwide (some 25 per cent of the world's prison population) are held 'on remand', awaiting trial or definitive sentence (Coyle, Fair, Jacobson and Walmsley 2016). Here it is legally inaccurate to speak of being punished for an offence: legal codes and human rights conventions affirm a presumption of innocence and in most cases no offence has been established. The allegation is the occasion for the detention, but the individual is detained to ensure they come to trial (and various other procedural safeguards) not 'for an offence'. Yet pre-trial detention and more generally the experiences of suspects and defendants are typically painful and burdensome to the extent that 'the process is the punishment' (Feeley 1992). It seems contrived to argue that this is not punishment: it is experienced as punishment and, at least in some countries, implemented as punishment by prison or jail staff who do not feel much need to distinguish between remand and convicted prisoners in their day-to-day practices and attitudes.

If remand is punishment before punishment, there are also examples of continuing punitive effects that persist beyond the allocated sentence – punishment after punishment, as it were. Those detained for public protection are a prominent example (Jacobson and Hough 2010). These are people who have committed offences (often, though by no means always, grave ones), but have now served the 'tariff' – the deserved minimum term awarded by the judge. Once that time has been served, they are no longer being punished 'for' the offence, but detained to prevent further offences. The uncertainties they experience, bewildered about how they might go about demonstrating that they are fit for release, add to the pains that beset other prisoners (Crewe 2011; Warr 2016). It is implausible to suggest that they are no longer being punished, a claim that would only be made in defence of the conventional definition.

Nor is it only in prison that such punitive hardships are experienced. There are a number of community measures where the rationale and justification are preventive, but which are nonetheless experienced as punishment. Parole and other forms of post-custodial supervision can be presented and defended as a continuation of punishment and/or as measures of prevention, but in either case are often experienced as punishment. An example is the supervision of sex offenders where measures to prevent reoffending, however justifiable, involve punitive restrictions and intrusions (Hudson and Henley 2015). More generally, the extended reach of the state in the cause of public protection has led to several measures and interventions that entail hardships and deprivations that are felt as – and at least sometimes meant as – punishment (Ashworth, Zedner and Tomlin 2013). This extension brings changes to the character and meaning of the criminal law, while some measures are put into effect outside the systems of due legal process and consequently lack the safeguards these normally provide (Hayes 2019: ch. 2). While a crime prevention strategy is presented politically as morally unimpeachable, 'Resort to the de-moralized language of prevention does not mean that a measure ceases to be stigmatic, burdensome, or punitive' (Ashworth and Zedner 2008: 41).

The detention of foreign nationals also calls into question the association between a punishment and an offence (Bosworth 2012). In many places, immigration detainees are held in confinement and experience their detention *as punishment*. Some have done nothing wrong at all (unsuccessful applicants for asylum) and others have committed no offence beyond unlawful entry into the country or overstaying, being held ostensibly because of concerns they may abscond (Guardian 2018). Some have been convicted of criminal offences, but nevertheless remain detained in the same conditions after the full sentence has been served. Many certainly regard this continuing detention as punishment – and perhaps a worse imposition than the sentence that constituted the original penalty (Warr 2016).

Nor is punishment confined to offenders. Innocent people routinely endure hardship as a direct result of punishment imposed on others. Most obviously, the partners and families of prisoners suffer the pains of punishment – notably, children whose mothers are imprisoned commonly suffer sadness and deprivation (Comfort 2007, 2009; Minson 2018). Walker (1991) described this as 'obiter' punishment. These hardships are not meant to be punishment, but they may be experienced in this way nevertheless. Collective punishment should also be considered. The punishment of groups (in response to actions carried out by one or more of their members) is contrary to most human rights conventions and, in war time, is a violation of Article 33 of the Fourth

Geneva Convention. Fabricant (2010) likened some intensive policing, involving indiscriminate aggressive actions against poor communities, to collective punishment. Didier Fassin provides powerful examples from the Philippines, where police have shot and killed numbers of people believed to be dealing drugs. Similar actions have been taken in Brazil as part of the 'pacification' of the favelas (Fassin 2018: 40). Punitive police raids in many countries are made against groups, sometimes in the firm belief that these are people who have done bad things but not been caught or, if caught, inadequately punished or simply inherently *punishable*. This is meant as punishment, experienced as punishment, regarded by the public and countenanced by the authorities as punishment. Again, the only reason to refuse to count this as punishment would be to defend the conventional definition.

## *iv.* It must be imposed by an authority

Unless the hard treatment is imposed by the competent authority, it would be more like revenge or retaliation. Yet sometimes the authority to punish is contested. Paramilitary groups or vigilantes claim that they are inflicting punishment – perhaps because they reject the authority of the state or accuse the formal authorities of failing in their duty to bring wrongdoers to justice; others who reject their right to punish will denounce their 'punishments' as reprisals, vengeance or mere gratuitous assault. The examples we have just seen of punishment by the police also put this criterion to test. For while the police are a recognised authority, their legal remit does not extend to behaviour of this type: they are acting *ultra vires*, exceeding their authority.

## *v.* Punishment is an act of censure or blaming

If the first four elements of the definition turn out to be a bit more complicated than anticipated, the fifth criterion – that punishment is always and unavoidably an act of censure or blaming – seems altogether necessary. Punishments can be envisaged that fail to meet one or more of the other conditions, but nothing could be punishment unless it expressed disapproval. Punishment declares that an act (or omission) is not to be done and that the responsibility for the wrong belongs to the punished. This has been conceptualised as censure, a central concept in modern punishment theory (von Hirsch 1993; Duff 2001; Bennett 2008; Du Bois-Pedain and Bottoms 2019). Censure is more than mere rebuke: it calls upon offenders to acknowledge their wrongdoing, perhaps to feel remorse and to do better in future. Punishment also attempts to communicate to others: a fitting punishment tells the victim that their experience is recognised and vindicated; a wider community is made aware such behaviour is wrong and punishment awaits those who offend.

Generally, the material form of the punishment ought to be intrinsically fitting to its communicative aim: 'Punishment speaks to the offender, not just through the words that are said to her, but through the material forms that it takes' (Duff 2001: 222).

Communications, however, can go (sometimes badly) wrong (Smith 2008). Sometimes the form of the punishment radically subverts the intended message:

> It is all very well to say that punishment affirms community values, but this piece of apriorism tends to shut out questions as to the material nature of the punishment and its relation to what it is supposed to be expressing. What if the punishment form, the medium, is cruel, degrading, corrupting, wasteful and divisive? What if its actual communication is in direct contradiction to the putative message? '(Whack!) Don't hit children smaller than you!'; 'Execute him! We must show the value we place on human life.'
>
> (Skillen 1980: 521)

Dissonance between what is meant and what expressed is more than ever likely when there are many audiences and the 'message' can try to carry several, complex and even perhaps mutually incompatible meanings. A sentencer may, for example, want to denounce a crime, to warn others against offending, *and* to try to effect positive change in the individual. Yet none of this may be what is understood by those who are subject to the punishment, while victims and their families and the general public may take other meanings besides. Nor is the message restricted to the formal pronouncement of sentence: how it is subsequently put into effect can variously support or undermine the sentencer's intention, although these further messages are normally only received by the offender. Skillen again draws attention to the hazards and limitations here

> [Hard treatment] 'expresses' a distorted sense of what is important. As far as the person punished is concerned, the 'hard treatment' rapidly becomes itself the focus of attention, an object of resentment and hostility. Remorse, which is pain at the wrong done, is overridden by pain at the treatment being received. What 'gets across', then, is a demoralizing sense of isolation, however this may 'work' as a deterrent.
>
> *(Skillen 1980: 523)*

Thus, while censure may be a necessary condition of punishment, it may not be assumed to be always communicated successfully to the offender, the victim or to others.

The definition of punishment, then, is contested and elusive. The degree to which this should trouble us depends partly on the reason for trying to construct a definition in the first place. For philosophers, a definition has been as a preliminary to an examination of 'the justification of punishment' and must therefore be accurate and neutral; the justification must not be buried in or smuggled into the definition itself. Some definitions of punishment already tilt the debates for justification in one direction or another (Bagaric 2001).

Yet perhaps the projects of definition and justification are too entwined to be undertaken without reference to one another (McPherson 1967). Sometimes 'they are being punished' is a sufficient explanation of (or even a justification for) what would otherwise be seen as gratuitous cruelty. Repressive regimes may contrive charges against political opponents and imprison them for their supposed offences to designate dissidents as criminals, their punishments deserved. Punishment professes legitimacy in this way, pre-empting accusations of oppression. When punishment fails to satisfy one or more of the conditions of the formal definition, it often seems more accurate to characterise it as *unjust* or improper punishment rather than not-punishment-at-all. Perhaps the true project of the conventional definition was less to define punishment in a formal sense, than to specify the conditions for its just imposition.

Among the practices that philosophers have been keen to distinguish from punishment is vengeance or revenge. This is perhaps a further example of the way in which definitions and justifications are bound up. Revenge is often considered to be a wrong so that, if punishment is to be justified, a boundary must be drawn. Some insist on the difference and seek to clarify the distinction (Nozick 1981; Ten 1987; Brooks 2012). Others accept that retributive punishment is revenge, but this is morally defensible (Wallace 1995; Barton 1999; Miller 2001). Revenge is argued to be a good thing or at worst neutral, neither good nor bad intrinsically, but taking its ethical character from the circumstances and the manner in which it is carried out.

Other practices on the boundary of the definition are various forms of rehabilitation or therapy (McNeill 2014). Some advocates of punishment have denied that therapeutic interventions amount to punishment, while many proponents of rehabilitation, even if it matches most of the criteria stipulated by the conventional definition, want to distinguish it from punishment – in the grounds for imposition, purpose or method. Another boundary may lie between punishment and restorative justice. Many champions of restorative justice deny it is punishment. But others (Roche 2013) have emphasised similarities and Duff (2003) has proposed that, far from being opposing paradigms, restorative justice and retributive punishment are better understood as two sides of a coin.

These border disputes put any definition to test. Boundaries turn out to be unavoidably contested and permeable. Friedrich Nietzsche (1996 [1887]: 60) wrote that 'only that which is without history can be defined' and the long, rich and variegated history of punishment explains why it defies definition. Yet the conventional definition also fails to delimit the proper scope of the study of punishment. It is possible, as we have seen, to insist that rehabilitative sanctions are 'not punishment' – perhaps because they are not meant as such or do not require 'hard treatment'. And perhaps pre-trial detention is not punishment since it fails to meet some of the necessary conditions of the definition. But no study of punishment could or should disregard the practices of rehabilitative agencies, among which prisons in many countries and probation services almost everywhere would aspire to be counted. Again, any account of imprisonment that failed to take account of the substantial numbers of prisoners on remand would be flawed as well as incomplete. The study of punishment should encompass the institutions and practices of the penal system, but also activities undertaken by agencies of enforcement, detection and prosecution where these are meant and/or experienced *as punishment*. This foregrounds meanings rather than the abstractions of definition. Here, Fassin (2018: 72) writes, 'we are not any more in the pure realm of ideas and the law but in the impure region of the obscure motives of crime and punishment – the world of Dostoevsky more than the universe of Bentham and Kant, so to speak'.

In this 'impure region', another uncertain boundary lies between punishment and slavery. Punishment and slavery are conceptually distinct, yet historically have been closely connected (Sellin 2016 [1976]). Enslavement has often been used *as a punishment* (Patterson 1982). McLennan (2018: 150) refers to the slave plantation as 'the single most important disciplinary institution of the 18th and 19th centuries in America'. Dreisinger describes how in Uganda and other parts of Africa in the colonial period imprisonment became an instrument of social control, confining people convicted of 'offences' like adultery in order to secure free labour for cotton production; generally, 'colonial powers adroitly manufactured reasons to put bodies behind bars', putting them to work for the profit of others (Dreisinger 2016: 107). Seventeen million 'blacks and coloureds' were imprisoned in South Africa between 1916 and 1986 and made to work in the gold and diamond mines (ibid.: 71). In a letter to Erving Goffman, Everett Hughes (1961) observed: 'I have been reading a great deal about Africa recently, and it is quite clear that in Africa they decide to punish the Negro and then seek the crime of which to accuse him.'[1] Punishment, race, poverty and debt are inextricably entangled: especially in the United States, it is never white people who have been enslaved, while debt (in different times and in various places) has led to imprisonment or debt-bondage.

Prisons provide a ready and tractable workforce and, at some times and places, this has been exploited, becoming an essential component of the national economy – most notoriously, perhaps, in the former Soviet Union (Applebaum 2003; Piacentini 2004: ch. 2).

Prison work is a complex area: most prisoners prefer to work, so long as this is something worthwhile and fairly acknowledged by (not necessarily financial) remuneration, but there are grave risks of exploitation (van Zyl Smit and Dünkel 2018; Johnson 2018). There are marked continuities between slavery in the *antebellum* southern states of America and modern penal populations, especially in terms of poverty and race (Western 2007; Alexander 2011; Campbell 2013). Loïc Wacquant (2000) refers to successive 'kindred institutions of forced confinement' which not only serve to segregate, materially and symbolically, an outcast group, but also to appropriate and exploit their labour.

The position of young people held in institutional settings also presents a problematic boundary. There is a considerable diversity, between and within different countries, among these institutions and their stated purposes – punishment, 'correction' or protection for their own welfare. Often these rationales are merged uncomfortably. But, whatever their avowed purposes, they may be experienced as punishment, especially when discipline is strict, detention secure and staff accordingly vigilant against absconding. A final example is the confinement of people believed to be mentally ill or with a learning disability. Institutions may be formally characterised as hospitals or treatment settings, but as coercive confinement and in the character of their regime they can resemble prisons. There is abundant evidence that detention and some procedures deployed as 'therapy' have been experienced as punitive (Porter 2002; Peterson 1982).

The boundaries, then, between punishment and its neighbouring territories are not always easy to delineate. On both sides of the boundary, there will be disputes about how some practices are to be characterised, but these questions cannot be resolved by appeal to a definition, however meticulously crafted. There are conceptual distinctions to be drawn and little to be gained by envisaging all these other areas as punishment. Nevertheless these reflections serve as a reminder that boundaries are permeable, and that studies of punishment can with profit pay attention to other adjacent social practices and institutions. Not all punishment involves hard treatment; not all punishment is of offenders for an offence; not all punishment is assigned or administered by the state and authority can be contested.

Perhaps the litmus test is not only what is meant or avowed by the punishers, but how it is experienced by the punished.

## Punishment's meanings

Shortly after his reflection on definition, Nietzsche wrote that punishment is 'overladen with utilities of all kinds', including

> punishment as a way of rendering harmless, of preventing further damage; punishment as compensation in any form to the victim for the harm done (also in the form of emotional compensation); punishment as the isolation of something which disturbs equilibrium, in order to prevent the disturbance from spreading; punishment as a means of instilling fear of those who determine and exact punishment; punishment as a form of forfeit due in return for the advantages which the criminal previously enjoyed (as, for example, when he is made useful as slave-labour in the mines); punishment as elimination of a degenerate element (… as a means towards maintaining racial purity or a social type); punishment as festivity, that is, as the violation and humiliation of an enemy finally overcome; punishment as a means of producing a memory, whether for the person on whom the punishment is inflicted – so-called 'rehabilitation' – or for those who witness its execution … punishment as a form of compromise with the natural condition of revenge …; punishment as declaration of war against an enemy of peace, law, order, authority …
>
> *(Nietzsche 1996 [1887]: 61)*

Some of this is readily recognisable; other elements are cryptic and even elusive. What is translated here as 'utilities' in English, as apparently in the original German *nützliche Einrichtungen* (though the reader should be warned that I do not speak this language), has too instrumental a connotation. Nietzsche bundles purposes set for punishment together with its effects and its meanings – what it represents for the punishers, the punished, and for everyone else. Punishment has to be *interpreted* and is therefore susceptible to different and conflicting interpretations.

Nietzsche's list could be added to. For example, punishment as a secular penance (Duff 2001); as an opportunity for commerce and industry (Lilly and Deflem 1996; Schlosser 1998; Christie 2000; Davis 2003; Ludlow 2017); as a source of cheap or free labour in itself (not just as 'forfeit') (van Zyl Smit and Dünkel 2018); as a means of imperial expansion, colonising lands and expelling indigenous people (Roscoe 2018; Anderson 2018); as a laboratory or testing ground for techniques of surveillance and discipline to be exported to a wider world (Foucault 1977; Melossi and Pavarini 1981); as tourist experience or spectacle (Brown 2009; Wilson, Hodgkinson, Piché and Walby 2017); as mass entertainment (Kohm 2009).

Philip Smith (2008: 26) writes, 'Objects and practices are never simply things and activities, never just utilitarian because they always carry with them a surplus of meanings, sometimes intended but often accidental, furtive, surprising.' And like almost all social practices, punishment cannot be understood without attention to the meanings that are intended and received. Nor, where different meanings are found or made, can it make sense to privilege any of these as 'the true meaning'. Smith (2008) argues that penal change often takes place, not when 'the evidence' points in a different direction, but when meanings are destabilised and new and unwanted connotations intrude. For example, public execution in Europe was abandoned when its meaning became confused and contested. The message of state execution was supposed to be a solemn didactic drama, but had become a carnival. The executions were more 'risible than solemn as they lurched chaotically between death and laughter' (Laqueur 1989: 309). This subversion could become politically menacing: 'the victim or the crowd could turn a controlled hanging into a public disputation of the state's justice and authority' (ibid.: 307).

Again, any confidence in prison is undermined if conditions are seen to be 'easy', but also if they are squalid and chaotic. Good order should prevail and where the conditions themselves come to be seen as source of contamination and danger, the meaning of prison is in jeopardy. In the southern states of USA, when attempts were made to revive chain gangs, resistance was provoked by their shameful associations with slavery and racism (Gorman 1997; Smith 2008). Arguably, probation and other community sanctions struggle to find public confidence not only because what they involve is poorly understood, but because their meanings are often uncertain and contested (McNeill 2018; see Chapter 3 below).

The policies and practices of punishment are communicative, although quite what they manage to communicate may be contested. But they are also *expressive*, disclosing values and social characteristics that may be no part of any intended communication and perhaps even unknown to the punishers. An example may be the age of criminal responsibility and the punishment of young people. While all countries make different provision for young people, arrangements differ and the age of responsibility varies markedly (Bateman 2012; Little 2018). This reflects (but also reproduces) attitudes towards children – the extent to which they are to be regarded as responsible agents, whether they are fitting subjects of formal criminal procedures and so on. Martha Grace Duncan (1996) is prominent among those who have examined punishment to make discoveries not only about penal practices but about how these practices illuminate psyche and culture. Punishment can also evince disrespect and contempt for groups of people. When punitive practices are discriminatory – for example, on grounds of race or gender – something is said about how those in power regards these groups. In trying to decode the language of punishment, it is these expressions as much as communicative intent that needs to be interpreted.

Meaning-making is all the more necessary and contestable when so much of the 'message' is expressed in symbol and allegory (Smith 2008). The rhetorical tropes and metaphors of political and popular discourse guide thinking and feeling towards some forms of interpretation, discouraging others (Simon 2001; Coyle 2013). How punishment is 'read' depends on an indeterminate number of factors. Meaning-making is likely to depend, for instance, on people's personalities, dispositions and prejudices; on their own experiences of themselves (or their family or friends) being punished or administering punishment; on how a case is presented to them; on the views of those around them; on the extent to which they able or willing to identify with the victim of an offence or an offender. Cinema and TV, books and magazines may prompt different thoughts about crime, punishment and their association. But minds are not open from the start – preconceptions about punishment always exert their influence – and what message is taken may be filtered by assumptions and experiences. It is not that these factors necessarily make people more or less punitive, but they mould what people understand punishment to mean, what they take its purposes to be and what fitting punishments should be like. These personal and cultural meanings mediate and may distort the intended messages of punishment.

Whether something counts as a satisfactory punishment – or indeed as a punishment at all – depends crucially on meaning. It depends upon the meanings of those deciding to impose the punishment and those carrying it out, but also on how it is interpreted by victims, by those undergoing punishment and the perceptions of a wider community. Meanings are commonly multivalent, in need of interpretation and disputable, but they can be decisive in shaping reactions to specific sentencing decisions and general attitudes towards penal policy.

## Punishment, shame and degradation

Punishment declares *the offender did this and this ought not to be done*, making this declaration not only to the offender, but commonly to others besides. Among the purposes of this censure, it can be claimed, is to call upon the offender's sense of moral responsibility to inspire better behaviour in future. An emotional impulse (as opposed to self-interested and moral motivations) towards this better behaviour is often said to be *shame*. Punishment has often been deliberately shaming and public. Foucault writes of a great transformation at the end of the eighteenth century in Europe (Foucault 1977; Cohen 1985). From the nineteenth century, confinement behind walls (asylums, workhouses, prisons) hid and segregated people, removing punishment from the public gaze. Local and extra-judicial shaming punishments mocked wrongdoers, making them an object of ridicule as well as of disdain. The *charivari* (or 'rough music') involved a noisy procession that derided and intimidated someone whose behaviour had somehow outraged the community (Thompson 1993). This may not have been 'criminal punishment', but its motivation and functions of communal denunciation were replicated in more formal practices (Sharpe 1990): the torture of the ducking stool, the humiliation of the stocks and the pillory involved the community in delivering the punishment – not simply witnessing it, although in shaming-punishment to witness *is* to deliver. While modern sensibilities are repulsed by the physical cruelties of being flogged or pilloried, these pains were, for those enduring them, often matched by the shame involved.

While this may seem only of antiquarian interest, there has been renewed interest in shame in recent times and attempts to revive shaming punishments – usually in the name of deterrence. The idle jingle 'name and shame' has become familiar. Such practices, sometimes referred to as 'Scarlet Letter' punishments (after the novel by Nathaniel Hawthorne), have included being made to stay in a public place wearing T-shirts or sporting placards that name the crime, and other humiliations (Book 1998). These public, ostentatious modes of punishment (Pratt 2000) have attracted criticism as inherently degrading and for their potential to let loose an unbridled and perhaps disproportionate response from the public (Whitman 1997). In modern societies, professional criminal justice personnel mediate – standing, as it were, between the community's emotional reaction and the punishment. This progressive bureaucratisation of punishment and the professionalisation of the people involved alters the cultural meanings of punishment (Garland 1990: ch. 8.) Shaming punishments, by contrast, expose the offender to the raw and maybe brutal emotions of public punitiveness and can deteriorate into bullying and tormenting.

The notorious Joe Arpaio, sheriff of Maricopa County, Arizona for many years, defended humiliating prisoners and filming them on 'Jail cam' on deterrent grounds (Lynch 2004; Smith 2011), but it is possible to discern uglier motives. Shame punishments can constitute deliberate degradation – an occasion for crude and unpleasant public ridicule and a venting of unworthy emotions. Defenders argue that only denunciatory public punishments are adequate to express outrage – or that they at least avoid the even more profound disrespect of incarceration (Kahan 1998; Book 1998). Opponents object that instead of trying to find punishments to match prison in their assault on respect for persons, the task should be to challenge the 'assumption that only dignity-violating sanctions will have the appropriate condemnatory weight' (Flanders 2006: 618; Markel 2001).

One difference between these practices and other pains of punishment is that they fundamentally depend on recognising the humanity of the person subject to punishment. Perpetrators of cruelty may neutralise their actions by erasing the very humanity of those they oppress, by 'othering' them (Glover 1999; Smith 2011). This insight has been applied to punitive attitudes and to criminal punishment (Bastian, Denson and Haslam 2013). Yet shaming punishment recognises the individual's humanity in order to exploit it: only through an awareness of someone's sense of dignity and self-worth can shame erode it and thereby bring its pains (Bloom 2017). Empathy rests on an understanding that brings with it the capacity to hurt (Bloom 2016).

Some punishments, then, are deliberately designed to shame and 'only' that, although all punishment shames. John Braithwaite (1989) distinguished between inclusive and exclusionary modes of shaming – the latter driving people away from mainstream society and into subcultural groups where their status can be regained through continued offending. Reintegrative shaming should induce shame to induce better behaviour: ashamed of their behaviour, people will resolve to do better. Restorative justice might engage with the offender's sense of moral responsibility, restoring peace with victims and the wider community. But the case for inducing shame rests on questionable assumptions. It is supposed, for instance, that offenders do not already feel shame, whereas the well-attested need to justify or to distance themselves from their conduct could plausibly be taken to imply that such feelings exist already (Sykes and Matza 1957). Nor is it clear that shaming people is the best or even a very good way of making them feel ashamed in the positive sense that should induce better behaviour. Shaming and the consequent perceived loss of dignity is a common incentive to violent rejoinders (Gilligan 2003). Scarlet Letter punishments are far more likely to provoke defiance, anger and resentment in the offender as well as disdain, suspicion and rejection from the rest of the community.

Punishment involves treating people in ways that would 'otherwise be instances of extreme disrespect or even cruelty' (Flanders 2006: 609). Thus, by stripping away aspects of respect as well as legal and civil rights, punishment *degrades*. Harold Garfinkel (1956: 420) wrote of *degradation ceremonies* in which 'The denouncer must make the dignity of the supra-personal values of the tribe salient and accessible to view, and denunciation must be delivered in their name.' The archetypal ceremony in modern societies is the criminal trial – especially pronouncement of sentence – the 'denouncer' the judge. Yet the trial is just one episode in a process of degradation. The keenness with which suspects may act to protect their anonymity demonstrates their awareness of the shame and potential for reputational damage that attends even suspicion (and even gossip). The process continues at the time of questioning, arrest and charge; when bail is granted or denied; at conviction and sentence; at admission to prison. Moral and social, as well as legal, standing is progressively diminished.

The processes of degradation are acted out and partly achieved through the design and deployment of physical spaces. The furniture of the courtroom, for example, elevates the judge and frames the defendant in a box, often behind bars.[2] The architecture of a prison expresses the debasement of the offender, as well as presenting its image of power to the outside world (Jewkes and Moran 2017). The design of probation offices can bespeak punishment and control, as well as managerialism (Phillips 2014; Tidmarsh 2019; Shah 2020). These physical spaces also mould practice, influencing the ways in which professional staff and 'service users' relate to each other and find meaning in their transactions. They are commonly deployed to express, to effect, and subsequently to confirm changes of status.

As people move through this process, they change status – suspect, arrestee, defendant, convicted offender, prisoner, parolee – each change marked by a ceremony or at least a speech act (*I arrest you; You are charged with* …; *You have been found guilty; I sentence you to* …). These may be regarded as *rituals*: they are patterned, self-conscious, solemn, stylised, prescribed, repetitive (Stephenson 2015). Like most other rituals too, they are performative. The judge announcing 'I sentence you to six months imprisonment' is not recording a decision, but enacting and accomplishing it. These successive enactments lower status, announced in word and ritual to the wrongdoer and the community. These changes of status are *accretions of shame* telling the community how the individual is now to be regarded and how they should think of themselves. Offenders are expected to manifest shame and disgrace by blushing, downcasting their eyes, bowing the head, covering the face in their hands, wanting to hide. These reactions are appropriate; other responses (defiance, laughing) are construed as a lack of shame, resisting the ritual and thus deeply offensive.

In common with most religious rituals, criminal justice rituals are tightly prescribed and officials are punctilious in respecting proper form. A miswording (for example, if the formal police caution is improperly administered) can wreck the whole enterprise. The comparison with religion is more than coincidence. As Durkheim insisted, the values that have been flouted by the crime and are vindicated in the punishment are *sacred* – even (perhaps especially) in a secular society – and responses must accordingly be ritualised. The novelist Adam Mars-Jones beautifully captures an aspect of the sacred and its principal ritual functionary:

> With a bow, the butler presents the judge with his wig, and the two of them adjust it on his head. The wig distinguishes sharply between professional administrator and ritual functionary. From this moment on, he is a job personified rather than a person working. There is exactly as much human-being left in him as there is bread in a consecrated wafer. He doesn't any more interpret laws; the Law finds utterance in him.
>
> *(Mars-Jones 1981: 106)*

'All rituals are potentially vulnerable to cultural failure' (Smith 2008: 37). Control of the meaning of a public execution, as we have seen, might be wrested from the authority and subverted. Famously (though perhaps apocryphally), Daniel Defoe was placed in the pillory but then pelted with flowers rather than rotten vegetables or stones, the crowd taking control of the ceremony and turning it into a celebration of his 'seditious libel' (Cavendish 2003). High-visibility jackets marking out individuals as offenders can become something to be laughed at by offenders themselves or regarded as a 'badge of honour' (Guardian 2009). The humiliation, then, sometimes fails, but more often it succeeds, and the degradation of the criminal justice process transforms a member of a community into someone 'ritually separated from a place in the legitimate order' (Garfinkel 1956: 423), someone worthy of punishment.

Among the purposes attributed to these practices is to unite a community in solidarity. Durkheim marks this as a passionate reaction against the *crime* – a salutary reaffirmation of binding values – but often the effect is to deprecate and denounce the *offender*. Jurists insist that punishment should be for the crime, not for character – for what someone did, not who they are. But even if this is observed up until the point of sentence,[3] thereafter it is the assessed character of the person that will determine their experiences – their allocation to prison, for example, or the level of supervision in the community.

Rituals of punishment 'separate', then, but they do more than make people distinct – they make them *lower*, they humiliate them.[4] Most rites of passage mark changes in status, moving people from one accepted standing to another. Sometimes the rite itself involves a degree of lowering, mocking or teasing, but that is neither the purpose nor the upshot: at the conclusion the individual has moved to an established and respected status (Turner 1995). There is commonly a raising: for example, from the inferior and patronised status of a child to adulthood. Criminal justice transitions by contrast involve de-grading. Stephenson (2015: 17) refers to rituals used to immunise warriors against the ordinary human revulsion against killing people. Rituals of punishment perform a similar function, inspiring attitudes of disdain or contempt to legitimise the pains to be inflicted. Conceptualising criminal justice as a succession of rituals also draws attention to the onlooker. Some accounts of punishment are, as it were, binary – the punisher and the punished, the treater and the treated. But the transitions of criminal justice do more than attempt to change the individual's self-conception; rather these rites signal to the community how these individuals are now to be regarded.

Rituals of prosecution and punishment, then, formally declare and effect a degradation, designating offenders as debased and worthy of the pains that the state imposes. This lowering can explain not *why* we punish, but *how we could* treat people in these ways. Their degraded status renders them deservedly punishable and asserts that this as an inherent property of theirs, rather than an artefact of the state's response to them. This is not an undesirable by-product of punishment, but essential to it: 'punishment only works if it succeeds in making the punished person feel like an inferior' (Whitman 2003: 20) and for others to look down on them. An overwhelming body of international law prohibits degradation – a prohibition that may reflect anxieties that punishment often approaches degradation, legal protection being necessary to avert it. But at the least punishment lowers and downgrades the individual relative to their former standing and to the status of others, even if human rights conventions protect them from forfeiture of human dignity.

The degradation and cruelties of punishment are usually assessed with regard to physical treatment – for example, squalid conditions of confinement. The Council of Europe's Committee for the Prevention of Torture attends to this especially. Similarly, the United States Supreme Court in *Brown v. Plata* (563 US 493 [2011]) focused especially on the insanitary state of prisons and lack of access to adequate health care. This judgment does not use the words *degradation* or *degrading* (which are not to be found in the Constitution), although there are references to human dignity and its inviolable value in a decent society. Yet while legal safeguards may offer some protection, it remains the case that many forms of punishment offend against human dignity. For example, most people just take for granted the right to choose when and what to eat, when to go to bed, who shares the room they sleep in, and the denial of these rights, however unavoidable in prison, amounts to debasement. Rights of autonomy are the basis of personhood (Griffin 2008) and many of them are violated by imprisonment. The degradation involved is not only physical, but involves a progressive loss of legal and social rights and of moral standing and in these respects legal protections are much weaker.

These lowerings are characteristic of (probably) all approaches to punishment. People have sometimes wondered whether offenders are to be regarded as bad (culpable wrongdoers), sad (disadvantaged and troubled lives) or mad (with pathologies requiring treatment). Yet while these are presented as contrasts, all carry and connote degradation and the condescension of others: to be damnable and pitiable is to be despised and looked down on; to be mad is to be not quite human, to be 'other' or alien – as in the old word 'alienist' for those who would now be called psychiatrists – and not just different but lower.

These are further respects in which punishment and slavery are proximate and indeed overlapping:

> to this day, the criminal law bears the traits of its origin in slave punishments ... To be punished means to be treated like a slave ...

> Slavish treatment meant not just a social but also a moral degrada-
> tion. The diminution of honour, which ineradicably inheres in
> punishment to this day, derives from slave punishments.
> *(Sellin 2016 [1976]: preface, quoting Radbruch; see also Davis 2003: ch. 2)*

Both slaves and offenders are degraded and made to be regarded as
worthy of the pains and humiliations heaped upon them. At least part
of the reason why people feel this need to humiliate others is concern
to elevate themselves by contrast. In time, however, debasing others
can itself become a source of shame and a stimulus to change (Appiah
2010). Speaking about white supremacy (which has an obvious relevance to slavery and a real if less immediately apparent significance for
crime and punishment), Toni Morrison (1993) observed, 'If you can
only be tall because someone else is on their knees, you have a serious
problem.'

## Summary

There have been three principal themes in this chapter. First, definitions
of punishment are inescapably contested. Many practices that fail to
meet one or more of the criteria of the formal definition are *meant, felt
and recognised as punishment.* Even if the conventional definition could
be agreed upon, moreover, it would not set the best parameters for the
study of the institutions and practices of punishment; the scope of study
should be open-ended. The discipline of criminology has accepted new
areas of research and fresh perspectives as their significance has become
apparent. For example, *zemiology* challenges criminology to extend
beyond the parameters of criminalised actions, which are just a subset of
social harms (Hillyard and Tombs 2017; see also Sumner 1990).
Equally, the study of punishment should not be confined to activities
and institutions identified by the conventional definition, but extend its
purview to any and all coercive and intrusive actions that are intended
to be and/or experienced as punishment. And when Fassin raises the
relatively neglected question *who gets punished?*, it invites a corollary –
*who does not?* By comparison, no study of health services would be
complete without attention to those who are unable to access them. A
great deal of social harm is not criminalised, not enforced or

inadequately punished and accounts that fail to reflect on this will be incomplete.

The second theme concerns the centrality of *meaning*. Dan Kahan insists that 'Theories of punishment that disregard meaning are certain not to make any sense' (Kahan 1996: 653). Much more use should be made of research methods that try to elicit the meaning that people make and find in their experiences, whether as agents of punishment or subjects of it (see Chapter 4). Again, meanings are taken in the context of cultural understandings about what punishment ought to be. Without an understanding of what punishment means to people, then, prospects of penal reform are likely to be frustrated.

The third theme is the lowering of legal, social and moral standing that punishment invariably involves. This has been characterised as a sequence of rituals – secular in most modern societies, although at times displaying a fitting emotional intensity as a passionate response to the violation by the offence of sacred communal values. In and through these processes, the offender is expected to bow the head in shame or remorse (Chapter 5 will discuss what it might take for someone to be able and allowed to raise the head again). The philosophical defence is that punishment is a communication of censure of an act, but in practice it is degradation of the person that is often expressed and given effect. Those subject to punishment are *lowered* and sometimes, international conventions notwithstanding, punishment approaches an absolute degradation. When this occurs, in seeking to shame the offender and with insufficient vigilance about the consequences, we risk treating people in ways that shame ourselves.

## Notes

1. I owe this reference to Tom Daems. Hughes suggested that this may be a key to a general theory of punishment – an intriguing suggestion which has not (to my knowledge) been elaborated.
2. One study found defendants confined in a box to be nearly twice as likely to be found guilty by a jury as those seated next to their lawyer (Taylor 2019).
3. Even here the principle is at least arguably compromised by attention to previous convictions (see Roberts and von Hirsch 2010). The 'recidivist premium' is morally indefensible (Tonry 2010), its persistence explained by the attribution of bad character.
4. Latin – *humilitas* – lowness.

# 2

# THEORIES OF PUNISHMENT

Chapter 1 considered the complications of defining punishment, interpreting its meanings and setting the scope of its study. Discussion next turns to theories of punishment. But what should a theory of punishment be like? One of the purposes of any theory is to explain, but there are many puzzles about punishment, attempts to unravel them daunting in their complexity. The prospect of a comprehensive theory to illuminate every facet of punishment is forlorn. Moral philosophy, on the other hand, uses the expression *theories of punishment* to explore justification – the justification for having punishment at all, who should be punished, how and how much. The purpose of this project seems less explanatory than normative. The ethics of punishment will be among the subjects considered in the Conclusion; in this chapter, discussion mainly attends to explanatory theories.

An explanatory theory of punishment could take as its starting point the question why people punish at all. Strawson (1962) argued that a community could not be envisaged in which there was *no* reprobative response to wrongdoing, though a further question is why this so often takes the form of retribution, repaying harm for harm (Renteln 1990). Perhaps such responses have evolutionary benefits, discouraging and deterring aggressors (McCullough 2008). Other reactions are also common: exhortations to do better, offers of guidance, making amends

DOI: 10.4324/9780429055829-3

and peace-making are usual and often coexist, more or less
tably, alongside retributive responses (Roberts 1979).

## Reading theories of punishment

How the social order influences the forms punishment takes at particular places and times has been a principal concern of the social sciences. Some studies have also examined how the institutions, practices
and motivations of punishment might have reciprocal effects on society.
These inquiries have been prominent in the works of Durkheim and
Foucault, of Cohen, Garland, Wacquant and Simon. It seems likely that
such studies might illuminate some of the most important characteristics
of any social order. In particular, punishment can contribute to a fuller
appreciation of the ways in which *values* are asserted, established, reinforced and reproduced, and of the mechanics of *power*.

Punishment is for an actual or alleged *wrong* and, in and through its
exercise, punishers make claims about values. The reactions of others
to our behaviour is one of the most influential ways people learn
what is expected and then internalise these expectations. Émile Durkheim argued that a consensus of values is a defining characteristic of
a community – what makes groups of people living together *into* a
community – and the criminal law can be regarded as an authoritative
statement of these values (Lukes and Scull 2013). A society corrobo-
rates its values in and through the responses to the violations that
crimes represent, strengthening social solidarity. Thus, 'the legal process serves as a highly dramatic method of affirming collective sentiments concerning the wrongness of criminal behaviour. Norms, once
implanted, do not thrive without replenishment and the punishment
of the offender symbolises anew the immorality of the deviant act'
(Sykes 1958: 38).

But the hard treatment involved in punishment lays bare structures of
power. Punishment is one of the very few instances where the state
deploys coercive force against its own citizens and others under its sway,
claiming a monopoly in the use of such force (Weber 2009 [1919]).
Definitions of punishment refer to its being *of an offender, for an offence*, and
again power must enter into an account of how these concepts are constructed. Some acts are criminalised while others, at least as harmful, are

not, so that criminalisation can be regarded as representing what powerful people take to be in their interests. For example, warfare, environmental damage, poverty occasioned by injustice or exploitation, violence against women and children in their homes, the miseries inflicted on asylum seekers and refugees, the industrial 'accidents' that occur when profit is put before safety – these all cause a great deal of death and suffering but are often kept beyond the scope of the criminal law or feebly enforced (Hillyard and Tombs 2017). Sometimes the failure of the state to repudiate harmful and wrongful conduct exposes the strength of powerful interests: rather than denouncing these wrongs by invoking the law, the state is eloquent in its silence.

Nor is it just the substance of the law that exposes power. Some people who have committed crimes are brought to justice while others who have done the same or worse are not, with similar inequalities in weights of punishment. Differences of power are manifest throughout these processes (for example, Dorling et al. 2008; Reiman and Leighton 2013). In all these ways, then, the study of punishment can expose power relationships. Yet power functions across other dimensions besides (Lukes 2005) and is made most effective not by force or coercion, but by presenting power as recognised authority (Tankebe and Liebling 2013) – another element of the received definition of punishment. The state must lay claim not only to the power to punish, but the right to do so and to practise in ways that must be shown to be consistent with the values that society professes. The deployment of punishment, therefore, is not only coercive, but also ideological. All modern states profess that theirs is a system of criminal justice – not (or not only) one of crime control. Legitimacy is fundamental to compliance with the law (Tyler 1990, 2006; Darley 2009) and a claim to the right to punish is a claim to rightful authority. Where these mechanisms fail and authority is unmasked as bare power, there will be at best instability, likely challenges to the law and its practices, and perhaps active resistance.

## Grand theory

The influence of criminal justice and punishment in legitimating power and illuminating the ways in which it operates, as well as its place in affirming, reproducing and reinforcing social values, has naturally made its study of interest to social scientists.[1] Some of the 'grand theorists' (Skinner 1985) have made a central place for punishment in their analysis, variously foregrounding social, economic, political, psychological or cultural influences that mould the contours of punishment. Yet punishment exerts a reciprocal influence. Durkheim sought to establish connections between systems of punishment and society, exploring punishment as a heuristic to illuminate forms of order and social solidarity. Michel Foucault's (1977) account of the origins of the penitentiary attempted to show how techniques of control through surveillance were developed in the prison and then exported and dispersed into the community. Foucault further argued that punishment and the claims to criminological and psychological knowledge with which it is in symbiotic relationship establish norms to which conformity is required – an exercise of power that inculcates *the mentality to be governed* (Lukes 2005). While punishment is less directly a concern of Marx and Weber, their respective analyses, concepts and specific insights have been put to use to try to understand punishment. There are disagreements among the grand theorists, but sometimes they are addressing different questions and it may be possible to use their insights in complementary ways.

There are, however, limitations in accounts at this level. Durkheim and Foucault, as well as many followers of Marx, attempt to determine the trajectory of the development of punishments over time. Much of this is valuable. For example, it is instructive to reflect that the beginnings of the measurement of punishment in terms of time spent in prison coincides with the introduction of wage labour calibrated by time at work (Garland 1990: ch. 5). Again, the relationship among forms of punishment, demography and the labour market merits careful inquiry and analysis (Rusche and Kirchheimer 2003 [1939]). But the historical accuracy of these narratives has been called into question. Garland (1990: chs 6 and 7) is among those who challenge the detail of Foucault's account, while Cavadino, Dignan and Mair (2013) similarly indict Rusche and Kirchheimer, scholars in the Marxist tradition, for plain historical error, so that the data adduced in support of these theories may be unreliable. Too much can be made of this criticism, perhaps. Sometimes – especially in Durkheim's work – these are less historical descriptions than a sketch of ideal types (or even speculative stages) in society's evolution, associated with forms and weights of punishment.

A more serious flaw is reductionism: one critical influence on the character of punishment is mistaken for the whole. In some versions of Marxism, for instance, it is as if the socio-economic order is the sole determinant, while other factors (for example, culture) are at best epiphenomena, resting and dependent upon socio-economics, or at worst irrelevant. Yet to understand how the socio-economic order works its way into policy and practice, into the meanings made and found in punishment, calls for theorisation at another level.

## *Hegemony*

Concepts of ideology and hegemony are of particular value in the attempt to understand how the socio-economic order may exercise its influence on punishment. Hegemony, associated especially with Antonio Gramsci, expresses the idea that the ruling class determines a dominant way of thinking, forming and directing the beliefs and values that prevail in a society (Forgacs 1988). For example, a neo-liberal society is marked by an individualism which holds people responsible for their own circumstances, actions and consequences, so shaping conceptions of both economic and punitive desert. Corporatist and social democratic societies have different notions of how people should relate to one another which may dispose them to recognise duties to those who are disadvantaged and to punish less severely (Cavadino and Dignan 2006b). Loïc Wacquant (e.g. Wacquant 2009) has made connections between the spread of neo-liberal economics, fuelling inequalities, and the rise of weights and forms of punishment that mark boundaries between groups, penalise the poor for their plight and immunise the powerful from any disquiet.

The idea of hegemony implies that not only are thoughts and feelings channelled in this way; concepts and critiques that may be brought to bear on these matters are similarly constrained. Hegemonic ideas become self-evident. Some beliefs and values are so ingrained that to question them becomes an act of desecration: emotional commitment makes them immune to criticism to the extent that opposing views are met not just with disagreement but with disdain (Lukes 2008). In many societies, prominent hegemonic beliefs are that punishment makes society safer by reducing crime; that it honours the experience of victims; and that it rights the wrong of the crime. Liberal penal reformers may stand accused of endangering society, letting down the victim or colluding with the crime (Canton 2017). To question these beliefs is an act of disloyalty, a defection from the 'hostile solidarity' formed against offenders (Carvalho and Chamberlen 2018). Just as the crime outrages the collective conscience, as Durkheim argued, a failure to feel and act in response to the crime in the established, hegemonic ways is similarly outrageous.

Parameters are thus set within which disagreement can take place – the boundaries of debate. There will, for example, be argument about whether punishment reduces crimes by deterrence or rehabilitation or incapacitation; or whether condign punishment alone can vindicate the suffering of victims or administer desert to the wrongdoer. But the wider question of whether punishment is the best resort in these endeavours is rarely allowed to emerge. Similarly, there are lively political debates about what purposes should be set for prisons and how their regimes should be ordered, but to raise questions about the existence of the institution itself – whether it could even in principle achieve these purposes, even aggravating the problems that it purports to solve – is to invite scorn or worse.

Hegemonic ideas of social and economic individualism or, on the other hand, collectivism work their way into conceptions of justice, desert and punishment; reciprocally and dynamically, the authority of the law endorses and legitimates these ideas. This partly explains why the criminal law in many jurisdictions struggles to deal adequately with corporate crime, even though commercial companies are responsible for so much avoidable loss of human life, personal injury, financial impropriety and environmental damage (Hillyard et al. 2004; Tombs and Whyte 2015). The law's insistence on provable acts and intentions of identifiable individuals struggles to deal with the decisions and omissions that lead to grave harms and misery, responsibility being diffused throughout the organisation with no individual palpably to blame (Box 1983).

Hegemony explains why the 'crime problem' is characterised as it is, the wrongdoings of the powerful resisting definition as crimes. The (over-)criminalisation of the poor, for similar reasons, acts as a distraction, diverting attention from the harmful behaviour of the powerful – a function that Thomas Mathiesen (2006) imputed to the prison. It is hegemony too that explains why ambitions to 'change the terms of the debate' so seldom succeed. There are things that people 'know' about punishment in which considerable emotional commitment is invested, so taken for granted that they are only exposed when challenged and even then prove impervious to argument.

## Change

That which is taken for granted is most likely to be exposed at times of change. The occasion for change might be the exigencies of the penal system itself – for example an overcrowded prison estate – but some changes occur in reaction or response to wider social change or cultural movements. In the eighteenth century, for instance, across much of Europe, broader cultural changes in sensibility affected attitudes to punishment and tended to mitigate some of the grosser physical forms of punishment (even if new methods introduced cruelties of their own) (Elias 2000; Garland 1990). An awareness that existing practices were brutal, arbitrary and inefficient excited Cesare Beccaria to propose more moderate and proportionate penalties with a clearer purpose.

An immediate stimulus for change may be an event – perhaps an appalling crime, but perhaps also a miscarriage of justice or revelations about conditions and practices. Here too hegemony helps to illuminate these processes. Events can be recruited to support reform, but they do not come with a label designating the kinds of event that they are or what lessons need to be learnt from them. A brutal murder of a child by other children could be taken as a sign that the system needs to be made tougher to deal with feral and unruly youth; or it could prompt reflections about whether children are neglected by their parents or the state (Green 2007). A prison riot can be seen as an outbreak of lawlessness, inviting more vigilance and strictness in the governance of the prison; alternatively, it can be interpreted, as by the Woolf inquiry into the prison riots in England in 1990, as an indication of a failure to persuade prisoners that they were being treated with fairness. Prison managers, staff and unions might take the event as an opportunity to lobby for increased funding – for more staff or higher salaries or better training. A grave crime committed by a recently released prisoner may be represented as an error of judgement by those taking the release decision or a failure of parole supervision, but could as well be taken as a sign of prison's inability to effect rehabilitation. Events have their impact, then, but how they are presented depends on the hegemonic interpretation and how this chimes or jars with the beliefs of the public. Similarly, an event that is not connected with crime in any obvious way – for example, an economic crisis or a pandemic – can have unpredictably wide effects, including after-shocks that unsettle a penal system.

Attempts to reform gain traction when arrangements are seen to be failing somehow, perhaps through doubts about effectiveness or efficiency, though more commonly through failures of *meaning* (Smith 2008). Yet allegations of failure are likely to be opposed, disagreements arising about a solution. Reform proposals encounter active resistance from those with an interest in maintaining the status quo or making changes of a different kind, for reasons of principle, pragmatism, perceived professional self-interest or perhaps economic gain. If the case for change is made out, defenders of those same interests will seek to mould reform in ways that favour their cause. The upshot is likely to be that the adopted policy will have been challenged, compromised or even distorted through these processes of contestation. As policies are put into effect, they may meet deliberate resistance. More often, perhaps, practitioners look to shape policies to their own interests, or simply to get the job done, varying, or even warping and subverting the plans of policymakers. Accordingly, 'If historians of punishment have provided any clear lessons, it is that reforms evolve in ways quite different from the aims of their proponents' (Feeley and Simon 1992: 463). Outcomes, then, can never be safely anticipated on the basis of these initial motivations nor can aims be inferred from outcomes.

The penal field is never settled and consensual, but always subject to contestation (Goodman, Page and Phelps 2017). The weary metaphor of a 'pendulum' is misleading: the process of penal change is never mechanical or automatic, like the workings of a clock; nor does reform follow a straightforward trajectory, only to return along the exact same path. Similarly, the history of punishment is not best organised into distinct epochs or stages, an approach that is likely to exaggerate change and conceal continuities. There is always more than a residue of past practices at times of change and, less obviously, some 'stages' fore-shadow those to come. These metaphors present punishment as a sequence of settled states, whereas in policy formation and imple-mentation it is always subject to contest. It is common, for instance, to counterpose times when rehabilitative treatment or punitive approaches dominate, but since the aspiration to reform prisoners 'can and often does perpetuate coercive social control, punishment, and oppression ... it is often incorrect to juxtapose reform against other purposes and outcomes' (ibid.: 54). Conceptions of 'reform' may themselves be contested: advocates of healthy minds in healthy bodies and spiritual edification through prayer and scriptural study are not at all natural allies of psychological therapies (ibid.: ch. 4). Punishment orientations too can differ markedly, some arguing that the rigour and discipline of imprisonment is sufficient, others urging that prisoners be subjected to hard labour and physical pain. There is abundant historical evidence that, at times when avowed policy was reformative, imprisonment still brought pain and hardship, while in times characterised as punitive there remained scope for personnel to make active attempts to help, even in the toughest prisons. Any regime can be resisted and subverted by staff or by prisoners.

Many purposes are set for punishment and there are times when ideologies have to compete not only with one another, but with logistics and cost. Principled efforts at reform might be distorted by (perceived or actual) practical imperatives. For example, a need to generate profit through commerce, to fund a prison or to enrich others, will lead to work activities quite different from punitive toil (hard labour for its own sake) and, on the other hand, from educational or vocational training designed to equip people for release. Staff may have priorities to keep themselves safe and manage burdensome workloads which matter to them more than the formal expectations of the insti-tution. David Rothman (1980) accordingly writes of tensions between 'conscience and convenience', in which convenience typically prevails.

The difficulties all this poses for an historical understanding are for-midable, since the experiences of practitioners are likely to be under-represented while those of prisoners, probationers and their families are usually altogether irretrievable. Historical reconstruction can come to rely on legislation and formal policy statements, privileging these accounts, risking 'mistaking radical shifts in rhetoric for radical shifts in practice' (Goodman, Page and Phelps 2017: 7) – words that echo Cohen's reflections on the uncertain relationship between the 'story' and the reality (Cohen 1985). Even at the height of the 'rehabilitative era' in prisons in California, for instance, the reality never came close to the aspiration and for all the talk of individual assessment, classification and treatment, there were neither the resources nor the professional expertise to make this happen.

Nevertheless, the story not only reflected the ambitions of proponents, but could be used to push developments in their preferred direction as the discourse achieved currency and impact, becoming 'a means of legitimation ... used to defend or promote practices in the face of opposition' (Goodman, Page and Phelps 2017: 93). Whatever the realities, these stories merit study in their own right: it is always worth asking who composed them, to what end and with what consequences.[2] They can contribute to the presentation and acceptance of policy (Annison 2021), feeding back into the self-awareness of an agency and staff, affecting their practice and the experiences of those subject to punishment. But perhaps the most radical consequence of the analysis by Goodman, Page and Phelps is that, since punishment is always subject to contestation and dispute, in its ambitions, practices and consequences, as well as in the perceptions of the punishers and the punished, it may be impossible to say what punishment 'is' at any time and place. What scope exists for explanatory theory when the *explanandum* defies specification?

## International differences

Examining international differences is a valuable project in its own right as well as having potential to illuminate the many interacting factors that go to shape punishment (Miethe and Lu 2005). Cavadino and Dignan (2006b) categorised different countries according to their political economy. They found that societies with neo-liberal economies make much greater use of exclusionary modes of punishment, and as neoliberalism has advanced, rates of imprisonment have increased. Social democratic and corporatist societies, by contrast, tend towards more inclusionary forms of punishment and much lower rates of imprisonment. These patterns of punishment reflect (and reproduce) respective hegemonic cultural attitudes. Plausibly, as we have seen, neo-liberal economics rests on a concept of strong individual responsibility and desert; other socio-economic orders might be more receptive to human frailty, wider conceptions of responsibility and a recognition of a collective duty to respond to wrongdoing.

Yet even if social economy sets the parameters of penal change, developments are modulated by social, political, cultural, demographic and other factors that have a force of their own. The 'new punitiveness' that has been said to characterise punishment in recent years (Pratt et al. 2005) has met robust opposition in much of Europe (Snacken 2010; Snacken and Dumortier 2012), demonstrating the importance of historical, legal and cultural dimensions. Again, while capitalism may favour the marketisation of punitive and risk technologies, there are countries where cultural traditions regard private sector involvement in the penal system as improper in principle. For that matter, while people may expect the state to keep them safe, history has shown some countries that among the threats from which they need protection is precisely the state itself.

Some important recent scholarship starts by identifying countries thought to be exceptional. These 'extremes in contrast can help exemplify and disclose the forces underlying penal change and orientation' (Brangan 2020: 600). The Nordic countries (Pratt 2008a, 2008b; Pakes and Gunnlaugsson 2018), the USA (Reitz 2017; Lacey and Soskice 2019; Garland 2020) and Scotland (Brangan 2019) have all been investigated in this way, prompting debates about the ways and extent to which they are indeed outliers – whether, for example, the claim of being a less punitive jurisdiction matches up to the reality – and what might account for any distinctiveness. Another source of understanding, underexploited but potentially rich, is policy transfer – deliberate attempts to introduce policies and practices established in one jurisdiction to another country (Jones and Newburn 2007; Canton 2014b). Whether innovations 'take' can illuminate the forces at work to enable or to resist them.

Most comparative studies have pointed to the ways in which a wide range of different, interrelated factors act to shape attitudes towards punishment, patterns of sentencing and penal institutions. These factors include geography, demography, historical traditions, crime patterns, poverty, inequality, and racism. One frequent finding is that systems turn out to be resolutely *local* (Tonry 2007): 'however many factors we incorporate into our theory, it will still not give us the whole story. Individual nations, and their cultures, histories and politics, can be just as quirky and esoteric as individual human beings' (Cavadino and Dignan 2006a: 452).

## *The Ghost Road*

Penal practice is typically contested and variegated (Rubin and Phelps 2017; Goodman, Page and Phelps 2017). Several interactions, bound up with a number of considerations of conscience and convenience, could be understood as constituting an *ecological niche* (Hacking 1999). A diverse, often conflicting and mutually influential set of social, economic, political and cultural factors collectively constitute a milieu in which penal institutions and practices emerge, operate and develop. The indefinitely many ways in which these factors interact accounts for local variation and idiosyncrasy, as well as making the development of penal policy and practice inherently hard to predict (Lacey, Soskice and Hope 2018).

In Pat Barker's novel *The Ghost Road* (the final book in her brilliant *Regeneration* trilogy), a group of soldiers in the trenches are pondering their situation during the First World War. One insists that the war cannot be explained by the official government rationale, but is 'feathering the nests of profiteers'. The novel's main character, Billy Prior, is asked for his opinion.

> What do I think? I think what you're saying is basically a conspiracy theory, and like all conspiracy theories it's optimistic. What you're saying is, OK the war isn't being fought for the reasons we're told, but it *is* being fought for a reason. It's not benefiting the people it's supposed to be benefiting, but it is benefiting somebody. And I don't believe that, you see. I think things are actually much worse than you think because there isn't any kind of rational justification left. It's become a self-perpetuating system. Nobody benefits. Nobody's in control. Nobody knows how to stop.
>
> *(Barker 1996: 143)*

This may be true of many human affairs. Actions are performed, sometimes with complex and ambivalent motives; consequences follow, some of which cannot be assumed to have been intended, further actions taken. Policies and strategies stray as they are put into practice, events taking a course of their own. The upshot can be arrangements that are not working in any way that had been anticipated and may be demonstrably unsuccessful, but in which people are enmeshed and which they feel (and perhaps are) powerless to alter. Again, attempts to bring about change are inevitably contested, so that either things continue on the same trajectory (even if the story changes) or the changes that do take place may be markedly different from anybody's ambition. To take a *Ghost Road* perspective is not to walk away from explanatory accounts: the many factors that go to shape policy and practice can be investigated in their own terms and in relation to their interactions. Each factor has its antecedents, but the meld, mixture and therefore the consequences defy any idea of single, unified strategy that can be straightforwardly achieved, even by the most powerful.

## Emotions

Among the most compelling influences on the trajectory of penal policy is its political salience (Lacey, Soskice and Hope 2018). Attempts to understand its sway in electoral campaigning in many countries must attend to *emotions*. Durkheim saw punishment not as an instrumental device to reduce offending, but as a *passionate* response to the violation of shared and sacred values. Criminal justice is suffused with emotions (Karstedt 2002); Sherman and Strang (2011: 145) suggest that 'The primary task of justice is to manage emotions.' Perceptions of policy and practice must in some way chime with these emotions on pain of failing in this 'primary task' and jeopardising legitimacy. Indeed, if it is to achieve the purposes that Durkheim supposed, it must have an affective quality of this kind.

There has been much recent attention to the ways in which emotions shape attitudes towards crime and punishment (for example, Bandes 1999; Freiberg 2001; Karstedt 2002; Murphy 2010; Loader 2010; Karstedt, Loader and Strang 2013; Nussbaum 2016, 2017). Their importance has long been recognised by politicians: in England and

Wales, the 'Platonic Guardians' (Loader 2006) strove to soothe emotions and to insulate penal policy from their influence, but the advantages of orchestrating emotional responses and even inciting them has been exploited politically. Many people feel strongly about punishment, often in general and certainly with regard to particular cases.

The place that emotion *should* occupy in guiding penal policy is less often considered. Sometimes the emotional has been explicitly renounced, even (perhaps especially) when it is being conjured deliberately (Canton 2014a). Part of the explanation, no doubt, is the suspicion that the emotional is precisely antithetical to the rational and therefore has no place in principled thinking. This idea that reason and emotion are opposed, and that reasoning is in all ways superior, is embedded in the Western philosophical tradition. Although he went on to argue that this opposition is mistaken, David Hume referred to the customary 'combat of passion and reason', remarking that the 'blindness, unconstancy and deceitfulness' of passion is set against the 'eternity, invariableness and divine origin' of reason (Hume 1967 [1739]: 413). A failure to subordinate emotion to reason, moreover, leads not only to folly, but to vice. Many of the classical penal theorists – Kant, Beccaria, Bentham – draw more or less explicitly on that 'combat', keen to extirpate emotion from thinking about punishment. Beccaria recognised connections between emotions and the cruelties of punishment he deplored, hoping for 'a body politic which, far from acting on passion, is the tranquil moderator of private passions' (Beccaria 1963 [1763]: 42).

Some professions are uncomfortable with the emotional. For example, judges might insist they are dispassionate in their sentencing decisions. Yet all the principal considerations that inform their judgements are guided by emotions. Deliberations about harm and responsibility, about desert and consequence, how much weight to give to previous convictions or adversity in the defendant's life, about most (perhaps all) aggravating and mitigating factors – all these reckonings draw upon moral intuitions inspired by emotions. And when relying on sentencing guidelines, regulations, standards and professional norms, practitioners are not so much setting aside the emotional as simply recycling the emotions of others.

This becomes less disconcerting when it is recognised that there is a degree of consensus among psychologists and sociologists that the notion that reason and emotion are distinct and in opposition to one another is flawed and misleading (Barbalet 2001; Haidt 2012). Decisions cannot be taken without the contribution of the emotions – and are all the wiser for it (Evans 2001; Damasio 2006). As Joshua Greene concludes:

> Reasoning frees us from the tyranny of our immediate impulses by allowing us to serve values that are not automatically activated by what's in front of us. And yet, at the same time, reason cannot produce good decisions without some kind of emotional input, however indirect.
>
> *(Greene 2014: 137)*

Even so, the sharp antithesis is a familiar rhetorical and political trope: our position is rational, considered, based on evidence; our opponents' is distorted by emotion, prejudice and ideology.

A better distinction is known as dual process theory. Individuals work with two modes of thinking. System 1 thinking is variously described as immediate, intuitive, unconscious and automatic; System 2 thinking is reflective, conscious, considered, analytic and slow (Kahneman 2011; Haidt 2012; Greene 2014). It should not be supposed that System 1 is emotional, System 2 rational: reason and emotion are involved in both modes. John Darley argues that demands for weighty punishment typically show System 1 in operation, but 'Circumstances … may provoke the individual into reasoning about the case, and the reasoning system conclusion can override the response dictated by the intuitive system' (Darley 2009: 4). Certainly recognition of the influence of System 1 in matters of punishment gives no grounds for abandoning reason. Where there is disagreement, disputants adduce *reasons* for their position: they are not reduced to passionate emoting.

A further insight of modern psychology, however, sharpens the challenge for System 2 thinking. While people tend to claim that they reached their conclusions through evidence and reasoning, Haidt (2012) and others argue that moral conclusions are often arrived at intuitively, with supporting evidence actively sought out subsequently (Kahan 2010; Greene 2014). 'People endorse whichever position reinforces their connection to others with whom they share important commitments' (Kahan 2010: 296). This is particularly apposite to punishment which, as Durkheim argued, encourages social bonding through reaffirming communal values. This selective deployment of evidence seems all the more likely where findings are inconclusive and in need of interpretation (as almost always in criminology and penology) and where emotions are often intense.

An immediate challenge is to discern *which* emotions are at work in shaping attitudes towards punishment – a task complicated by the deficiencies of any vocabulary of emotion, the problems of framing and perhaps reducing emotions to neatly bounded concepts. As Hannah Maslen (2015: 5) writes, 'The messiness of emotional experience precludes the consistent application of sharply delineated ascriptions of different emotions.' It is possible to distinguish conceptually between (say) embarrassment and shame, regret and remorse, sadness and loneliness, but these pairs of emotions are phenomenologically close and shifting. Nor are emotions individual and discrete; often (perhaps typically) they interact and work dynamically. There are, moreover, meta-emotions – 'emotional reactions to emotional experiences' (Barbalet 2001: 23) – for example, feeling guilty about feeling envious, ashamed of being angry or scared. Despite these formidable complications, the attempt should be made to disentangle the emotions that animate the will to punish; or, on the other hand, those emotions that may constrain crueller impulses and may be more supportive of other responses to wrongdoing and subsequent reconciliation. Without this understanding, the prospect of engaging with and maybe influencing these emotions in the cause of penal reform is likely to be frustrated.

Several emotions are at work in shaping attitudes to punishment, both in general and in particular cases (Freiberg 2001). Often too these emotional responses are complex and ambivalent, partly due to psychic tensions that arise during childhood socialisation (Garland 1990: 64ff.). Discussion now turns to three emotions: *anger, fear* and *disgust,* all salient if not always explicit in debates about punishment. Once more the problem arises that these, while conceptually distinct, are often very close as experienced: I may be frightened of something just because it is so disgusting and want to make my distance from it; or angry because I feel frightened. At the same time, these may provoke quite different behavioural responses: anger prompts confrontation, disgust distancing, fear (famously) fight or flight. An awareness of the influence of these emotions illuminates aspects of punishment that are otherwise (even more) puzzling.

## Anger

Retribution is associated with anger above all and it is anger that is most evident in political debate about punishment. When Garland says 'the emotional temperature of policy making has moved from cool to hot' (Garland 2001: 11), it is anger that the thermometer is registering. Anger towards offenders prompts a zeal for punishment and an intuitive reaction that offenders should get what they deserve (System 1) exerts far more influence than, notably, evidence about effectiveness in reducing reoffending (System 2) (Carlsmith, Darley and Robinson 2002; Sherman and Strang 2011). Johnson (2009) found that anger about crime is significantly associated with punitive attitudes, even after controlling for fear and other relevant factors. Anger is the most prominent of public reactions to grave crimes or when sentences are considered insufficient. And many will feel that this is altogether fitting, especially when crimes are grave.

Martha Nussbaum (2016) argues that anger is always a response to a perceived wrong: where there is no wrong, there is no place for anger. (People do get angry with objects, but this is infantile.) And it involves a wish for some kind of retributive payback. This wish is a conceptual component of anger:[3] 'anger', absent a wish for payback, isn't anger at all, but something else – perhaps grief. While anger can have an initial value in signalling that a wrong has been done, it is problematic morally. Nussbaum accepts that anger may be more or less *well-grounded* – directed at the proper target (the wrongdoer), with the appropriate focus (the wrongful act), and proportionate – but even then it is unjustifiable. It may galvanise people to action, 'But once they get going, they had better not follow anger's lure all the way to fantasized retribution' (Nussbaum 2016: 39), for payback represents a magical thinking that imagines the past can somehow be undone.

The conjuring and indulgence of anger often obstructs the reflection and learning that should take place following a grave crime (Green 2007). It diverts attention from the specific needs of victims and from considered strategies to reduce the chances of recurrence. Anger is 'especially poisonous when people use it to deflect attention from real problems that they feel powerless to solve' (Nussbaum 2017). It is grief in particular that she has in mind: it is easier to indulge anger than to deal with overwhelming loss. Anger instils a sense of control, but this is bogus. Even if this anger could ever be satiated – for example, parents' reactions to the murder of a child – there is still the loss and the grieving to undergo. Anger is a stage of grieving (Kübler-Ross and Kessler 2005), but one to go beyond: to remain locked in anger and punitive obsessions brings further pain.

There are other aspects of anger to note. First, few people believe they act at their best in anger – even when they regard their anger as entirely justified. Second, it is inherently given to excess: when people 'boil over', there is no telling where the spillage may end up. Third, expressed anger provokes a reaction from its target. This may be shame or self-pity, but is quite as likely to be defiance or a reciprocal anger (Gilligan 2003). None of these responses is likely to encourage better behaviour.

There is, though, Nussbaum argues, one way in which payback 'makes sense': as a downgrading of the wrongdoer as redress for the downgrading of the victim that the crime represents. She rejects this ethically, but there is a connection here with the idea of punishment as degradation. Chapter 1 argued that processes of prosecution, trial and punishment can be regarded as a succession of rituals of degradation. Whatever view is taken of its moral propriety, this degradation evinces anger. The anger that crimes so often provoke can be moderated and articulated in terms of justice, framed to look like just retribution rather than angry revenge. The harms of a crime can be assessed more precisely, attributions of responsibility made in more nuanced ways in the attempt to assign fair punishment. Here System 2 thinking works to limit and channel the immediate reaction of System 1. But anger's influence persists.

## Fear

Unlike anger and disgust, fear has received considerable attention in mainstream criminology. Fear of crime in itself causes distress, damage and inconvenience to many individuals and communities. Fear has a powerful political salience, parties claiming their penal policies will make us safer than those of their opponents. Commercial companies may hint that some fears are well-warranted, that there are real dangers against which their products are the best defence. Many people seem quite willing to tolerate any costs, amount of intrusion into their personal lives (CCTV, face recognition technology, online monitoring) or disruption of routines (airport security) when assured that this is what it takes to keep them safe. This is all the more likely where the disruptions and intrusions are borne by others: 'if indulging in fear is costless, because other people face the relevant burdens, then the mere fact of "risk", and the mere presence of fear, will seem to provide a justification' (Sunstein 2005: 208, quoted by Zedner 2009: 148). Where fear propels penal policy, the 'relevant burdens' – long sentences for deterrence or incapacitation – are indeed carried by 'the other'.

Expressions of fear of crime should always be taken seriously and not scoffed away as 'irrational' (Newburn 2017: ch. 14). Grave crimes are rare and those most frightened of (say) violent crime are often among those least at risk, but comforting statistical aggregates mask specific vulnerabilities, associated, for example, with gender, race or poverty. Nor is it irrational to be frightened about an event which, however improbable, could be catastrophic in its consequences. Yet expressions of fear of crime need to be interpreted. Crime has a singular capacity to *stand for* something. This may be a breakdown in law and order and the collapse of authority, the threat of the feared 'other', a reminder of personal vulnerability. But it is also a ready proxy for other insecurities and concerns that have little or nothing to do with crime (Tyler and Boeckmann 1997; Taylor 1998). Ontological insecurity may impel a search for a convenient scapegoat, so that anxieties about crime and an insistence on punitive responses are most likely to arise at times of social change and insecurity. 'Enter street crime, a blessing disguised as a curse. Street crime offers a way to channel public anger and anxiety away from amorphous social and economic threats and toward criminals, who, in their own, much more concrete ways, threaten our wellbeing' (Scheingold 1995: 165). Other studies have explored connections between fear of crime and economic concerns, one study concluding that 'Public insecurities about crime were associated not with the level of crime in a country but rather with the degree of social security provided in a country through its welfare state provision' (Hummelsheim, Hirtenlehner, Jackson and Oberwittler 2010: 16).

Nor do the steps taken to allay fear always have that effect. Fear may change behaviour: 'Fear constrained people's lives. The important factor about these constraining behaviours is, however, is that instead of reducing fear of crime, they constantly reminded people of their vulnerability. Constraining and cautious behaviour actually increased fear' (Bourke 2005: 334; see also Zedner 2009). And just as anger 'spills over', fear can spread: inchoate and amorphous anxieties may go looking for suitable targets. It may also be contagious as people become more fearful in response to concerns expressed by neighbours and friends.

It is not clear that there is a direct correlation between fear of crime in general (or of personal victimisation) and punitive attitudes (Maruna and King 2004). Costelloe, Chiricos and Gertz (2009) interviewed people in Florida finding that fear of crime did 'predict' punitiveness, although that this was entangled with economic worries and anxieties. King and Maruna (2009) found correlations between punitiveness and (general, more than personal) economic anxieties, as well as with factors that crime represents – for instance, unruly youth. Fear, then, may influence punitive attitudes – even if it is sometimes fear of something other than crime.

Fear, articulated in the language of risk management and public protection, is an accepted and respectable way of advocating punitiveness. Conjuring the spectre of increased danger is a familiar tactic to resist liberal penal reform. This can mask other reasons for advocating punitiveness, including political advantage, professional and commercial self-interests (Goodman, Page and Phelps 2017: ch. 6). As well as concealing such interests, the discourse of risk and public protection can obscure emotional impulses towards punitiveness – notably, anger and disgust. Since anger and disgust could be seen as unworthy and unreliable guides to policy, public protection is adduced to defend punitiveness, obtaining political traction through sentiments of fear.

If fear of crime is, to begin with, a System 1 (intuitive and immediate) reaction, System 2 deliberations often take place in the language of *risk.* One way of understanding the dominance of risk in contemporary penal thinking (O'Malley 2010), then, is to regard it as a means of taming fear. Jonathan Simon's *Governing through Crime* (Simon 2007) thesis is predicated on the evolution of a culture of fear. Public protection – 'the dominant theme of penal policy' (Garland 2001: 17) – calls for ostensibly dispassionate, 'scientized' and (ideally) quantified assessments of risk as a precondition of its management and reduction. Risk technologies are now embedded at the heart of criminal justice and assessments of risk significantly determine the experience of individuals in the penal system. Fear also contributes to marked increases in prison populations, with sentences lengthened on an incapacitative rationale, confinement seeming to promise a security no other intervention can match. Fear propels preoccupations with security and preventive measures. Whether or not these 'are' punishment, many such measures are experienced in this way. Affecting the lives of everyone, they make a difference to how people live, sometimes trespassing on human rights and occasioning disappointment and frustration when they fail (Zedner 2009).

An increasing awareness that the penal system, or even the wider system of criminal justice, cannot ensure safety from crime (Garland 2001) might have led to a *reduction* in punitiveness (Zedner 2009). Perhaps the admixture of other emotions may help to explain why it has not. The archetypal response to fear is 'fight or flight'[4] and where 'fight' ensues fear becomes hard to distinguish from aggression and anger. For that matter, anger is often an expression of fear: homophobia and xenophobia often give rise to anger and aggression (the etymology of these words is the Greek word for fear). Situational and social preventive/reductive measures are more effective, but fail to satisfy the anger that crime evokes.

In conclusion: emotions of fear are an essential safeguard against dangers. Yet fear can notoriously also induce panic and other counter-productive responses to increase risks and introduce further dangers besides. Expressions of fear call for reflection and interpretation. Responding appropriately to these fears should take people's own perceptions seriously, but also help them to explore the dimensions of their concerns and, crucially, what would count as a solution.

## *Disgust*

Fear can be made respectable in political discourse by framing it in terms of managing risk, public protection and reducing crime. Anger is less easy to talk about, although it can be presented as righteous outrage expressing solidarity with victims. Although disgust is often apparent when crimes and punishments are talked about, it is even harder to avow. That which disgusts us may also make us fearful and angry, but disgust is conceptually quite distinct. Anger is hot; disgust typically chilly and distancing. When angry, you want to confront someone and (at least) give them a piece of your mind; when they disgust you, you want to keep away. Anger is directed at a perceived wrong; disgust is anxious about contamination (Nussbaum 1999).

Harms and threats arouse anger and fear, but some crimes violate a community's most sacred values, a desecration evoking disgust. A grave wrong contaminates a community, calling for specific actions or rituals of purification. *Cleansing* through punishment is a recurrent metaphor in justifications of retribution. Some crimes prompt disgust, the language in which they are spoken about disclosing this distinct emotion, with words like *scum* and *filth* used to vilify offenders (Duncan 1996). Some readings of prison history foreground the principles of cleanliness and good order that the architecture and regime of the prison were designed to instate (Evans 1982; McGowen 1995; Smith 2008). Moreover, holding people in squalid and insanitary conditions, without (any or sufficient) access to toilets and showers, as in many prisons and penal camps, makes it easier to regard them as disgusting and warrant further ill treatment (Duncan 1996).

The influence of disgust makes sense of some practices that are otherwise puzzling. For example, in most places a record of previous offending is taken to merit a weightier punishment: reoffenders have shown that their crimes are no temporary aberration but reflective of their character. Efforts to explain this without recourse to emotions are unconvincing (Tonry 2010). Anger (perhaps as exasperation) and fear (past behaviour taken as evidence of the future) have their effect. But abhorrence occasioned by disgust may also be part of the explanation.

Nussbaum (1999, 2004) insists that disgust has no place in a principled response to wrongdoing, while Whitman (2003) recognises that attitudes of disgust will invariably assault the dignity of the offender and lead to cruelty: perhaps it is psychologically impossible to avoid the inference that those responsible for the worst wrongs are themselves disgusting. Others have argued, however, that disgust has a proper contribution to make to moral and legal reasoning: ' repugnance is the emotional expression of deep wisdom, beyond reason's power fully to articulate it ... Shallow are the souls that have forgotten how to shudder' (Kass 1997: 20). Dan Kahan (1998) holds that disgust is the only appropriate response to the cruelties of some crimes: this alone matches up to the violation of our deepest moral commitments. He argues that disgust cannot be eradicated from criminal justice, even if that were desirable: it could only be forced 'underground', where its destructive influences would become all the harder to discern and challenge.

Fear is content merely to escape, whereas disgust 'puts us to the burden of cleansing and purifying, a much more intensive and problematic labor than mere flight, one that takes more time and one at which we fear we may not have quite succeeded' (Miller 1997: 26). In that case, another possible response to disgusting things or people is removal. This has a long history as a penal strategy through exclusion, banishment, galley-slavery, transportation and death – the eliminative ideal (Rutherford 1997). *This is someone who does not belong among us.* Reviewing Miller's (1997) book, Kahan writes:

> The social function of disgust ... is to construct and reinforce status rankings. Disgust sensibilities police social boundaries, determining who deserves esteem and admiration and who loathing and contempt. By feeling it and acting on it, individuals prevent subversion of the norms that keep the low in their proper place and assure the high their own pre-eminence.
>
> *(Kahan 1998: 1633)*

Chapter 1 should again be recalled, where criminal justice was characterised as a sequence of degradations: disgust, even more than anger, debasing the offender.

Disgust in itself is rather disgusting; it is not easy for people to articulate these sentiments. Disgust accordingly often disguises itself as something more respectable. Haidt and colleagues explored moral attitudes by setting out scenarios and asking respondents for their reactions (Haidt 2001, 2012). One hypothesis was that, among Western, well-educated, middle-class respondents, avoidance of harm is a decisive moral consideration: so long as an action does not do any harm, anything goes. To test this, harm was written out of some scenarios, which were designed to evoke *disgust*. The immediate (System 1) reaction prompted an aversive reaction, but since personal disgust seemed insufficient for moral condemnation, once engaged in debate at the level of System 2, respondents reintroduced harm into the scenario – even though it had been expressly written out. A form of confabulation takes place to rationalise (to ourselves as much as to others) what is essentially a reaction of disgust. This behaviour is unacceptable: it must therefore (my reasoning insists) be harmful.

Disgust may, for good or ill, be a response to the gravest crimes, but the term seems altogether too strong to describe reaction to more mundane offences. Disgust may be fitting for atrocity and cruelty, but hardly for minor theft or the use of drugs. Nevertheless, there are aversive reactions even to less serious crimes that cannot be adequately explained by reference to other emotions. Offenders may be spurned, reviled, disdained, despised, mistrusted, suspected or held in contempt. While these reactions fall short of disgust, they are related. And they all involve *a looking down* – the status ranking to which Kahan refers.

While anger and contempt often coincide phenomenologically, they are distinct:

> Whereas anger leaves open the possibility to repair the relationship, this option seems further away in the case of contempt … a lack of intimacy, a lack of control, and a dispositional attribution of negative behavior make the experience of contempt on top of one's anger more likely … the feeling of superiority over another person often present in contempt can be a mental means of gaining control that one does not otherwise have.
>
> *(Fischer and Roseman 2007: 113)*

This study found contempt would be more readily experienced in reaction to 'out-group members' – those believed to be (or now reconstructed as) 'other'. Attitudes of disgust may also be gendered:

what is regarded as merely gross or vulgar when done by men may be seen as disgusting if done by women. Brutal crimes against children, for example, attract an especially strong aversion when committed by women who are expected to show care and nurturing. Some women in prison report they were viewed with disgust by prison staff for their perceived betrayal of their motherhood (Baldwin 2021).

Contempt or disgust, more than anger or fear, lies behind a reluctance to seek or even allow an 'end to punishment' (see Chapter 5). This attribution of *being worthy of contempt*, moreover, seems especially difficult to shed and can even be seen as an intrinsic and inalienable characteristic. Thus, Zebulon Brockway at the Elmira Reformatory in New York invented a new category of prisoner – 'the degenerate', inherently debased and degraded, and elsewhere categories of women prisoners were identified as irredeemable (Goodman, Page and Phelps 2017: ch. 3). Resort to these ideas is by no means unusual in the history of the prison: even (perhaps especially) at times of confidence in rehabilitation and reform, there is found to be a residual class of the recalcitrant and incorrigible, for whom incarceration and eugenic sanctions are considered the solution (Garland 1985).

In summary, disgust and related sentiments are commonly at work, although often masquerading as fear or as righteous retribution. When people who have committed some of the gravest crimes are being considered for release, opposition is often articulated as fear by people who are in no position to make any considered assessment. Plausibly, they are implying an inherent and immutable characteristic like evil (or a secular equivalent like psychopathy) and calling upon all members of their community to share their sentiments of disgust. If that is right, these reactions will be entirely untouched by assurances of safety.

## Sadness, care and compassion

One universal emotion[5] that has received insufficient attention in discussions of punishment is sadness. Crimes, especially grave crimes, bring enormous distress and pain to people, to which a seemly response would be sadness. Sometimes, as more is discovered about background and context, this sadness is felt not only for the victim, but perhaps for all affected by the crime – including the families and associates of all concerned and the perpetrator. Reducing someone to their worst behaviour, to the status of offender, affords a reassuring insulation against a recognition that punishment heaps pains on top of the abuse, trauma and deprivation that have scarred the lives of many who commit crimes. Once rid of the idea that compassion is 'zero-sum' – that in the rhetorical opposition between offender and victim the more compassion for the one, the less is available for the other – it becomes easier to extend this reaction to encompass the wrongdoer as well.

Sadness and grief, as Nussbaum observes, can be overwhelming and may appear too passive, but their replacement by anger and its bogus promises of control can lead to further pain for the victim as well as to rash and unjust allocations of punishment. Sadness can be reflective and measured. It could encourage a community to consider how the outrage it feels can be turned into something of value – to support the victim, to do as much as possible to ensure such things occur less often and to reflect on what it is about their society that allows people to behave in such ways. Maybe sadness should be cultivated as a wholesome and salutary response to the miseries of crime.

Perhaps this is all too bleak. Might there not be some emotions with a more positive valence shaping attitudes towards punishment? After all, anger here is felt mostly on behalf of others, evincing a decent compassion for victims. It remains problematic, however, why concern and solidarity should be expressed through a zealous endeavour to harm wrongdoers, rather than focusing on the needs of victims. There are, to be sure, organisations and individuals dedicated to giving emotional and material support to victims, while no doubt always and everywhere many victims have been helped by the spontaneous reactions of families, friends and neighbours. Formal state-established mechanisms, however, have in many countries come much later in time and with a much lower priority than punishment. And they are rarely sufficient, almost never matching the enormous amounts societies seem prepared to invest in punishment.

While emotions urging punishment are mainly negative, other emotions are at work to constrain punitive excess – perhaps especially the 'moral emotions' (Haidt 2012; Canton 2015). Care for others can sometimes be urged on behalf of offenders or perhaps for their children who may be damaged by weighty punishment of their parents. Fairness encourages a proportionality to moderate severity, although its potential here may be limited (Lacey and Pickard 2015). Conceptions of liberty and aversion to oppression, notably as articulated in human rights conventions, can also curb punitive excesses. These constraining emotions may operate at the time of imposing the sentence, as the punishment is being carried out and when it has been formally fulfilled. The countervailing positive emotions, however, usually struggle to counter the will to punish, impelled by anger, fear and disgust, each with its inherent tendency to excess and to spread.

## Concluding remarks

This chapter has considered explanatory theories of punishment. Punishment is more than its material forms and understanding must involve attention to the several meanings found and made in its institutions and practices. Sometimes these difficulties are evaded by privileging one set of meanings over others, the hegemonic accounts of policymakers and legislators suppressing the experiences of others, especially the punished.

Reflections on the place of grand theory followed Garland (1990) in commending their value, seeking complementarity and synergies among accounts that are often unhelpfully put in competition by their most enthusiastic proponents, but also in recognising their limitations. Such accounts need to be supplemented by 'bridging' theories to explain how macro-level social structures engage with thoughts and feelings. For policy makers and penal agents:

> Economics matter. Crime trends matter. Racial, ethnic, and gender inequality matter. Wars, depressions, moral panics about gruesome violence – they all matter. But they do not matter in a vacuum. People make them matter. And people make them matter in particular ways (and not others) in the face of opposition from other actors who have competing visions of crime, punishment, justice, rights, freedom, and a host of other ideologically inflected issues.
>
> *(Goodman, Page and Phelps 2017: 123)*

The concept of hegemony helps to explain how some ideas succeed in commanding the support and confidence of a wider community, shaping the meanings they find in punishment. There may be a stimulus to change when the institutions and practices of punishment fail to chime with expectations of what punishment ought to be like. In these circumstances, the legitimacy of penal practice, forms and weights of punishment are called into question.

Emotions are key to understanding the meanings of punishment and accordingly to accepting or rejecting claims to legitimacy. Politicians have never doubted the emotional salience of punishment, sometimes looking to calm these feelings, but often provoking them to their own ends. Academic commentators recognise this salience too, although they differ in the degree to which they think emotions should have a place. Yet once the false polarisation between reason and emotion is jettisoned, it becomes easier to acknowledge that emotions do and should influence scholars, lawyers and practitioners. It is a truism that, unacknowledged, these emotions are likely to have unhappy effects, but where they are accepted and appraised (System 2 putting System 1 to test) wise policies and decisions are much more likely to result. Wisdom lies not in pretending that emotion has no effect but in questioning the counsel it seems to offer. Anger, fear and disgust can be valuable alarms, but, especially unexamined, poor advisers on action.

As practices become formalised, institutions are created, together with personnel to undertake their tasks, introducing other economic, political and social priorities which shape trajectories of penal development. These institutions are influenced by the character of the wider social order, by the social economy and by contemporary understandings of organisational governance. Purposes are avowed for institutions, although they may be compromised or even subverted in implementation. Convenience, or institutional or occupational self-interest, more than principle or purpose may determine the practices of punishment (Rothman 1980). Yet the argument here is that the emotional forces are always more than residual: where punishment fails to match up to these impulses, it will be said to fail, with calls for changes that better respond to anger, fear and disgust.

## Notes

1. David Garland's (1990) account is masterful. Other shorter but well-judged reviews can be found (Carrabine et al. 2014: ch. 15; Cavadino, Dignan and

Mair 2013: ch. 3; Scott and Flynn 2014). See further Simon and Sparks (2013) and Focquaert, Shaw and Waller (2021).

2. There are parallels here with Colin Sumner's accounts of censure. Often little or nothing can be said about 'criminals', but much can be learnt from a critical scrutiny of who is censured, how, by whom and with what consequences. (Sumner 1990; Amatrudo 2017).

3. See Nussbaum (2016: 22). This is not necessarily (of course) a desire for violent revenge personally exacted, but does expect that the wrongdoer experiences at the least some kind of discomfort – a deserved comeuppance of some sort – if only the guilty or shameful sense of having done wrong.

4. Another option might be separation through penal incapacitation, which could be seen as a hybrid of fight (forcible detention) and flight (distancing from danger).

5. Anger, fear and disgust are three of the six emotions argued to be universal since Darwin's *The Expression of the Emotions in Man and Animals* (Darwin 1872). The other three are happiness, sadness and surprise. People have refined this set of emotions but fear, anger and disgust appear on most lists.

# 3

# THE INSTITUTIONS AND PRACTICES OF PUNISHMENT

The last chapter ended with the proposition that the emotions of anger, fear and disgust are the principal motivations towards punishment. Forms and weights of punishment are not determined by this alone, but these emotions drive the will to punish and continue to affect the way in which practices are regarded, shaping attitudes towards them and moulding and constraining initiatives towards change when perceptions of failure brings institutions into disrepute (Smith 2008). Hegemonic ideas shape not only reasoning about crimes and punishments, but emotions too, insisting that certain harmful acts (but not others) must be deplored and that only particular weights and forms of punishment constitute an adequate response.

Yet there are other influences at work and, indeed, other emotions. Compassion, sentiments of fairness, aversion to brutality and fears about an over-mighty state can serve to mitigate some of the crude brutalities that have so often been used as punishment. There are also other responses to wrongdoing and wrongdoers that encourage the making of amends or offering tutelage and guidance towards better behaviour. These can involve hard treatment and coercion, but are not reducible to those effects and cannot be explained just by anger, fear or disgust. As forms of punishment are deployed for such purposes, the pain is by no means eradicated: a shift from punishing the body to training the mind might be not so much a project to punish less as to punish more effectively (Foucault 1977). For some, the delivery of pain remains at the centre of punishment (Christie 1981). Punishment also serves to *control* in a number of different ways – by coercion, but also by affirming moral standards and setting normalising routines.[1] This is among the purposes set for punishment for which emotions cannot fully account.

DOI: 10.4324/9780429055829-4

This chapter offers a critical discussion of the institutions and practices of punishment, a review that should expose the strengths and limitations of an explanation that foregrounds the emotions. At first sight, such an account seems much more plausible for some forms of punishment than for others. For example, anger seems necessary to explain how it is that so many brutal and even ingenious means have been devised to inflict pain (Newman 2008; Roth 2014). Torturous punishments have often involved excessive cruelties: 'Even in the supposedly most civilised forms of dispensing justice, a dark side remains' (Fassin 2018: 87). Fear and disgust, as much as anger, may lie behind the 'eliminative ideal' (Rutherford 1997) – primal acts of reprisal that expel the wrongdoer. Exile, galley-slavery and transportation involve the infliction of pain, but (unlike corporal punishment) also entail distancing and hence purging.

The death penalty is the ultimate elimination. This has been abolished in most countries and the numbers of people put to death has tended to decline even where it is retained. International human rights conventions, awareness of abuse in implementation, and miscarriages of justice have all lent momentum to these trends (Hood and Hoyle 2015). Less encouragingly, life sentences are increasing – and not only for those who would formerly have been put to death. Perhaps as many as half a million people across the world are serving formal life sentences (van Zyl Smit and Appleton 2019). Whole-life sentences (without parole), the functional equivalent of the death penalty, are also becoming more common, especially in the UK and the USA. The prison, then, is the modern institution that most plainly gives expression to the urge to exclude.

## Prison

Prison is at once altogether familiar and utterly strange (Davis 2003). When punishment is discussed, imprisonment is likely to be the first sanction to come to mind and is always prominent in political debate. Media reports, books, cinema and television provide both 'true' and fictional portrayals of prison. Yet very many people have never entered a prison, even more never detained, so that in their consciousness prison may remain both dread and mysterious. Imaginings about prison can be at least as powerful in moulding attitudes as glimpsing its realities.

Some prisons bespeak their authority in their external architecture, with an imposing façade and high walls. They express the power and majesty of the state, evoking awe among onlookers as surely as did the judicial processions of eighteenth-century England (Hay 1975). Others seem designed merely to intimidate, with ugly razor-wire fences, sometimes guarded by armed personnel. Some look more like dilapidated industrial units, rusty factories or ramshackle army barracks. Others again resemble farms or college campuses or small towns, or the sinister ordinariness of the high-rise Metropolitan Correctional Center in Manhattan (see www.bop.gov/locations/institutions/nym/index.jsp). None is welcoming; none a place you can just walk into or out of.

Prisons everywhere are all the same and everywhere different. While some characteristics are common and perhaps universal, prisons across the world and over time have differed in any number of ways (Skarbek 2020). They are 'dark mirrors, grand social doppelgängers, profound microcosms: life-distilled, caricatured, intensified' (Dreisinger 2016: 21), varying accordingly with the societies in which they are found. Among the factors that shape the character of a prison are: a conception of its purpose; a society's culture, including legal traditions and practices as well as political expectations; the relative affluence of a society and its willingness to commit resources to penal institutions; the degree to which a country is concerned to comply with international norms; the openness of institutions to external inspection and responsiveness to the findings; the authority or bare power of criminal justice professionals to determine its character.

These factors themselves change over time and are inflected by their mutual influences. Culture is not static, changing in response to circumstances, events, new ways of thinking and the influences of other cultures. The wealthy state of California allowed conditions in some prisons to deteriorate into squalor and was unable to afford the improvements the Supreme Court insisted on (US Supreme Court 2010; Schlanger 2013). Transitional democracies may seek to present themselves both as more responsive to public opinion and more accountable to international standards, with uncertain effects on numbers in prison and the conditions in which they are held (Canton 2006).

And within any country prisons will vary with size, the age and upkeep of the establishment, numbers, gender, catchment and length of stay of prisoners, staffing and many other variables.

There are probably more than eleven million people held in prison across the world (Coyle, Fair, Jacobson and Walmsley 2016) and few people seem able to imagine a society without prison. Yet criminologists and campaigners commonly denounce prison as a failure. The question they then frame is why it persists, often concluding that prison somehow serves the interests of the powerful (Foucault 1977; Reiman and Leighton 2013). To speak of failure, however, is to suppose a purpose and the purpose which is assumed and which prison so emphatically fails to achieve is reducing reconviction. Yet a number of purposes have been declared for confinement in prison: to hold people to stop them running away as they await trial or sentence or to prevent them committing crimes;[2] to coerce them into paying debts or fines; as punishment (Morgan and Liebling 2007).[3] And indeed prison mostly succeeds in its custodial, coercive and punitive uses. The aspiration to reduce reoffending is, historically, a later arrival and changes in the use and character of prison have rarely been influenced by evidence of its effectiveness in this respect. Prison, politically and in the public awareness, most conspicuously fails when people escape.

As prison detains, so it segregates. There is a clearly delineated boundary between the inside of the prison and the outside world, marked by walls or fences. There are in-between spaces – between the barrier at the entrance to the campus and the outer gate, the 'decontamination chamber' between the outer and inner gates – where someone is neither within nor yet outwith the prison. Like the visits room, these liminal spaces challenge the idea of a totally closed institution, suggesting that the walls and fences are more permeable, more porous than is sometimes supposed (Moran 2013). Even so, and while passage in and out of the establishment is policed with variable strictness, there is always a boundary and any blurring of it risks a subversion of the idea of the prison. Even an open prison (a somewhat paradoxical notion) has a clear demarcation between inside and outside.

If the most fundamental requirements are detention and segregation, prisons can fail by being so disordered that they seem no longer under the control of the authorities. Rioting in particular affronts the sovereignty of the state and subverts the meaning of imprisonment, especially when it spills beyond the walls or disorder is visible as in rooftop protest. But prisons may also be denounced for failure when they are seen as squalid and anarchic. Evans (1982) discusses Newgate, London's infamous prison in the eighteenth and nineteenth centuries, which came to be regarded as a warehouse of vice, filth and corruption. He juxtaposes the chaotic appearance of Newgate and the neat, unsullied façade of the new (1842) Pentonville, which aspired to clean away the very vices that were believed to burgeon in Newgate.

John Howard was outraged by filth, disease and contamination within the prison, which could even spread beyond the walls.[4] Within the prison, systems of segregation and classification originally seem to have been mainly an effort to avoid contamination – a constant threat from that which evokes disgust (McGowen 1995). As these systems came to be refined and bureaucratised, younger people were separated from old, women from men, repeat from first offenders. While a rationalised case can be stated for all these separations (security or 'treatment' requirements), the avoidance of contamination, in one sense or another, is a persistent concern. Movements for reform accordingly accelerated when prisons came to be seen as producers of disorder and contagion rather than order. Their production of immorality and filth undermined their intent to signify shame and hardship. 'They were semiotic disasters because they didn't look like prisons should' (Smith 2008: 63).

Prisons can also fail in their meaning because they are seen as lax or permissive – for example, the lazy journalistic trope of prisons as holiday camps or hotels, 'the country club prison' (Smith 2008: 85). Protests about indulgent regimes or conditions chime with the long-established and widespread insistence on 'less eligibility' – living in the workhouse or the prison should never be preferable to even the meanest living conditions of the law-abiding (Morris and Rothman 1995). Comfortable prisons, just like chaotic and squalid ones, don't 'look like prisons should'. Thus, while the eliminative ideal may rest content with secure segregation, the character of the institution will have to be seen to match up to the expectations required by the emotions of punishment.

The elimination that prison constitutes is usually temporary and the recognition that the great majority of prisoners will one day be released carries with it an implication that they should be 'better' (or at least no worse) than at the time of their imprisonment. It has long been an aspiration that prisons, and similar institutions like the workhouse, should effect such change and in the modern era success in this respect has been a principal criterion of evaluation. And it is precisely in this respect that they are commonly denounced as failing. Yet how might prison 'improve' people? Almost every factor known to be connected with desistance – family and other personal relationships, employment prospects, settled accommodation, sufficient resources – is damaged by imprisonment. As Carl Cattermole pointedly remarks, 'the cause of so many crimes is either trauma or poverty, and prison makes you poorer and more damaged' (Cattermole 2019: 11).

Nevertheless, the avowed intention to bring about positive change is part of prison history. Thomas Mathiesen (2006: 40) argued that 'Work, school, morality and discipline have run through the centuries as main pillars of thinking' – core themes in accounts of prison's reformative ambitions. Work may be variably burdensome or welcomed, depending upon the nature of the tasks, whether any profit generated is at least adequately remunerated or seized by the prison or an outside contractor so that workers are exploited (Davis 2003). For some, even the dullest work routines can feel preferable to the tedium of the cell. Education can be rewarding in terms of personal development, artistic expression and creativity (Dreisinger 2016), but may also be experienced as limiting, with the curriculum and learning environment restrictively controlled, obstructing other ambitions – 'particularly those that encourage individual prisoners to acquire autonomy of the mind' (Davis 2003: 57).

As for morality, at the birth of the modern prison, religious instruction, prayer and introspection were to be the means of reform, with obedience to orders and anticipation of surveillance designed to effect changes in behaviour to support moral progress. 'Treatment', including offending behaviour programmes, is perhaps the modern counterpart and this too can be beneficial or (and/or) an imposition, increasing the weight and tightness of imprisonment, aggravating its better-known pains (Crewe 2011; Sykes 1958). This is especially so if release is contingent on attendance at such programmes and when it is by no means clear what is expected of participants. The legitimacy of programmes in such circumstances is profoundly compromised. Crucially, anything that is valued by a prisoner can be co-opted in the interests of control, often spoiling any benefits that might be gained. Work and education opportunities may be granted or withheld as part of some form of incentive scheme; recreation and even family contacts can be used as instruments of control (Goodman, Page and Phelps 2017; Booth 2020a). Needs or rights can be constructed as 'privileges', contingent on good behaviour, and this can be seen as manipulative – and resented.

There are also persistent tensions among reformative ambitions and practical exigencies – between 'conscience and convenience' (Rothman 1980). For example, institutions need to be funded. Prisoners must be accommodated, fed, clothed, their basic needs met; staff must be paid, their work too often poorly remunerated. And if prisons are expected to pay for themselves, keeping up the establishment can compromise the intentions of policy. The 'silent system' insisted on no communication between prisoners, but once workshops were introduced to generate income, there had to be opportunities for people to speak to get their job done (Goodman, Page and Phelps 2017).

A central theme of the Woolf inquiry[5] into the rioting that had taken place in 1990 in prisons in England is that there is a plain connection between security and good order: disorder compromises security, as well as the safety of staff and prisoners. Yet Woolf also insisted on the importance of *justice* and the need for prisoners to feel that they are respected, their interests taken into account. Sometimes the report speaks as if these elements of security, control/good order and justice are in tension. Understood in this way, justice is always likely to be vulnerable. This became all too apparent when the promises of reform and enhancement of justice heralded by the Woolf report were derailed by high-profile escapes that led the Home Secretary to reassert security and his own conception of discipline (Dunbar and Langdon 1998). But the report also recognises the symbiotic relationship among these principles: just as good order supports security, a prison in which people are and feel treated fairly will be better ordered and hence also more secure. Legitimacy is central in securing consent and cooperation (Tyler 1990, 2003; Jackson et al. 2012; Tankebe and Liebling 2013).

There are compelling reasons, then, why the prison should strive to act justly. Regimes that depend upon coercion or repression are dangerously unstable. Where staff walk the landings and corridors, it is in everyone's interests for steadier relationships to be cultivated. Recognition of the humanity of prisoners can also elicit a sense of care or at least provide constraints against abuse. Fairness, at least in principle, is stoutly defended by the courts and it will always be relevant to denounce unjust treatment. Attention must therefore be paid, not only to the morality of the prisoner, but to the 'moral performance' of the regime (Liebling 2004). This matters not only, and perhaps not mainly, because of its contingent effects on reoffending, but because justice is owed to everyone. The perception of staff and prisoners is now established as an important criterion of evaluation, HM Prison and Probation Service conducting annual 'decency' audits (Gov.uk 2020; Liebling, Hulley and Crewe 2011).

Prisons can be deplored for their chaos and squalor – including inadequate sanitary arrangements, poor diets and limited or no access to health care – but also for cruelties and tortures: Supermax prisons (Lippke 2004; Haney 2003; Shalev 2013), Abu Ghraib and Guantanamo are perhaps the most prominent recent examples. Sometimes reports emerge to disquiet even the most punitive. Forced sterilisation has a long history in US and is said still to occur (Hunter 2017). The shackling of women during pregnancy and even in childbirth has been said to be 'endemic' in USA, with women of colour especially vulnerable to such abuse (Ocen 2012; Yearwood 2020). In 2019, a baby died in an English prison after a mother gave birth alone in her cell (Wood 2019). Prisons have been described as 'the largest providers of residential care for frail elderly men in the country' (Hill 2017), with HM Inspectorate of Prisons (2018) drawing attention to the social care needs of elderly prisoners: the incidence of dementia was admitted to be unknown, but there are numbers of elderly, infirm and bewildered people in prison. In the USA, mortality rates are disturbingly high, partly reflecting the poor health of many prisoners and problems of addiction (Russo, Woods, Shaffer and Jackson 2019; Sainato 2019). The systemic failures to meet the needs of vulnerable people, with fatal consequences, are attested in other countries too, including England and Wales (Inquest 2020). Sometimes, then, individual stories or investigative reports raise awareness of the essential humanity of people in custody and tears the fabric of the comforting insulation that protects society from recognising the miseries of incarceration. It becomes harder to reduce people to 'prisoners' when they can be seen as mothers, as children, as somebody's elderly relatives, as sick and vulnerable.

There are, to be sure, many influences on the character and development of prisons. For example, as the private sector extends its reach into the penal field (Bean 2020), it will have its own expectations about prison conditions, regimes and staffing. Staff associations and trade unions can exert pressure to defend their members' interests (Page 2011). Yet, to the extent that politicians are willing to take account of (and exploit) the views of the public, all these developments must take place within parameters set by ideas of what punishment and the prison ought to be like – parameters informed at a deep level by the emotions of punishment. Some of the harsher implications of anger, fear and disgust are mitigated by emotions of justice and care, but they retain their force. Prison distinctively satisfies these particular emotions: it imposes hardship to satisfy anger; it offers a level of security to assuage fear; and (critically and distinctively) it promises a separation, a distancing which, in the absence of recognised methods of cleansing, is the only remedy for disgust.

## Community sanctions and measures

Compared to prison studies, there has been markedly less scholarly inquiry and research into community sanctions and measures so that 'the supervision of adult offenders in the community has become something of a neglected and under-theorised zone' (Robinson 2016: 101). This is the case even though in most Western countries there are appreciably more people subject to community sanctions and measures (CSM) than in prison (McNeill 2018: ch. 3; Phelps and Curry 2017), while an awareness of their potential impact on wider aspects of society through the 'dispersal of discipline' might have been expected to prompt much further exploration and analysis (Cohen 1985). There is even a difficulty in naming these punishments. A common expression is *alternatives to custody*, but this is problematic for its implications: first, that imprisonment is a standard against which other sanctions are to be benchmarked; second that CSM take the place of imprisonment. The term CSM, favoured by the Council of Europe, is adopted here, although this expression introduces difficulties of its own – partly because 'community' carries different connotations and even denotations in different languages (Lacey and Zedner 1995) and partly too because of conceptual uncertainties about whether community could or should mean anything more than not-in-prison (Nelken 1994).

The aspiration that CSM might displace custodial sentences has naturally beguiled policy makers struggling to manage large prison populations, often held in cramped, sordid and unhealthy conditions, offensive to international standards of human rights. Yet the relationship between rates of imprisonment and its 'alternatives' turns out to be much more complex. Any displacement from imprisonment may be offset by a significant *widening of the net* (Cohen 1985), while recourse to prison when CSM conditions are breached also inflates prison numbers. A recent enquiry concluded that prison and CSM populations *both* rose in Europe during the period under study – growth that cannot be explained by an increase in levels of offending – and argued that the availability of CSM has had that net-widening impact (Aebi, Delgrande and Marguet 2015). Statistical aggregates can obscure local and specific states of affairs, however: sometimes CSM may have contributed to a reduction in prison populations; at other times it has tended to increase them or made no demonstrable difference either way (Phelps 2013; McNeill 2018).

CSM involve requirements – to do or refrain from activities, to attend at appointed times, to stay away from certain places or people, sometimes to reside where directed and almost always to notify changes of address. And people may not comply with such conditions. This introduces challenges of enforcement and compliance, matters that imprisonment does not have to confront – or not, at least, in the same way. The best prison regimes try to engage prisoners, but an uncooperative and recalcitrant prisoner is nevertheless being punished in ways that are recognised by the courts, the public and by prisoners themselves. But ignoring or compromising the requirements of a CSM without consequence looks like impunity. To establish CSM as credible punishment, requirements must be regarded as demanding or 'tough' and they must be rigorously enforced. But these two factors combined are likely to lead to increased violations and weightier consequences for default.

In the USA, nearly 30 per cent of admissions to state and federal prisons in 2017 were for violations of parole or probation (Bronson and Carson 2019) and a good half of all such admissions were for technical violations (missed appointments, for instance) rather than for further offending or even increases in assessed risk (Ocen 2019). The repertoire of responses to breach is limited and in consequence numbers of people in jails and prisons have been sent there because of failure to comply. It can be too readily assumed that a failure to respect the conditions of supervision is deliberate and reprehensible, although sometimes it is allowed that their 'chaotic lifestyles' can make a difference. In truth, there are many places on the spectrum between 'won't' and 'can't' and increasingly sophisticated understandings of compliance should lead to practices that are fairer, more responsive to the many reasons for non-compliance, and fewer violations (Bottoms 2001; Weaver, Piacentini, Moodie and Barry 2021). Legitimacy matters: those under supervision are much more likely to comply when they can see that what is asked of them is fair, even when requirements might appear intrusive or burdensome (Robinson and McNeill 2008; Ugwudike and Raynor 2013; Dominey 2019). Yet this insistence on securing compliance, cooperation and even 'coproduction' in the setting of objectives and the management of CSM does not always sit comfortably alongside political and public conceptions of what punishment ought to be like.

In many countries, probation agencies are primarily responsible for the implementation of CSM (sometimes in partnership with independent/'non-governmental' organisations or even for-profit companies), although not all countries have agencies that perform these 'probation' tasks. In Europe, attempts have been made to set standards for practice grounded in the European Convention on Human Rights and countries trying to establish probation systems have drawn on models from other jurisdictions (Canton 2009). Yet for all these pushes towards harmonisation, differences persist (Ruggiero and Ryan 2013; Robinson and McNeill 2016). Variations in organisation, personnel and activities have diverse origins, including national resources, legal and cultural traditions, historical contingencies, systems of governance (favouring centralised or more local arrangements), demography and geography. Another variable is the extent to which agencies are securely embedded in the penal system or are a newcomer, still striving to make their place in a judicial setting that may be wary of its pretensions. Their significance to a general public (if they are known and understood at all) may also be affected by perceptions of their authority and their beneficiaries. Are these agencies answerable to the prosecuting authorities and the courts, to the state, or to the local community? Are they more than an adjunct to a prison system? These considerations may all make a difference not only to the performance and effectiveness of CSM, but to their meaning and legitimacy.

Because of their difficulties in finding political champions or gaining public confidence, and their struggles to demonstrate effectiveness – in terms of reduced reoffending or in reducing prison numbers – their persistence has been said to be 'improbable', perhaps attributable to their capacity to adapt to changes in emphasis in penal policy (Robinson, McNeill and Maruna 2013). At different times, CSM have been presented as rehabilitative, punitive, reparative or simply as a convenient means of managing crime. The concept of rehabilitation itself has adapted to these differences of emphasis, capable of being presented as benign concern for an individual's welfare and/or as in the service of reducing risk for the benefit of victims and wider society (Robinson 2008).

While for some purposes of exposition and analysis it makes sense to consider CSM as a bloc, as it were, a distinct set of practices, there are important differences among them. There is a need for a more granular account to try to identify differences of nuance and significance among the different forms of CSM, chiming or jarring in their different ways with the emotions of punishment. Discussion, then, turns next to some of the most common forms of CSM.

## *Probation supervision*[6]

That one response to misbehaviour might be to offer the benevolent influence of a wise head – to guide and to counter temptations, fecklessness or influences of the wrong sort – is probably familiar always and everywhere. To this extent, the work of probation's pioneers was in beginning to formalise practices of this kind. Histories of probation conventionally begin with accounts of people of humanitarian vision with a distaste for avoidable punishments who encouraged courts to place offenders under supervision instead of sending them to prison or imposing financial penalties they were often unable to pay (Panzarella 2002; Vanstone 2004). Assurances to the court of mentoring or tutelage averted more punitive responses, especially for young people whose characters are usually believed to be malleable and who may be permitted some mistakes as they start to find their way in the world.

In the United Kingdom, the Probation of Offenders Act 1907 empowered the court to 'make an order discharging the offender conditionally on his entering into a recognizance ... to be of good behaviour and to appear for sentence when called on at any time during such period, not exceeding three years'. Recognizance means an undertaking, bond or promise, with an implication that further misbehaviour or maybe a failure to comply with supervision could have punitive consequences. The probation officer would support and encourage the probationer – 'advise, assist and befriend' them – to help them to honour their promise, but responsibility rested primarily with the individual, who would be called to account if this promise were broken.

The word *probation* denotes testing or proving and probation typically combines a conditional suspension of punishment with personal supervision. These two components have been given varying emphasis at different times and places: in the Anglo-American tradition, supervision used to be the defining characteristic; elsewhere, especially in countries with a civil rather than common law tradition, conditional suspension of punishment has been emphasised (Harris 1995).

In the Anglo-American tradition, probation began with an avowedly Christian mission, but throughout the twentieth century, it became progressively more scientific, secular and professionalised. Although scientific conceptions of the 'causes of offending' – and consequently of fitting and effective responses – had to some extent been present from its beginning (Garland 1985; Vanstone 2008), probation drew more and more on the social sciences. Offending was increasingly understood as an expression of a psychological flaw or malaise and in that case a promise to do better will not be enough: there will have to be intervention or treatment to 'address these causes of criminality' (Vanstone 2004;

Canton and Dominey 2017: ch. 2). Change was now to be effected by the skills of the probation officer: formal interventions, more than the probationer's promise to the court, became its focus. This shift of emphasis also contributed to the pretension of probation officers to the status of a profession (Bochel 1976).

What all this amounted to in practice is not easy to capture. Sometimes probation was regarded as a method in itself, although a diverse range of approaches were employed. There might, for example, be very practical assistance (in finding work or accommodation, or navigating systems of welfare benefits), combined with general support and encouragement. Various forms of psychological therapies were also attempted under the generic term *casework*, seeking to uncover and then treat the concealed traumas or anxieties that were supposed to lie behind much offending (Raynor and Vanstone 2002).

As probation tried to establish itself as a provider of interventions to reduce reoffending, it struggled to demonstrate its effectiveness. This began to change as promising results from research in Canada and USA showed that 'programmes' (structured sequences of intervention), properly targeted and delivered, had significant success. Interventions based on cognitive behavioural principles became widely accepted in Anglophone countries and parts of Europe as the way in which probation could demonstrate its effectiveness (Worrall and Hoy 2005; Lösel 2012; Canton and Dominey 2017: ch. 7). Strong claims were made for the model known as RNR (after its foundational principles of risk, needs and responsivity which were to guide the nature and intensity of intervention) (Bonta and Andrews 2007). Any disappointment in results might be attributed to poor implementation or to a political reluctance to allow practice to be led by evidence (Polaschek 2012).

More recently, a 'desistance paradigm' has become influential (Maruna 2001; Bottoms et al. 2004; McNeill 2006; Farrall and Calverley 2006; McNeill and Weaver 2010; Weaver 2015). This connects practice with 'criminal careers' studies, investigating the beginning, duration and cessation of offending in people's lives – with obvious relevance to enhancing probation's work (Rex 1999). While RNR aspires to change individuals, desistance emphasises the value of 'social capital': changes in people's thoughts, feelings and behaviour will not be enough unless they have opportunities to acquire the relational and material opportunities to sustain law-abiding lives (Farrall and Calverley 2006). Desistance research accordingly insists less on the need to 'change people' than on giving them chances to flourish. The role of probation might be in endeavouring to ensure their fair access to the resources they need and offering motivation and encouragement.

Desistance scholarship also emphasises the central place of relationships: 'desistance is co-produced between individuals-in-relation' (Weaver 2015: 212). This is not a matter of one person's influence upon another, but rather of the bonds and 'reciprocal orientations' among people in intimate relationships, families and friendship groups that enrich human lives. While the relationships that matter most are personal ones, the professional relationship with a probation officer or criminal justice social worker can be important (Rex 1999). Some people recall not only the practical help provided, but also the sense of personal interest and concern that they experienced and appreciated (Farrall and Calverley 2006).

Some aspects of desistance research challenge RNR, although there also seem to be opportunities to deploy the insights of these paradigms in complementary ways (Ward and Maruna 2007; Porporino 2010; Maruna and Mann 2019). Identifying differences, McNeill (2006) argued that while RNR sees professional intervention as decisive in reducing reoffending and protecting the public, the desistance paradigm prefers to regard such involvement as supportive and helping – a potentially valuable, but necessarily subordinate and ancillary contribution to an endeavour which must be 'owned' and led by individuals themselves. There is, perhaps, no small irony that after a century of development this conception of its proper place might return probation to somewhere close to its origins – helping people to honour their promises to the court not to offend, with professional treatment just one possible support to that process.

Irrespective of evidence of effectiveness, probation's foregrounding of personal relationships and its historic mission to 'advise, assist and befriend' seem at odds with what is expected of punishment. Probation agencies have sometimes attempted to address this by insisting on demonstrable burdens that supervision involves (Brownlee 1998). But success in persuading the public of probation's punitive weight or even its potential in this respect has been limited (Allen 2016).

And the more probation tries to emphasise its toughness – making increased demands with stern responses to infractions – the more it undermines some of its core objectives by bringing people to prison and obstructing desistance (Hyatt and Barnes 2017). Nor do probation staff understand their work in this way, often resisting the political characterisation of their work as punishment.

Probation has often struggled to gain public understanding, much less support, or to find political champions. Its meaning and significance are elusive: people know (or think they know) what it's like to be imprisoned, but it is hard to imagine the position of someone on probation (McNeill 2018). Even the most intensively supervised people spend almost all their time away from direct scrutiny, carrying on with all their usual activities so that the impact of probation is obscure. To the punitive-minded, the idea that offending results from psychological flaws or shortcomings in thinking looks like making excuses for bad behaviour. At the same time, rehabilitation, which probation more than any other agency has affirmed as its mission, has been impugned by others as a project of control. In symbiosis with the carceral project (Foucault 1977), probation has contributed to 'normalisation' and been charged with collusion with injustice by constructing the social inequalities that give rise to crime as individual pathologies.

In many parts of Europe and the USA, probation has increasingly been drawn into a system of corrections, adopting technical and bureaucratic processes, striving to demonstrate its efficiency but perhaps losing its soul in the process. It can be seen as a remote state agency, valued mainly for its contribution to managing swollen prison populations. In England and Wales, this has been aggravated by the replacement of many small local offices with large 'reporting centres'. But a different vision might instead bind probation to the communities it ought to serve, operating as 'hubs' alongside other community agencies, nurturing relationships and enabling people to have fair access to the resources that they need to accomplish desistance (McNeill 2018; Phillips, Albertson, Collinson and Fowler 2020). This vision has been most fully realised for women, even if many of the initiatives have been developed outside the formal probation service. With less direct emphasis on offending behaviour and interventions, the predicaments of women have been approached more holistically. '… the creation of a national network of community-based programmes and centres is undoubtedly one of the major achievements in demonstrating care for women in conflict with the law', with many positive evaluations of their effects (Gelsthorpe and Canton 2020: 63).

In England and Wales, recent preoccupation has been with governance – who should be running things, how services should be commissioned, how workloads apportioned and remunerated. Yet perhaps the prior question is what all this is *for* – a question that has to be answered in terms of meanings as well as set objectives. Perhaps its essence is the belief in the possibility of personal change, through help, encouragement and social inclusion. In this respect, probation makes statements. But perhaps the statements it makes – if heard at all – fail to chime with the emotions of punishment: this is not what is expected of punishment. In the following chapter, it will be seen that these benevolent intentions do not always correspond with the experiences of those subject to supervision. But this is less apparent to a suspicious public or politicians who protest about the lack of 'credibility' in this conception of community supervision. Since probation's credibility in reducing reoffending at least matches the success of prison, the problem lies in its meaning.

## Community service

If research into CSM has generally received less scholarly attention, community service has been especially overlooked in recent years. This is all the more to be regretted since the number of people undertaking community service is, in many countries in Europe, considerably larger than that of people subject to probation supervision[7] (Aebi and Hashimoto 2018). Community service involves undertaking work as a punishment and in some countries is known simply as unpaid work. Taken up in many countries over the past fifty years, part of its success is that (in contrast to some forms of community supervision) it is readily recognisable as a fitting response to crime – an actual or symbolic means of *making good* (Cornwell, Blad and Wright 2013). Intuitively, perhaps, there is something distinctively appropriate about making good for a wrong through toil.

Community service can be regarded as a burdensome punishment, as a form of symbolic reparation to the community, and perhaps as rehabilitative (Canton and Dominey 2017: ch. 12). These objectives can fit together but may also be in tension, making community service versatile but vulnerable to appropriation by those with a fixed or exclusive view of its purpose. Its meaning is contested, ambiguities nicely captured by the expression *community payback*, which could be taken as a punitive/retributive characterisation (*we'll pay you back for that*) or as reparative (*paying a debt to make amends*). The acceptance and success of community service may hinge on the meanings found in it, which can be conveyed through the kind of work undertaken. Work regarded as hard and burdensome will 'say' something to courts, victims, the offenders involved and the public; tasks that are of genuine value to the community convey something else; work that is of rehabilitative benefit will express something else again. Many schemes try to incorporate these several elements. Further variations of meaning relate to how the work is overseen and what follows if the order is ignored or work undertaken unsatisfactorily.

Whatever the perceived values or burdens of the work, the meaning of community service may also be affected by local social and cultural factors. For example, the feasibility and character of community service will depend on:

- a cultural view of what counts as punishment or as making amends;
- attitudes towards labour and the extent to which it can constitute either punishment or reparation;
- popular and judicial attitudes about what constitutes socially useful activity;
- an employment context (the availability of and remuneration for work); and
- a welfare state or other provision that enables people to give up time and labour without prejudice to their own and their dependants' well-being.

The manner in which community service is introduced, presented and subsequently develops can shed light on these and other important dimensions of the social order. For example, some of these considerations are *gendered*. The hard manual labour that may be regarded as suitable punishment for men, for instance, may in some cultures be seen as less appropriate for women. In the earlier days of the scheme in the United Kingdom, there was a marked gender difference with disproportionately fewer women receiving these orders (McIvor 2007; Worrall and Hoy 2005: 120), and while the numbers evened out, differences remained between the genders in how the sanction was used, the type of work assigned, age profile and likelihood of completion (McIvor 2007).

Community service affords an unusual opportunity to match a punishment to a crime. For instance, people who had painted graffiti could be required to clean walls; fly-tipping could lead to rubbish clearance or litter-picking. There are constraints here, including risks of humiliation, but community service could in principle adapt punishments to crimes in ways that could not be done by probation or imprisonment. In some countries, the public are invited to propose suitable tasks, while sometimes the talents and preferences of individuals are taken into account. Yet the larger a scheme becomes, the harder it becomes to assign work to suit the individual. Once risk factors and practical matters (like employment and family responsibilities) have been considered, assignment can end up being a matter of routine.

Community service achieves 'modest but important benefits' (McIvor 2016: 123), both for individuals and the communities where work is undertaken. At its strongest, it can represent a much richer meaning of *community* than other CSM. At the same time, community service acts out the tensions in the purposes set for punishment. No theory of punishment seems adequate to explain the trajectory of community service. It has not been significantly determined by evidence of effectiveness (for instance rates of reconviction), so much as political decisions about how it should be represented to courts and to the public. Here too principles are modulated by practical considerations of expediency, costs and system management which seem to have much more explanatory power than the grand theories. These factors are themselves shaped by wider social considerations, but they are more than dependent variables. The different meanings imparted can in turn mould the development of a scheme. For instance, protest about community service taking a particular form and failing in its punitive meanings might induce change and lead to other initiatives. The emotional sets parameters for the development of community service, then – feelings about what constitutes a fitting punishment, the meanings that are found and made in general and in particular cases, by policy makers, sentencers, practitioners, offenders, victims and the general public.

## *Electronic monitoring[8]*

Legend has it that it was Spiderman's experience of being tagged by a baddy with a device to keep track of his movements that prompted a judge in the USA to ponder monitoring offenders electronically (although a further inspiration for the same judge was the tagging of livestock) (Burrell and Gable 2008). The judge thought home detention might be monitored and devices have become widely used for this purpose. An ankle bracelet is linked (using radio frequency technology) to a transceiver installed in the individual's place of residence, a monitoring centre alerted if the person leaves the premises at any forbidden time. The duration of the electronic monitoring (EM) order and the hours of restriction can be matched to the seriousness of the offence as a punishment and/or to manage risks through these controls. Unlike Spiderman being tracked by his adversaries, those early (and still most commonly used) devices cannot otherwise disclose the individual's whereabouts.

More recently, technological developments have made possible the use of devices that use global positioning systems (GPS) to determine a precise location (introduced in England and Wales in November 2018). GPS tracking seems to have several advantages over radio frequency devices, although the equipment is more expensive and has technological frailties and limitations. Its main use in England and Wales has been to check if people have entered areas forbidden to them – exclusion zones (Hucklesby and Holdsworth 2020). It can also provide evidence of absence from or presence in specific locations, to provide a convincing alibi against accusations of other crimes – or maybe to overturn one. Even the radio frequency technology can at least ensure that someone is where they are required to be at specified times or, if not, that this would immediately be detected. This promise of certain detection of non-compliance, adding to EM's credibility in support of other community sanctions and measures, is perhaps its most conspicuous advantage. EM cannot prevent someone going out, although knowing this would trigger an alarm may act as a deterrent. Much depends, however, on what happens when this alarm goes off. Responses can vary within and between countries. These include immediate checks by phone, home visits, advice about future compliance, warnings, formal reports or breach action which may lead to eventual custody. In some overburdened systems, there may be no response at all.

A common aspiration is that EM might reduce the size of the prison population, concerns about which have significantly determined its use in many countries. It has been used as a bail requirement (perhaps as an alternative to custodial remand) and a condition of early release, as well as a community sentence. But it does not follow that the technology somehow makes these things possible and that the prison population would be higher but for their use. It has been political decisions that have determined their use in these ways. In some European countries, it seems that EM may have contributed to reducing rates of imprisonment when used relatively sparingly, but jurisdictions with high use of EM also have high prison populations (Hucklesby et al. 2016). The relationship is uncertain, but there is little compelling evidence to support the original ambition.

A critical difference between the use of these devices and the deployment on Spiderman is that individuals know (have to know) they are tagged. Since tagging requires less active agency than most other CSM, it could be assumed that assent is irrelevant. Yet the individual's reaction to the tag matters. Any enduring value from EM is thwarted unless understanding, legitimacy and compliance are cultivated. This is of particular significance if the technology is intended to support rehabilitation, which was part of the original vision and at various times has been adduced to justify its use (Hucklesby 2008; Nellis 2016). At first sight trying to ensure someone's whereabouts is a strange type of 'rehabilitative intervention'. The tag neither knows nor cares about an individual's thoughts or behaviour: staying put is enough to comply. Still, the rationale of the panopticon was that prisoners, not knowing when they were being watched, would conform their behaviour as if they were under observation, so acquiring proper routines of behaviour and thinking that would become soon familiar and then automatic. Perhaps EM could work in this way; it could be desistance-supporting, if not exactly rehabilitative, replacing 'bad habits' with better ones (Hucklesby 2008).

EM is most effective in reducing reconvictions in combination with supportive interventions (Graham and McIvor 2015) and its relationship with other CSM, especially probation supervision, remains a topic of inquiry and debate (Nellis 2016). Detaining someone at home could be regarded simply as punishment, although its acceptance as such, by courts and by the public, is likely to depend on its being recognised as hard treatment. For some, confinement to home will be a burden, frustrating their wishes to go out at certain times, although this will vary with age, affluence, employment and recreational preferences. EM can also have an impact on other members of the household, who may find themselves confined with someone irascible or violent, or subject to intrusive home visits from monitoring agencies. Strained relationships can deteriorate further (Hucklesby and Holdsworth 2020).

When first envisaged, electronic tracking technologies were cutting edge if not futuristic – available to the foes of Spiderman and James Bond (*Goldfinger*), but not for ordinary folk. Years on, these technologies are utterly commonplace. All kinds of objects and commodities are tracked, as are (in many countries) domestic pets and livestock. Our smart phones, moreover, disclose not only our whereabouts, but reveal much about our habits, lifestyles, consumer preferences and even political inclinations – information which can be gathered, collated and used for commercial and political purposes. Unlike the 'carceral project', where mechanisms developed in penal institutions were then exported to wider society (Foucault 1977; Cohen 1985), these are technologies that have been developed mainly for different purposes and then put to use in the penal system. Their contemporary ubiquity makes penal monitoring at once seem less like punishment (what hardship for offenders to be tracked if everyone is?) and for just the same reasons stirs fewer anxieties about privacy, which at one time troubled some people about EM. It remains the case that EM poses several ethical challenges that call for principled responses (Nellis 2015).

Arguably, electronic monitoring was originally a technology in search of a purpose – something done because it was possible. It is a penal practice first enabled and then driven by technological, economic and commercial interests (Paterson 2007). As with other sanctions, its subsequent development has rested not so much upon any demonstrable effectiveness in reducing reoffending (unsurprisingly, the evidence is complex and uncertain: Belur et al. 2020) or because of its impact on the prison population. While its trajectory has had less to do with public reaction, its use and acceptability are shaped by its ability to engage with the emotions that punishments are expected to satisfy. Specifically, it may be difficult to persuade courts and the public that either home detention or location tracking are hard enough treatment to amount to the punishment that outrage demands or that it can assuage fear, with incapacitative and controlling effects that fall well short of the security that prison is felt to provide.

In summary: different CSM encounter problems of their own, but a common difficulty is in explaining their meaning and point to courts and to the public. In particular, they often fail to meet public expectations of what punishment ought to be like. They are felt to be insufficiently burdensome to count as punishment, thus failing to match up to the anger that many crimes arouse. Again, even the most intensive surveillance fails to provide the same level of assurance of safety as prison does, so failing to calm fears. The distancing that the sentiment of disgust demands is also not achieved: 'they' are still among 'us'. In that case, while some commentators take pride in CSM because they succeed in holding people in the community, this is precisely among the messages that many people don't want to hear.

Public doubts notwithstanding, the hazards of CSM are increasingly being recognised in research. Aware of the miseries of imprisonment and beguiled by their own worthy intentions, champions of CSM have advocated their wider use and they have expanded to a point where researchers identify a phenomenon of 'mass probation' (Phelps 2013, 2018; Phelps and Curry 2017; McNeill 2018). The upshot has been often disproportionate sentencing (where CSM take the place of lighter penalties like discharges), even as their limitations (at best) in reducing prison populations are becoming all too apparent. So far from becoming a plausible response to 'penal excess', CSM are coming to be regarded as part of the problem (Hayes 2015, 2019; McNeill 2018). Driven by political imperatives to discover 'what works' and to demonstrate effectiveness, probation agencies have been set objectives framed in these terms. And when this project fails (or cannot be shown to succeed) this can be used as a stick to beat these agencies. But it is their communicative shortcomings and their failure to match up to emotional expectations of what punishment should be that make them politically vulnerable.

## Financial penalties

An altogether common sanction that does not involve imprisonment (save sometimes in default) is a fine or other financial penalty. If the prison is likely to be at the centre of most people's penal imagination, financial penalties are at the very edge. Yet while relatively few people have been in a prison, very many have had to pay fines, which are levied not only by the state for crimes, but by many organisations for infractions of regulations. The fine is by far the most common criminal punishment, accounting for at least 70 per cent of sentences in the lower courts of most countries (O'Malley 2013: 388), 78 per cent in England and Wales (Ministry of Justice 2020), and 84 per cent in Germany (Bögelein 2018).

The feeling that a person who has committed a crime has incurred a debt to be repaid is common and deep-seated (Radzik 2009). In most modern forms of punishment, however, the 'repayment' is metaphorical. Imprisonment may be represented as 'paying a debt to society', but it is an odd repayment that puts the creditor to further expense through the costs of prison or a CSM. At other times and places, crimes and wrongs have been understood to incur a financial obligation, with further consequences in default. Punishment and debt have thus been yoked together through practices like penal slavery, peonage, debt bondage and debtor imprisonment (Atwood 2008).

Making payment, in compensation or as punishment, is a very old and well-established response to wrongs, both civil and criminal. Some historical accounts suggest that coming to understand an action not as a private wrong against an individual but as a 'crime against society' was part of the state's assertion of a monopoly of the power to punish. It was also a way of raising income, diverting payments formerly paid to victims in compensation into the Crown's coffers (Johnstone and Ward 2010). This is an aspect of the dispossession of the victim that commonly accompanies the formalisation of penal practices (Christie 1977). Not all places or times make the familiar distinctions between fines, compensation or damages and sometimes payments have carried all of these meanings. As ever, in attempting interpretation, it is necessary to beware of anachronism or cultural misapplications. Nevertheless, as Fassin concludes, 'Punishment used to entail a debt to repay; it has become a suffering to inflict' (Fassin 2018: 47).

Fluctuations in the use of fines have been variously associated with levels of actual or perceived poverty (Rusche and Kirchheimer 2003 [1939]), changes in a society's means of production (Bottoms 1983) or in patterns of consumption (O'Malley 2009), and in ways and standards of living (notably the use of the motor car; O'Malley 2013). Yet connections have also been suggested with shifts in confidence about the ability of other sanctions to achieve 'correction': when this is thought feasible, fines tend to decline; where there is scepticism about the effectiveness or value of correction, fines may become more favoured again (ibid.). For the fine, in contrast to many other penal sanctions, professes no reformative ambition: it attempts to regulate unwanted behaviours with no pretensions to understand or influence anybody's character beyond an assumed deterrent effect.

Von Hirsch (1993: 9) identified the difference between a tax and a fine: 'the fine conveys disapproval or censure, whereas the tax does not'. Yet the pragmatic Bentham referred to a financial penalty as a *licence paid in arrears*. For the crimes of the affluent and powerful, a financial penalty can look like no more than a business overhead. Even in the worst cases of pollution or disregard for health and safety leading to injury or death, penalties can be disproportionately minor where there is even prosecution at all (Tombs and Whyte 2008). In a capitalist economy, even wrongdoing can be assigned a monetary value. The minimisation of censure has been compounded by the proliferation of on-the-spot fines, where there are compelling disincentives to contest the penalty and the right to require the state to prove wrongdoing is bypassed.

Fines might have retributive potential although, while it must look heavy enough to be recognised as a punishment, it must still be payable by people with limited means. This consideration, and the retributive requirement for equality of impact, entails that the amount and rate of repayment ought to accommodate differences between rich and poor. Bentham recognised this, at one time regarding the fine as an optimal punishment (O'Malley 2013), and modern unit or day fine systems try to incorporate the principle (Easton and Piper 2016: ch. 7, §3.1).

The fine is not the only or even the most burdensome of financial demands. The association between punishment and money has the plain consequence that the burden of prosecution and almost all forms of punishment weigh disproportionately on poorer people. In various ways, poverty can bring it about that this person but not that one is prosecuted, convicted or imprisoned, while in some places, corruption allows the rich to evade justice altogether. As Dreisinger puts it, 'In various incarnations all over the world, money and justice are bonded together in unholy matrimony' (Dreisinger 2016: 115). A range of fees, costs and surcharges may be levied throughout the criminal process (Harris, Evans and Beckett 2010), while poverty significantly intersects with race, gender and other dimensions of difference to compound social injustices.

Some states in the USA have experimented with charging fees for costs of incarceration (Wacquant 2002), although these have sometimes fallen into disuse when costs of recovery far exceed any revenue. Sometimes people subject to CSM have been made to pay for their supervision, varying the meaning of the punishment with an intimation that the offender is a 'customer' purchasing supervision from a 'provider' (Teague 2016). Requiring people to pay such costs might be regarded as no more than what is deserved, but that people should incur a double punishment in this way has been argued to be wrong in principle (Beckett and Harris 2011). Default can result in imprisonment, leading critics to deplore a return of debtors' prisons (Natapoff 2018), bringing distress to individuals and families, obstructing desistance and aggravating prison over-crowding in order to make money for private companies. Metaphors of debt carry the implication that pains suffered are always the fault of the debtor (Graeber 2011). Similarly, the pains of punishment are blamed on the offender, shielding against any unease that these pains fall upon others (for example children), or persist beyond anything that might be considered retributively just.

Deflecting attention away from the character of the agent and towards the act, the fine lacks the emotional pull of other punishments.

Nevertheless, there is likely to be dismay and indignation where fines are felt inadequate to match the seriousness of a crime. On the other hand, sentiments of fairness and compassion may be engaged where impositions and consequent hardships are seen as excessive or borne by the wrong people, even though these effects are commonly invisible to the public.

## Conclusions

To understand what punishment 'is' it is necessary to attend to the forms that it takes, how these practices are represented, how received and interpreted by their several audiences. The perceptions of politicians and sentencers are not all that matter: especially in a democratic society, penal policy cannot disregard public attitudes and their implications for legitimacy. Perceptions feed back into practices and have their effects, even though these are mediated by other influences besides. Decisions are significantly influenced by the degree to which types of punishment match up to expectations of what a punishment ought to be like and this commonly weighs much more than arguments made for 'effectiveness' – where evidence anyway is invariably complex and contestable (Hamilton 2021). If imprisonment, for example, persists despite its conspicuous failure in almost all the formal objectives set for it, it may be because of its distinctive capacity to answer to those emotions that drive the will to punish: anger (through the imposition of hard treatment), fear (by promising a security that no non-custodial sanctions can match) and disgust (by the segregation of wrongdoers).

Many discussions offer 'a deterministic kind of social theory ... in terms of a deep background of historical and structural change rather than a foreground of ongoing activity and interpretation' (Smith 2008: 37). But Smith warns that to see changes driven by refinement and transformation of power loses the importance of symbol and agency, of meaning and feeling – immediate influences on attitudes, policies and practices. Smith persuasively applies the argument to the death penalty and to imprisonment, while this chapter has attempted to extend these insights to CSM and fines. This is not to minimise the importance of social economy or the instruments of power: the concept of hegemony connects class interests and power with the cognitive and emotional commitments that shape attitudes. But emotions have their own claim, not reducible to other factors. Even if they were so reducible, any explanation which loses sight of meaning is to that extent insufficient.

Several emotions are at work, sometimes impelling penal practice in different directions, and a range of other forces besides channelling its development. These include contingencies like the emergence of new technologies, sometimes fuelled by commercial expansion, and considerations like the size of the prison population which have shaped the trajectory and character of CSM, despite the limited evidence to show their potential to reduce prison numbers. As policy works its way into practice, it can be subject to adaptations, compromises and even subversions. There are disputes about the origins of probation, for instance – whether its avowed benevolent intentions should be accepted at face value or whether this masks a 'real' project of exercising control, all the more insidious for its pious pretensions (Young 1976; Vanstone 2004). Yet whatever the original motivations (whose?), practices soon liberate themselves from the intentions of their founders until their association with their original ambitions becomes complex and even tenuous. This is why motivations cannot be inferred from effects – nor indeed outcomes from motivations.

Practices are formalised and institutions established, which acquire interests and objectives of their own. As this has occurred, 'the emergence of a powerful penal bureaucracy has done much to remake modern punishment in its own image' (Garland 1990: 188). Policy makers and institutional representatives articulate their mission in the language of rational, utilitarian purposes, as bureaucracy requires, although the emotional forces persist, however sublimated or repressed. Practice is further modified as practitioners, as individuals and in association with colleagues and with other agencies, try to undertake their work and to realise (and sometimes resist) policy instruction.

This chapter has enquired into forms and institutions of punishment and the meanings found and made in them. Yet the endeavour to understand what punishment is and means also requires an appreciation of the perspectives of those who undergo it, as well as those involved in its administration and delivery. It is to these (historically neglected) questions that the next chapter turns.

## Notes

1. Sometimes critics of punitivism conflate pain delivery and control, but they are separate projects and ones that may be in tension. Pain delivery is a weak means of control, while the most effective forms of control involve the recruitment of consent rather than threats.
2. The familiar political claim that people cannot commit crimes while inside blithely overlooks the very high rate of offending that take place in prison – not only against other prisoners and staff (O'Donnell and Edgar 1998; Howard League 2014, 2015), but even a continuing involvement in 'outside' criminal activity (see Chapter 4).
3. While these distinct rationales are important on legal grounds and for historical exposition, no doubt compulsory confinement has always been experienced as and commonly intended to be punishment. As Fassin (2018) insists, this may be enough to qualify as punishment, whatever the philosophical definition (see Chapter 1). Even as the pains of detention have always been recognised, loss of liberty as a punishment may depend upon some prior conception of a right to liberty, an ideal which Davis (2003) suggests emerged from the Enlightenment.
4. An anxiety expressed in recent times when prisons in some parts of the world are recognised as a source of infectious disease (e.g. Sarang, Platt, Vyshemirskaya, and Rhodes 2016).
5. The report has (to my knowledge) never been available online and copies are hard to get hold of. Prison Reform Trust (1991) offers a succinct and reliable summary. See also Morgan 1992.
6. While this section considers community supervision under the generic term 'probation' (a community sanction imposed by a court), much of the discussion also applies to parole (the licence period after leaving prison – see Chapter 5). There are other terms in use for the practices here denoted as probation.
7. Counting is complicated by the many different forms of supervision used across Europe.
8. This section considers devices to determine an individual's location. It does not discuss other technologies – for example, voice verification, reporting booths or remote alcohol monitoring. For the use of various devices, see Nellis, Beyens and Kaminski 2013; Nellis 2016; Hucklesby and Holdsworth 2016; Belur et al. 2020.

# 4

# BEING PUNISHED

This chapter considers what punishment means to those subject to it. As Lori Sexton insists, 'Punishment is not just something that is done – it is something that is done *to* people and experienced *by* people' (Sexton 2015: 115, emphasis in original). Her research investigated the perceptions of the punished. The thoughts, feelings and behaviour of penal agents matter too. Indeed the interactions and dynamics between the punished and the punishers fundamentally affect their respective experiences. Wherever such interactions occur, meanings are found and made, imposed and resisted, negotiated and compromised.

Punishment has been said to have a communicative intent, addressing several audiences. Beyond the pronouncement and publication of the sentence of the court, however, the communications of punishment will be heard only by those undergoing punishment and those closest to them. Yet the meanings that legislators or sentencers might have hoped to convey to offenders could be radically undermined in implementation. Formal accounts articulated in policy statements and in law set out various rationales and intentions, but it may not be assumed that any of this accords with the experience of the punished and the punishers. The endeavour here, then, is to appreciate the experiences and interpretations of those subject to punishment rather than relying on the official accounts. Without some such understanding it is impossible to gauge the extent to which punishment achieves the purposes set for it. Other

DOI: 10.4324/9780429055829-5

consequences that are no part of anybody's stated purpose but may damage the justice or efficacy of punishment may be elusive but just as necessary to comprehend.

## Being punished

The history of punishment has been excessively, however understandably, reliant upon published and thus accessible documentation. Legislation and policy statements, however, are declarations of aspiration – how legislators and policymakers think that punishment ought to be undertaken – and these ambitions have often been thwarted or at least compromised in practice. There are other accounts to be heard besides. Defendants and offenders, their families and friends, victims of crime, courts, probation and prison staff and the wider community all have perceptions of what the penal system meant to them, ways in which they were respected, felt let down or simply ignored. These experiences, however multifarious and elusive, are quite as much a part of its history as the more formal accounts and go to make up part of what punishment was and is.

There are several reasons why much more needs to be understood about how punishment is experienced. Since retributive justice rests on ideas of fair and proportionate punishment, there is a need for a fuller understanding of what these are (Hayes 2016). The pains, effects and significance of incarceration vary considerably (Tonry 1996). There may, for example, be vulnerabilities associated with age; responsibilities of caring may bring additional upset to the offender as well as their dependents; illness and disability may aggravate the pains of imprisonment; cultural sensibilities may make confinement additionally distressing; loss of accommodation or employment commonly add to the weight of imprisonment and are all the heavier for those with fewer protective resources. Similar variations in impact arise for financial penalties and community sanctions. These considerations have a plain relevance to judgements about a deserved punishment (van Ginneken 2016a; Hayes 2018).

Some insist on the central relevance of subjective experiences to a just determination of sentence, while others substantially reject these arguments (for penetrating discussion and references, see Hayes 2016,

2018). Yet since the impacts of all punishments are most severe for the most vulnerable and those with least resources, a failure to take this into account risks compounding social disadvantage in the name of justice. This debate cannot even get off the ground unless efforts are made to discover the true effects and no one is better placed to bear witness to this than the punished. Relatedly, censure theory, foregrounding the reprobative character of punishment (du Bois-Pedain and Bottoms 2019), must have regard to offenders' perspectives. Censure communicates and how such communications are heard and understood by its audiences and especially by the offender must form part of its account (Duff 2001; Rex 2005; Schinkel 2014).

Attention to the lived experiences of the punished also brings opportunities to enhance the quality of penal interventions. Much (not all) of the criminological tradition has regarded offenders more as objects than as subjects, inquiring into causes rather than the reasons that are usually looked for when trying to understand human behaviour – reasons that agents themselves might seem uniquely placed to explain.[1] This 'correctional perspective', where the urge to suppress crime interferes with a proper understanding, risks 'losing the phenomenon – reducing it to that which it is not' (Matza 1969: 17).[2] The idea of offending as a symptom of some underlying pathology encourages that perspective. Individuals' articulation of their difficulties might be over-interpreted, even taken as just a symptom of their 'real' problems, and not taken seriously in its own terms. All this encourages a dismissal of offenders' own accounts as unreliable and self-serving. David Matza's (1969) proposal was for an 'appreciative' inquiry, respectfully heeding individuals' accounts of their behaviour and experiences, without condescension, collusion or romanticisation – which he also warned against.

To engage people actively in processes that often make such a difference to their lives is a moral duty. Where the views of the punished are disregarded legitimacy is eroded and reductive effectiveness potentially undermined (Sherman 1993). Key decisions should be discussed with those undergoing punishment; their preferences will not always prevail, but they should be and feel heard. This is one component of the procedural fairness that underpins compliance with the law – complying because this is recognised to be the right thing to do, apart from any instrumental/prudential incentives, costs and benefits (Tyler 1990; Tankebe and Liebling 2013). Soliciting the views of service users has become common practice for many agencies, but the institutions of punishment have been late to come to this. Individual voices have sometimes been able to make themselves heard through campaigning and writing, but have rarely been able to exert their due influence on policy and practice. This neglect betrays and upholds an attitude that their opinions are unworthy and suspect – a *testimonial epistemic injustice*.

Testimonial injustice may be said to take place when 'the hearer makes an unduly deflated judgement of the speaker's credibility, perhaps missing out on knowledge as a result; and the hearer does something ethically bad – the speaker is wrongfully undermined in her capacity as a knower' (Fricker 2007: 17). Miranda Fricker centres her discussion on credibility deficits associated with gender and race, but this applies no less to the punished: this is a manifestation of an *identity power* that is exercised to suppress people who, regarded as offenders, are defined in terms of and reduced to their worst behaviour. It is a structural operation of power that persists irrespective of the behaviour of individuals. The injustice is also 'systematic', a term which Fricker uses to mark an association with and grounding in a wider set of injustices. This functions to the detriment of all parties – not only (and most saliently) offenders whose experiences are discounted or trivialised, but also policymakers and practitioners whose work could only be enhanced by attending respectively to these perspectives. This testimonial injustice could be understood as precisely the opposite of hegemony (Chapter 2). Hegemonic discourse sets an agenda, proposes how people are to think and feel about crime and punishment, suppressing alternative accounts. This too is 'systematic' in Fricker's sense, reflecting and reinforcing a structural operation of power.

When the experiences of people subject to punishment have been examined, it turns out that its pains do not always take the form or intensity that might be imagined. Sexton (2015: 120) distinguishes between objective and subjective hardships:

> The objective component, which I call the punitive referent, is the object, event, or condition being experienced as punishing. Punishment, in contrast, is determined by the prisoner's subjective

assessment of why the punitive referent is, in fact, punishing. ... punishment is what a prisoner makes of a punitive referent.

For example, prison beds may be hard and lumpy and the food horrible (the concrete objective components), but account must also be taken of what all this means to the prisoners. Squalid conditions express a disdain that carries symbolic weight quite apart from its intrinsically unpleasant qualities, saying much about how society and the institution regard you and perhaps how they think you ought to regard yourself.[3] Punishments 'representative of larger losses or injustices' (Sexton 2015: 125) weighed especially heavily. While concrete pains and privations can be grasped readily enough, the more abstract and symbolic dimensions require a degree of imagination and empathy which emotions of anger, fear or aversion make many people reluctant to exercise. Yet Sexton found these abstract pains were regarded by prisoners as relatively more severe than the tangible and visible pains of the 'punitive referent'.

## *Prisoners*

Segregation stands as a defining characteristic of prison: it serves to exclude prisoners from a 'general public' who are presumed to be comforted by their absence. It also starkly and painfully separates them from those who love and miss them. Yet the separation that imprisonment constitutes is not total (Cunha 2014) and prison walls may be more porous than is commonly supposed (Skarbek 2020). Visitors come and go, staff return to their homes and arrive back for their next shift, while letters, TV, radio, Internet and newspapers open up channels to the world. Much of the lived experience of prison is deeply affected by the ways in which the world is envisioned – by the hopes, dreams, worries, fears and fantasies about the outside, by longings and doubts about personal relationships, by anxieties and maybe ambivalence about anticipated release.

The prison in turn has its effects on the outside world. Ben Crewe (2016: 83) observes 'street culture ... has itself been deeply imprinted by norms and values from the prison that have been re-exported and integrated over many years'. Even the reassurance of incapacitation is unsettled by learning that in California 'prison gangs are the de facto government for street gangs across the state', while gangs in Brazil have a 'powerful reach into the free world' (Skarbek 2020: 6). In England too, concerns have been expressed about prisoner involvement in crime outside (Milmo 2020) and no doubt the same would be found in many other jurisdictions.

Even porous walls are still barriers and the prison walls that effect separation at the same time create a distinct grouping or community. There has been extensive research into this 'society of captives' (Sykes 1958) – the relationships that are formed, the culture and character of the prison, how order is established[4]. Many prisoners themselves have written about prison (Nellis 2012), often challenging or even subverting the dominant discourse (Morgan 1999). Few of these works have made much difference to practice – a plain example of testimonial injustice. Yet while some accounts are lurid and sensational, much can be learned from these writings that might inform policy (Nellis 2002).

Recent scholarship has also explored sensory phenomena, the immediate and vivid experiences of the sounds, sights, touches, tastes and smells of the prison (Herrity, Schmidt and Warr 2021; https://sensorycriminology.com). While prisoners and staff may become habituated, newcomers and visitors are struck by strange sensory experiences – rattles, clangs and shouts, the visual drabness of the wing, distinctive and often unpleasant smells. Less obvious, although all too plain to prisoners, are sensory deprivations – the scarcity of opportunities to hug, or of calming sights like green spaces and even the sky, which may be reduced to no more than Oscar Wilde's 'little tent of blue' (Wilde 1999 [1897]). These somatic experiences are powerful in shaping what it is like to be in prison and haunt memories.

The prison is faced with all the practical, material, economic and social concerns that any other community has to manage. There is a need for accommodation, food, health care, personal safety, work, education and passing the time. In relatively affluent countries, some of this is provided, although this cannot be taken for granted everywhere (Skarbek 2020). Yet custodial confinement poses distinct problems. The roles of prisoners and custodians generate tensions and there has been extensive research into the question of how order is established and maintained (for overview, Crewe 2016). The management of routines, of space and of time are fundamental to maintaining security and order.

Even though in the final resort imprisonment is irreducibly coercive, recourse to force is dangerous for everyone and is neither reliable nor sustainable as a means of ensuring order. Staff may therefore strive to cultivate consent or at least acquiescence, best achieved by treating people fairly. Relationships among prisoners may be fraught; individuals, thrown into an inescapable and often unwanted intimacy, must contend with all the usual demands of life, aggravated by the unique frustrations of imprisonment. The prison community may be splintered into gangs, groupings and clusters, sometimes hostile to one another, and marked by status hierarchies based on (among other things) individuals' offence type, perceived character and command of resources. These dynamics and their consequences vary with an indeterminate number of other considerations – for example, the social distance among prisoners, the size of the establishment, the turnover in population, the extent to which officials are the main providers of resources, administration and governance (Skarbek 2020). As in any community, alliances form, some ad hoc, some more enduring. Exchange and barter are usual, sometimes requiring high levels of trust. Reputation, of individuals and of groups, matters, and 'Gossip, ostracism, and shaming are common tools of social control' (ibid.: 13).

As well as sustenance, adequate material resources and personal safety, people have needs for a sense of self-worth and affirmation of personal identity, for friendship and companionship. Gresham Sykes famously identified the 'pains of imprisonment' – deprivations and frustrations around 'social acceptance, material possessions, heterosexual relationships, personal autonomy, and personal security' (Sykes 1958: 106). The experience of imprisonment may also include a 'tightness' – an internalised power that 'operates both closely and anonymously, working like an invisible harness on the self' (Crewe 2011: 522). This feeling may come from not having a certain release date or bewilderment about what may be required to advance it – and from associated anxieties of undergoing psychological assessment, involving arcane processes with results that can determine the conditions of confinement as well as the time of release. It also arises from a 'responsibilisation' for making and demonstrating one's own rehabilitative progress. This entails self-government, with prisoners often uncertain about the boundaries of permissible behaviour, how conduct will be assessed and with what consequences.

Such uncertainty provokes anxieties and teases hopes (Warr 2016, 2019), aggravated by the inconsistency that Sexton (2015) found was especially resented. With so many doubts about what is expected of them, and receiving little or no explanation for crucial decisions, people are likely to make comparisons between their treatment and those of others, especially anyone believed to have been favoured unfairly. This, perhaps, applies particularly to release decisions, but extends to the application of regulations – what Carl Cattermole refers to as CRAP: Confusing Rules Applied Patchily (Cattermole 2019). Discretion may be associated with discrimination: black prisoners in England are appreciably more likely than white to be on a basic regime without privileges, held in segregation and have physical force used against them (NOMS 2015; Phillips and Bowling 2017). Nevertheless, Liebling, Price and Shefer (2011) found the wise deployment of discretion can be appreciated by prisoners and by staff.

The material hardships of imprisonment interact with and are compounded by ineffable psychological pains, which 'carry a more profound hurt as a set of threats or attacks which are directed against the very foundations of the prisoner's being' (Sykes 1958: 79). Constraints on independence are a significant aspect of this assault on the self. For example, in women's prisons, infantilisation and limits on autonomy threaten self-respect and identity as adult women (Carlen 1983: 39–44). In a very different cultural context, Dreisinger found in a Thai prison a 'kind of maternal authority structure' that often treats women as 'naughty children' (Dreisinger 2016: 153), reflecting and reinforcing the patriarchy of wider society.

Motherhood, fundamental to the identity of so many women, is neglected by the systems of the prison, where women may be denounced and shamed for their failures as mothers. Yet motherhood is a constructive identity that should be nurtured as one basis for desistance, as well as benefiting children (Baldwin 2021). The pains and deprivations that harm children by the incarceration of their parents, especially their mothers, are well attested, undermining safety, trust and confidence (Condry 2007; Baldwin 2015, 2021; Condry and Smith 2018; Minson 2019; Booth 2020b). Such effects on children, in other circumstances, might be expected to attract public outrage. That it does not is attributable in part to their 'systemic invisibility' (Knudsen 2018) but also perhaps because their suffering is felt somehow deserved, at least vicariously, as the sins of the parent are visited upon the children, who are contaminated by association (Minson 2018). Hardships of separation could be mitigated by enabling reliable and rewarding family contacts. Yet the experience of visiting can bring distress as well as joys (Booth 2018; Cattermole 2019) and even telephone contact may not always be reliably provided (Booth 2020a).[5] Intersections of gender, race and class aggravate the miseries for mothers and children (Condry and Minson 2020), with consequences that can persist long after release and sometimes damaging relationships irreparably. Being a parent, a partner, a friend are among those aspects of selfhood that are under assault in the prison. Stripped of freedom, autonomy and identity, prisoners may struggle to hold on to a sense of self-worth.

Sometimes mutual support among prisoners mitigates these hardships. Shared experiences can create solidarity, companionship, friendship, trust and even love and belonging that traumatic experiences may have denied them before. Yet, as in any community, relationships may sour and people nevertheless have to rub along together. Equally, valued relationships can be suddenly ruptured by moves – especially the practice of 'ghosting', where prisoners are moved without warning or explanation to other establishments, sharply and poignantly fracturing friendships (Cattermole 2019).

Yet prison sometimes represents a safe place, a sanctuary from violence, perhaps especially for women (Bradley and Davino 2002; Bucerius, Haggerty and Dunford 2021), but some men too (Schneider 2021). One of Megan Comfort's (2008) respondents saw his prison sentence as 'the best seven years I could'a done'. Prison may provide health treatments or educational programmes that might not otherwise be available. Even as the absence of other and less perilous sanctuaries and portals to opportunities may be regretted, these experiences are part of the picture too (compare Wacquant 2002). Alice Goffman (2015) writes of how women, in an intensively policed Philadelphia neighbourhood, sometimes hand over their partners to the police, using jail tactically to save themselves from domestic violence, or to protect their partners from street violence or drug misuse. Some seek positive meaning in their imprisonment, finding a different perspective not only on the pains of imprisonment but on the traumas that have scarred their lives, as well as taking advantage of the opportunities the best prisons provide. Some engage actively to try to create another – and what they regard as a truer – self (van Ginneken 2016a; Crewe and Ievins 2020). Thus, while some accounts of prison presume a life disrupted or wrecked by imprisonment, the reality is that for many no such life existed and to this extent imprisonment might offer a stable and even rewarding experience.

Plainly the meaning of a prison sentence will depend upon its length, the stage of the sentence, the age and circumstances of the individuals concerned, the character of the regime, as well as other factors besides. For those who serve a number of sentences, it is less the impact of any single term than the cumulative effect that is so crushing, adding up to so much lost time and even a sense of a life wasted (Armstrong and Weaver 2013; Schinkel and Lives Sentenced Participants 2021). Strategies adopted to cope with longer sentences can have an enduring and deleterious effect, diminishing a capacity to thrive in the community (Hulley, Crewe and Wright 2016; Warr 2019). What this means to individuals is far removed from the communications that censure theory supposes to be imparted (Schinkel 2014).

## Community sanctions and measures

The experiences of people subject to various forms of community supervision have been canvassed infrequently and (mostly[6]) anecdotally. And while the surveys, questionnaires and structured interviews agencies use are straightforward enough to administer, they may miss the complexities and nuances of what it's like to be under supervision. Recently, creative methods have been used to gain an appreciative understanding of the processes of desistance and the part that community supervision may play. Fitzgibbon and Healy (2019) asked probationers to take photographs to capture aspects of their experience, reflecting on these in focus groups; the *Distant Voices* project explores experiences through song (www.voxliminis.co.uk/projects/distant-voi ces; see also Crockett Thomas et al. 2021). Such methods, for all the complexities of interpretation, can illuminate experiences that elude more conventional approaches, engaging with the ambivalence, doubts and confusions that often mark the process of desistance and attitudes towards agencies of criminal justice.

No doubt probation staff have always had their own ideas about how their work has been received and discussed it with their clients, but these accounts have rarely been collated or analysed. Sue Rex (1999) drew attention to the opportunities that were missed by neglect of probationers' experience, making creative connections between the findings from 'criminal careers' research (McAra and McVie 2017) into desistance and probation's objectives in reducing reoffending. Inquiring into probationers' views, Rex found that it was active engagement and the professional relationship that mattered and were particularly appreciated. Encouragement and indeed explicit direction were often welcomed, even though social work has been chary of any suggestion that people should be told how to behave. Sometimes a sense of obligation to the probation officer was generated – a normative incentive to comply – and was felt to contribute to reduced reoffending, with formal monitoring playing no more than a minor role. Appreciation of the relationship, especially when marked by mutual respect and reciprocity, is shared by both RNR and desistance approaches, and has been emphasised in a number of studies (Burnett and McNeill 2005; Anderson 2016; Canton and Dominey 2017: ch. 7; Dominey 2019).

Other positive experiences of supervision have included appreciation of being encouraged, not being judged, being listened to and recognised (McCulloch 2005; Barry 2007, 2016). King found that supervision played an 'important role in developing motivation and self-confidence within probationers, and by helping to develop particular skills and capacities that are likely to be of assistance during the desistance process' (King 2013: 147). Dominey's (2016) respondents spoke of practical assistance, a 'helpful environment' and support for personal change, although there were other, less positive experiences and, for many, probation supervision was found to be mainly a business of being checked and monitored.

There has been positive testimony from those who have undertaken community service. An early local survey found that some had found so much fulfilment that they continued their work voluntarily after completing the hours of the order (Flegg 1976). Workers' perception of the worth of their tasks made a difference: work could be demanding, even tough, but so long as work was found to be worthwhile, there were fewer enforcement problems and rates of reconviction were lower

(McIvor 1992; see also Zeleskov Doric, Batricevic and Petrovic 2015). Attempts to make community service more visibly punitive, however, or managerial requirements to routinise work placements may affect workers' experience and the worth they are able to find (McIvor, Beyens, Blay and Boone 2010).

At the same time, different accounts have emerged. Ioan Durnescu (2011) has written about the 'pains of probation', while many respondents in Western's study of people on parole (Western 2018) found supervision to be intrusive and inducing a constant sense of precariousness. Hayes (2015) found that probationers reported a number of different 'pains', variously eased, aggravated or left untouched by supervision. McNeill (2018) argues that when community supervision is imagined (when it can be envisaged at all), it is the meetings with the supervisors that comes to mind, losing the reality that being supervised is by no means confined to these occasional encounters; supervision, rather, can be something that is experienced all the time.

The pains of community sanctions and measures (CSM), then, can include constraints on freedom, intrusion and sometimes financial burdens, but feelings of humiliation and the threat of enforcement action are especially onerous. McNeill borrows Crewe's metaphors of depth, weight and tightness to capture the sense of being enmeshed in a web of control or wearing 'an invisible collar'. Women have expressed 'feelings of being overwhelmed, inconsequential, powerless, constrained, under surveillance and stigmatized' (Fitzgibbon and Healy 2019: 21). These stresses may have their impact on other people too. The effect on children of their mother's imprisonment is well attested, but this is less often studied in the context of community supervision. Having a parent with the feelings just described can only be damaging for children. Yet other experiences can be found: for some, the very 'existence of the probation order itself seemed to create a supportive, protective structure, a positively experienced constraint on their behaviour', a safety net more than a collar (Weaver and Armstrong 2011: 16).

Longitudinal studies are instructive in appraising the meaning and effects of probation supervision. Preoccupations with targets, with 'successful completions' and short-term research into reconviction may elbow aside attempts to understand its significance in the longer term. Farrall and Calverley (2006: ch. 3) found many respondents indifferent, dismissive or scathing about their recent experiences of probation, but interviews at a later date revealed something much more nuanced. Later events sometimes enable people to recall probation exchanges, finding a new sense and value in these conversations. For example, some key phrases and ideas from supervision

> somehow get 'lodged' in the minds of probationers and recalled sometimes long after supervision is ended, creating a slow 'chipping away' of attitudes … Doubtless maturation is at work here too, but were it not for the key phrase having been delivered, then it would not have been there to have been remembered.
>
> *(Farrall and Calverley 2006: 65)*

The supervisory relationship, then, is often marked by change and ambivalence. Both those under supervision and those who supervise them may be variously rewarded, disappointed, satisfied and frustrated. In this respect, supervision is no different from many other human relationships. Importantly, to acknowledge positive experience is not to minimise attendant pains and hardships; nor does recognition of these burdens exclude possibilities of benefits and support (Hayes 2015). In one study, many reported that probation was experienced as a punishment, but this did not mean it was of no help. As one person put it, 'Punishment, yeah – in my eyes. It helps you. It's a punishment that helps you' (Dominey 2016: 114).

Communicative theories need to understand how CSMs are experienced as punishment – not just in terms of their benefits or burdens, but for the meanings that are found and made. Rex (2004, 2005) found that while all respondents readily grasped the idea of 'the messages of punishment', offenders were less concerned than others (staff, magistrates, victims) about normative messages of their wrongdoing: 'The picture that emerges … is of offenders being less keen to identify and receive penal messages than other groups were to transmit them' (Rex 2004: 125). The question she then raises is:

> if the aim of punishment is morally to persuade offenders to desist, is this sort of moralising comprehensible to those who are supposed to be doing it or to those who are at the receiving end? If not,

why might that be the case? Does it mean that the theory is 'wrong', or that the conditions for its implementation have yet to be satisfied?

*(Rex 2005: 51)*

Part of the difficulty may be that not enough was being done to attend to the social context of desistance. With probation staff concentrating on offending behaviour programmes, with a predetermined idea of offenders' 'criminogenic needs', there was a reluctance to allow them to participate actively in the determination of their problems or solutions to them (Rex, 2005; Farrall, 2002; McNeill and Weaver 2010). There was a dissonance between the form of the punishment as experienced and the message it was intended to impart, undermining coherence and legitimacy.

Perhaps community punishment fares little better than prison in its communicative ambitions: 'there is not even an agreed language for communication: punishment means very different things to different people' (van Ginneken and Hayes 2017: 74). While the 'material form' of punishment can be stipulated, how it is put into effect determines the individual's experience. For example, monitoring and ensuring compliance may be accepted as legitimate, deriving authority from the court's decision, but both these activities may be undertaken officiously and intrusively or, on the other hand, in ways that express an interest in, concern for and care about the probationer's rights and well-being. These modes of supervision can communicate quite different messages with varying consequences for the quality of the experience, for compliance and cooperation and perhaps for the chances of reoffending.

## *Electronic monitoring*

Comparisons have been made between the hardships of being monitored electronically and the pains of imprisonment or of other CSM. Some burdens can be similar – restrictions, constraints, sometimes financial burdens (people may have to pay to be monitored) and the immediate impact on family members. Electronic monitoring (EM), however, can occasion distinctive domestic tensions – the frustrations stemming from watching those around you being able to do things and go to places denied to you and the temptations that arise from this. These are among the psychological harms reported by those subject to EM and other members of their household (Gibbs and King 2003). A small-scale study of in Canada found a common experience of 'stuckedness' (Gacek 2019). This is a time of waiting at a place and at times chosen for you by others, a sense of time passing, of missing out, and other ways of living and opportunities lost. Gacek speaks of a carceral 'web' – a metaphor that, in his exploration of the pervasiveness of punishment, McNeill's respondents often used. Nor should the physical effects (the discomfort of the 'bracelet' device) be disregarded or the anxieties and shame felt when other people may see it (Payne and Gainey 1998).

The aspiration that EM might displace people from custody has led to comparisons with imprisonment, with expressions like an 'electronic ball and chain' (Gibbs and King 2003), although Nellis (2009) has argued that EM should be conceptualised as a technique of surveillance as much as a means of confinement. Even though the most common form of monitoring can only determine presence at or absence from a particular place, there may well be feelings of intrusiveness, of privacy invaded. Loraine Gelsthorpe reports a case of 'a man who cut off his electronic tag because it "made him feel like a dog"' (Gelsthorpe 2007: 495).

This affective dimension is an ineradicable part of what it means to be punished (Nellis 2009). And as GPS technologies develop, enabling the monitoring station to determine a precise location,[7] these feelings may become more intense. While these appliances 'tag' the body rather than working on the mind, existing technologies and foreseeable developments will enable devices to induce the kind of response attributed to the panopticon: uncertain whether under surveillance, people may behave as if they were – at least to the extent of confining themselves to particular locations. EM imposes a significant degree of self-regulation, while there are likely to be circumstances in which people become doubtful about what is expected of them, leading to that sense of 'tightness' that both Crewe and McNeill argue marks the experience of prisoners and those subject to other CSM. Just as the more 'concrete' (Sexton 2015) pains of other punishments do not always turn out to be the most acute ones, so too with electronic monitoring. The burden varies not only with individual characteristics

(Payne and Gainey 2002), or with the physical conditions in which one is confined and the inclination to leave the house, but may depend on more abstract and subjective feelings besides.

As with imprisonment and traditional probation supervision, however, other experiences are reported. A study from Belgium found positive effects as well as negative ones, at least some respondents believing that EM supported their reintegration (Vanhaelemeesch, Vander Beken and Vandevelde 2014). Many preferred EM to what they imagined to be its alternatives, especially imprisonment. Anthea Hucklesby (2008) found that some who were tagged felt this had led to changes of habit and lifestyle, helping them to avoid 'antisocial people' or places, as well as to reduce their use of drugs. Positive changes in personal relationships and lifestyles were also reported and some commented on a longer-term deterrent effect (they would not want to be tagged again). Other respondents, however, remarked on damage done to intimate relationships and that the restrictions had been an obstacle to finding or retaining employment. Effects like these, more than the duration of the order, can determine the experience of EM (Hucklesby, Beyens and Boone 2021). Unsurprisingly, the experiences of offenders and other members of their household are mixed. There are pains, not all of which might have been anticipated, while any benefits may come to be appreciated at a later time. (Graham and McIvor 2015; Hucklesby and Holdsworth 2016; Nellis 2016). Pains and benefits can coexist and neither should be exaggerated or minimised in defence of or accusations against this mode of punishment.

The logic of EM disregards the value of a human relationship: the consent and cooperation of the individual could be regarded as substantially irrelevant, in contrast to the best forms of probation supervision which tries to engage active participation. Yet for EM to have its best effects, it needs an individual's understanding of how it might bring advantages. The Council of Europe accordingly advises that EM be used in combination with personal supervision, rather than as a substitute for it, even as it recognises its use as a stand-alone in many jurisdictions (including England and Wales) (Council of Europe 2014: Basic Principle 8).

Where EM does stand alone, human engagement reverts to the operators of the equipment, who may or may not see their role as something more than ensuring that the technology works and responding to violations. Still, experiences of EM are 'inextricably linked to the individuals operating it – the technology is only as effective as the people working with it' (Hucklesby 2013: 242). Compliance was greater where the EM requirement was accepted as a fair imposition, but also where there was some contact with the monitoring agency. Contact with monitoring staff takes place when the device is initially fitted and finally removed, but is likely to occur otherwise only at times of suspected violation – a time when (mutual) anxieties and suspicions are likely to be high. Violations, often minor, are by no means uncommon and the way in which monitoring staff respond can either undermine or enhance the legitimacy of EM.

## Financial penalties

A first thought might be that the experience of a financial penalty would depend mostly, if not entirely, on the size of the amount. For some people, this burden, bearing down not only on them but also on households that are already impoverished, perhaps with the threat of imprisonment for default, is likely to be the dominant consideration. There are, however, other considerations that might make a difference to the meaning of a financial penalty. In principle, the sum of money could disappear into a state coffer; or go into a general fund for victims of crime; or to the victim of the specific crime in compensation. Or perhaps, and most alarmingly, fees might be levied to pay private companies for the 'services' they provide. It is plausible to think that the meaning of this penalty, how it is experienced by the individuals and how regarded by others, might correspondingly vary.

Nicole Bögelein (2018) interviewed people who had failed to pay their fines (although for that reason alone, they may not be representative of all who have been fined). She found that some regarded the financial penalty as a (more or less) fitting punishment for their wrongdoing, while others declined to undertake that kind of moralising reflection, simply seeing it as a financial encumbrance. The size of the amount and the hardship this occasions can overwhelm any censuring message to the point where it is not heard at all. Exploring the proliferation of financial penalties in the USA, Beth Colgan (2018) cites cases of people faced with impossible choices between paying the court or providing for their families, with insult to their dignity, a consequent rejection of the court's legitimacy and predictable criminogenic consequences. Yet for affluent and especially corporate offenders, a fine can be seen as an overhead – a matter of commerce and nothing to do with right and wrong.

The fine is by no means the only punishment that entails financial encumbrance. In many countries, imprisonment impoverishes the families of prisoners – sometimes through the absence of the 'breadwinner', but also because of costs of travel for visits and a felt obligation to lend material support to the prisoner (Schenwar 2014; Western 2018; Skarbek 2020). In parts of the USA, probationers are required to pay a fee towards the cost of supervision, risking the transformation of probation and parole into income generation for private profit (Teague 2016). Those unable to pay are hounded by warrants, summonses and pursuit by private collection agencies, debts increasing with interest charged (Martin, Sykes, Shannon, Edwards and Harris 2018). Sexton's distinction between the punishment and the punitive referent has relevance here once more. Whatever the state takes itself to be attempting to communicate, these consequences express disdain for those in poverty.

Financial penalties have a unique characteristic. No one can serve your sentence of imprisonment for you or undertake your community service; but money is anonymous (O'Malley 2013) and with the fine the law is indifferent to who pays the price – just so long as it is paid. But even if the offender pays in person, the consequent financial deficit can fall heavily on others – notably dependents, who are likely to be further impoverished. To disregard these effects is to overlook a critical aspect of the moral performance of financial penalties.

## Implementing punishment

It is through human engagement that penal interventions might have their worth to the individuals concerned. This is among the most important reasons for the need of a deeper understanding of the attitudes and conduct of personnel who implement punishment. Their motivations and the meanings they bring to their work constitute another dimension of what punishment 'is' and it is to this topic that discussion now turns.

## Prison officers

John Howard maintained 'The first care must be to find a good man for a gaoler; one that is honest, active and humane' (Howard 1929 [1777]: 25), immediately insisting on sobriety as the first virtue. The rights and well-being of prisoners, the character and legitimacy of the establishment fundamentally depend on the ways in which staff go about their work. Neglect in researching this area has been made good in recent years by studies that try to understand what motivates prison officers, what they make of their role and tasks and the meanings and values they find in their work (Arnold 2016 and references there cited).[8]

Officers' tasks include peace-keeping, monitoring, providing services, mentoring, as well as responding to requests and demands from prisoners, colleagues and managers (Crawley 2004). The priority of security is emphasised to all staff from the beginning. The good order of the establishment is another priority to ensure the prison functions as it should, protecting everyone's personal safety and minimising stress. The Woolf report also insisted on the importance of justice (see Chapter 3), which in this context is often less about *what* is done than *how* staff go about it. Prisoners and staff recognise authority must sometimes be exercised, but whether this is done officiously or even aggressively or, by contrast, with respect and regard for the dignity of individuals makes a decisive difference. It is on such differences that justice and legitimacy may depend.

During their acculturation to the prison service and to particular establishments, officers are encouraged to develop an 'intense peer solidarity' (Arnold 2016: 270) – an unfailing willingness to 'be there' for their colleagues, perhaps especially at times of personal danger. Solidarity and the nature of the job bring it about that their occupational culture and values are worked out collectively (Liebling, Price and Shefer 2011). Whatever a new officer's understanding and motivation for their work, it will be modulated in and through their exchanges with colleagues and observations of one another's practices. Another important arena is the officers' mess. Many professions have their canteens or coffee rooms – backstage areas to which outsiders have no access and where people can variously grumble, joke, debrief and seek advice and support. 'Canteen culture' has sometimes been deprecated for its role in transmitting prejudices, but is of indispensable importance in binding colleagues and helping people to understand how to go about demanding work.

Such interactions, more than initial basic training, cultivate shared attitudes and values. As a profession, perhaps, prison officers are reticent about their occupational values, but if values are what is *done* as much or more than what is *said*, in the best settings honesty, integrity, fairness, a wise use of discretion, resilience and compassion are in evidence every day (Arnold 2016: 273). Liebling, Price and Shefer (2011) found that most officers could readily identify the characteristics of a 'model officer'. On the other hand, overcrowding, inadequate resourcing, inept management and grim working conditions may lead to behaviour of a very different kind. And even when the circumstances are more auspicious, the marked imbalances of power and the artificiality of a division between custodians and inmates is inherently a distorted and unnatural form of human association which is at risk at bringing out the worst in both staff and prisoners.

The job can bring enormous strain and there is much evidence of the toll that it can take on people's well-being, their own intimate relationships and work performance (Crawley 2004). The trauma and stress of experiencing or witnessing violence can make it hard to 'switch off'. The emotions generated by these stresses are not always easy to talk about and have to be managed within the parameters of the 'feeling rules' of the prison (Crawley 2004). Some of the less functional responses include detachment, hardening of attitudes and cynicism – all of which have negative consequences for the quality of the relationships on which the prison community fundamentally depends. The prisoner's life is suffused with emotions of all kinds – traumatised backgrounds, the complex matter of managing day-to-day transactions, the impact of separations and communications with the outside world. All of this has direct emotional consequences for staff so that 'Far from being an "add on" to prison life, emotions – and their management and mobilisation – are actually pivotal to the way in which organisational order in prisons is achieved and undone' (Crawley 2004: 251).

> ... rehabilitation tends to be seen as a theoretical, distant, and somewhat irrelevant by-product of successful performance at the tasks of custody and internal order. A released prisoner may or may not commit another crime in the free community, but that crude test of the prison's accomplishments in the area of reform lies far away. Within the walls, in the clear-cut scope of the custodian's responsibilities, the occurrence of escapes and disorders is a weightier concern.
>
> *(Sykes (1958: 38) observed:)*

This is an example of how the priorities of policymakers and managers may not coincide and even sometimes be in conflict with the main concerns of practitioners. Nevertheless, rehabilitation is much more than 'treatment' and programmes. Indeed any programme must be supported by the institution's regime and general culture if it is to have its benefits. Where staff in their routine work fail to demonstrate the respect due to others, the core lessons that programmes are intended to impart – the need to consider the interests of other people – will be undermined. Where officers work with justice, however, they will to this extent be advancing rehabilitation all the time.

Some of the more negative cultural attitudes towards 'offenders' are reinforced in the course of occupational acculturation. Crawley (2004) gives examples of contemptuous and ugly expressions that prison staff sometimes use to refer to those in their charge, including many words that plainly evince disgust. Yet every day officers encounter individuals who, whatever their original offence, are ordinary people and often people in distress. This can evoke a sense of care. While care may not always be an explicit objective of the Prison Service (Tait 2011), the prominence of indices of humanity, respect and caring that prisons use to evaluate their moral performance acknowledges the value of relating to prisoners in these ways (Liebling 2004). Sarah Tait identified some staff who would not have seen their task as caring:

> But they were also paternal and protective, with a keen eye for detecting exploitation. 'Care' was a complex and loaded term for most of these officers; however, prisoners identified them as caring

and enjoyed their sociability and humour. They provided a reliable and trustworthy presence on the wing, and prisoners could count on their responsiveness and straightforward approach.

*(Tait 2011: 446)*

Just as (intended) care may be mistrusted as bogus or manipulative, so too there are occasions when behaviour towards prisoners comes across as caring. Treating people with respect and kindness, even when those individuals find this difficult to acknowledge, much less to reciprocate, is worthwhile for its own sake and is one of the ways in which prison officers find value in their work. Many take satisfaction and justifiable pride from specific acts that, however seemingly modest, make a valued difference to the lives of vulnerable individuals.

## Probation

In England and Wales, and no doubt in many other countries in the Anglo-American tradition, a sound and honest character seems to have been the main quality originally required of a probation officer. People who shared a belief that wrongdoers might be helped to change their ways through support and mentoring were likely to have been attracted to the work (Bochel 1976). This has been a persistent and resilient belief, surviving government attempts to cast probation as more punitive and/or controlling: the motivation of applicants to the service has continued to include a commitment to trying to help people in distress and support them in efforts to lead a law abiding life, the work valued because it is 'people centred' (Annison, Eadie and Knight 2008; Deering 2010). For all the differences among them, probation staff interviewed in one study 'shared a belief in the worthwhileness of working with offenders … [which] always included a belief in the capacity of the individual to change for the better' (Mawby and Worrall 2013: 39). For many practitioners, probation is more than 'just a job'. It is even possible to speak of a 'vocation' – a calling to enter a profession committed to helping vulnerable people and supporting them in attempts to change (Mawby and Worrall 2013; Raynor and Vanstone 2018).

This commitment has made for a natural alignment with social work, an alliance strengthened when both occupations, becoming more secular and more 'scientific', espoused social casework as their defining professional skill. Many probation agencies in Europe still identify strongly with social work (van Kalmthout and Durnescu 2008). There have been insightful studies attempting to identify the skills needed to undertake probation work (Ugwudike, Raynor and Annison 2018; Raynor and Vanstone 2018; Raynor 2019). Much depends upon the ways in which these skills are put into practice: an emphasis on technical skills or a bureaucratic orientation risks eclipsing the central place of relationships, even though warm, open and enthusiastic relationships are at the heart of effective practice (Dowden and Andrews 2004). In these respects, probation and social work remain very close.

In parts of the USA, as rehabilitation has fallen into disfavour, surveillance and enforcement have even more emphatically displaced earlier social work orientations, although some staff reject a sharp opposition between their 'controlling' and social work roles and 'synthetic' officers have tried to combine those duties (Miller 2015). Nevertheless, Joan Petersilia observed that:

> Parole agents have also become less 'kind and gentle.' Parole departments in most large urban areas have developed a prevailing culture that emphasizes surveillance over services. ... Training often provides minimal training on casework practices and service referrals, but numerous classes on arrests, searches, and other topics stressing law enforcement. Such training increasingly reinforces the image of parole officers as cops rather than social workers.
>
> *(Petersilia 2003: 11)*[9]

In the mid-1990s social work was explicitly repudiated in England as the way to understand probation practice and a social work curriculum was rejected as suitable training for staff. This was not because the knowledge, skills and values of social work failed to equip probation staff to do their work, but because the association of social work with 'caring' was felt by politicians to be incompatible with their presentation of probation as an agency charged with delivering punishment in the community (Brownlee 1998). The original historic mission to 'advise, assist and befriend' was replaced by the stated purposes of enforcement, rehabilitation and public protection (Worrall and Hoy 2005).

Yet much as politicians try to jettison social work and connotations of caring, they keep insisting their way back into practice (Smith 2005). In line with their original motivations to join, staff have often been tenacious in their defence of values like respect for persons, helping and encouragement as ways of bringing about change, reluctant to accept their work as 'punishment'. These commitments have sometimes risked setting practitioners at odds with their managers, as well as with politicians and the general public. Fergus McNeill (2018) portrays a practitioner who finds tensions between the motivations that brought her into the job in the first place, strengthened by a social work training (in Scotland), and the modern managerialism that has worked to oust it. As policy has variously insisted on stern enforcement or the meeting of bureaucratic targets, these tensions have become ever more acute for some practitioners, especially those with a career-long commitment (Mawby and Worrall 2013).

Governance arrangements should support staff in delivering best practice, but may be experienced very differently. Even before the disruptions of Transforming Rehabilitation in England and Wales, newly qualified officers were to be heard expressing disappointment about the ways in which constraints associated with their role were inhibiting their potential to make a difference to people's lives (Annison, Eadie and Knight 2008; Gregory 2011). During periods of reorganisation and 'marketisation' in England and Wales, a prominent concern has been that the fragmentation of services might militate against the relationships on which so much has been found to depend (Robinson, Burke and Millings 2016; Dominey 2019). Changes in management structures, in political priorities and expectations, and in the public's attitude have had their effect on staff morale and the coherence of the profession (Deering and Feilzer 2019; Tidmarsh 2020). The size of workload can make it difficult to engage constructively, prejudicing the quality of work and also the well-being of staff (HM Inspectorate of Probation 2021a). Again, 'the tyranny of the computer' (Mawby and Worrall 2013: 43) can be deeply discouraging for those who had anticipated more personal contact. Writing before the time of greatest upheaval, Mawby and Worrall found many more positive testimonies. Some staff thrived on the turbulence and continued to find ways of engaging clients and bringing meaning to their work. Many took pride in knowing this was work that needed to be done and not everyone could do it.

Probation's occupational culture(s) may be defined by their professional values which have been marked by strong continuities, even amid all the change (Worrall and Mawby 2014). Compliance and cooperation with supervision depend upon trust and mutual respect (Robinson and McNeill 2008; Ugwudike and Raynor 2013; Canton 2014c): officiousness, scolding and punitive posturing meet only with resentment and resistance (Weaver, Piacentini, Moodie and Barry 2021). Encouragement, kindness, good humour and attempts to establish warm relationships are not only reductively more efficacious, but are part of what it takes to get the job done at all. The resilience of probation's traditional values, then, may be a function of the inherent demands of the work as much as the application of principle (Robinson, Priede, Farrall, Shapland and McNeill 2014; Ainslie 2021).

Some of these commitments have been strengthened by an increasing awareness of the disadvantages that have burdened the lives of so many under supervision and the traumas that have scarred them. Regardless of its reductive effectiveness, respectful attention and concern for those life experiences is a moral imperative (Anderson 2016). Recognition of this may confuse policy preoccupations with punishment, but these realities may not be dismissed just because they bring discomfort.

## *Electronic monitoring personnel*

Much more needs to be known about the work of electronic monitoring staff and the meanings they bring to their tasks. The frequency and quality of contact with staff can contribute to achieving the potential of the technology, so that even if the principal concern is about EM's reductive effectiveness, 'A narrow evaluative emphasis on bottom-line "outcomes" will obscure the contextual differences "on the ground" that shape and inform such results, and hence fail to illuminate how surveillance technology achieves its effects' (Ibarra, Gur and Erez 2014: 441).

The way in which the monitoring occupation has grown and the character of the agencies involved have militated against the formation of a formal training programme and Hucklesby (2013) found that their 'working orientation' falls short of a cohesive 'occupational culture'. She went on, however, to identify three types: *probation workers*,[10] who try engage respectfully and constructively; *pragmatists* (the majority) who do the job fairly and non-judgementally, while nevertheless withholding trust from those who are tagged and keeping an interpersonal distance; and *technicians* who withhold empathy and trust, striving to make contact as brief and formal as possible. They variously emphasised different aspects of their work – punishment, efficiency and a principled concern for the offenders under supervision (compare Rutherford 1993).

Many staff develop interpersonal skills which they put to good use. Often working alone and visiting homes at night-time, staff are concerned with their personal safety, devising practical strategies to minimise risks including interpersonal skills to avert conflict (Hucklesby 2011). In one study, a respondent described how he has often walked into a scene of domestic tension, aggravated, perhaps, by his arrival and the constraints of EM (Paterson 2007). Others have been moved by the obvious poverty and misery of some households. Whatever their presumptive working credo and irrespective of the extent to which they believe that it is any part of their role to sort things out, staff will react as people to people and draw upon their own personality and life experiences accordingly.

## Some conclusions

The experiences of people subject to punishment are fundamental to our understanding of what punishment is. Accounts and justifications that neglect this dimension are at best incomplete and most likely flawed. Legitimacy and endeavours to support desistance depend upon the meanings of punishment found and made in its implementation. Misunderstanding, injustice and ineffective intervention are among the consequences where this is ignored.

Some broad conclusions may be drawn from this review. First, experiences are variegated: the pains and benefits of punishment vary with individuals, according to their wider circumstances, individual temperaments, time of life and an indeterminate number of other variables. Generalisations about what punishment means are therefore hazardous. Second, most experiences include a degree of pain or hardship – sometimes severe. Often these are specific physical sufferings or deprivations; others are more abstract, involving shame, emotional pains and various assaults on self-respect and identity. And it is these dimensions of punishment that often weigh the most heavily (Sexton 2015; Hayes 2015). Not everyone summons their imaginative empathy to understand how distressing this is likely to be – or is willing to make the attempt, perhaps because of the emotions that crime and punishment arouse.

Third, however, the experience of suffering and the possibility of not only consolations but active benefits are not mutually exclusive: both can take place at the same time or at least during the same sentence. Fourth, time makes a difference, although not always for the better. This is a dimension that can elude researchers who, most usually, capture a snapshot – a picture that, however authentic, can only represent a particular moment. People in prison may focus on the immediate pains, but later find a different significance and meaning in the context of their lives. For instance, what is now recognised as a life-saving intervention to prevent perilous drug misuse was experienced quite differently at the time. The best prison autobiographies not only describe the experience of imprisonment, nor even just the background leading to prison, but also situate these experiences within their lives, elaborating the meaning prison had for them then and later. Nor should time be overlooked in understanding the significance of probation supervision (Farrall and Calverley 2006).

Prison can be oppressive, damaging or futile, although more positive experiences are sometimes reported. CSM impose specific demands, while the sense of being under surveillance and vulnerable to enforcement processes represents another level of burden. Officious, condescending or perfunctory behaviour by probation staff may be experienced as insensitive or over-bearing. The assignment of worthless or humiliating community service tasks may be harder than any taxing labour involved. Financial impositions bring material hardships but may also have this expressive function, while limited or non-existent financial support on release from prison makes clear how society regards former prisoners and belies claims about rehabilitation.

Changes in policy and in organisational governance can constrain or even shape how punishment is delivered and experienced. A policy shift from penal welfarism to managerialism made a difference to the experiences of some prisoners in Scotland (Schinkel 2014), while changes in governance have affected probation practice in England and Wales (Burke and Collett 2015; Dominey 2019; Deering and Feilzer 2019; Ainslie 2021). Yet often the effects of policy on practice are far from direct or straightforward. Practitioners have to find ways of getting the job done; they may need to adapt policy instruction for this reason alone. Policymakers, by contrast, are likely to be much less directly aware of the practical consequences of implementation or, evidence notwithstanding, persist with policies for political reasons.

Staff can respond to policy in different ways – sometimes, for example, to ameliorate the harsher consequences of punitive or managerial imperatives. Leonidas Cheliotis (2006: 330) refers to 'the power of human agents to resist and reverse unfortunate turns', although also, more pessimistically, to block or spoil more auspicious opportunities. Prison policy has often been thwarted or distorted in the process of its implementation by practitioners trying to do their work in a decent manner or, as it may be, in pursuit of their own interests (Goodman, Page and Phelps 2017). McNeill (2018) exposes the uncomfortable tensions when practitioners and their managers have different conceptions of the work. Staff's understanding of the significance of their work often comes not from management or the mission statements of the organisation, but from their experiences at work and exchanges with colleagues: especially in stressful jobs, people are sustained as much by their colleagues as by anything else (Knight 2014) and it is through their work together and reflection upon it that they discover its worth and meaning.

Staff typologies have been constructed to explore the various motivations that attract staff to their occupation and sustain them in their work (for example, Scott 2008; Tait 2011; Hucklesby 2013; Mawby and Worrall 2013; Worrall and Mawby 2014). Such typologies are best regarded as ideal types, highlighting particular aspects of attitudes and performance. But motivations are dynamic, often mixed and influence each other in complex ways. A former prison officer remarked that they could move from one 'occupational category' to another during a single shift, never mind the course of a career (personal communication). Again, some staff regard their work as a vocation (Mawby and Worrall 2013), but over time the words of this calling may be heard differently or even become inaudible. Cynicism may corrode the original passion and people may become jaded or stale, stuck in jobs from which they can find no escape for the most practical reasons. Staff may report feeling 'marooned' amid organisational restructuring (Burke, Millings and Robinson 2017). Even those who are most sincere about their commitment have financial obligations that may at times become especially important to them, constraining career options. Conversely, individuals who choose their occupation for reasons of job security or adequate income, are likely to seek worth and meaning in their work, bringing a fulfilment they had not anticipated, as well as enhancing the quality of their practice.

This account of the experiences of those administering punishment is at risk of over-generalisation. There should, for example, be no assumption that the experience of women prison staff is the same as that of men (Wood 2015). The experiences of staff from minority ethnic groups may be distinctive, with implications for their interactions with people in prison or under community supervision (Bhui and Fossi 2008). Race, gender, social class, age and experience intersect in any number of ways to affect experiences and attitudes. With regard to race in particular, prejudice, ignorance and unexamined assumptions may lead some staff to treat some individuals unfairly, compounding the pains of punishment with a further assault on identity. Diffidence too can be a factor – fretful about doing the wrong thing, staff may behave in ways that result in the wrong thing being done (HM Inspectorate of Probation 2021b).

What penal staff and what those subject to punishment make of their experiences are elusive and ambivalent, yet constitute most fundamentally what punishment 'is'. This chapter has considered first of all the experiences of those subject to punishment and then of those who put punishment into effect. Yet this structuring can lose the interactions between these groups: whatever attitudes, preconceptions and intentions are brought to their encounters, it is in and through their relationships that meanings are negotiated, found and made. There is always a hazardous gap between the intentions of penal agents (which may in any case be mixed) and the experience of the punished. Staff who would not describe their work in this way may nevertheless be experienced as caring (Tait 2011); on the other hand, commitments to beneficence, however sincere, may mask practices that are sometimes experienced as coercive and punitive.

Whatever their original motivations and preconceptions, practitioners soon meet individuals who are not reducible to their crimes or to entries on a spreadsheet, but are traumatised, frightened, bewildered, frustrated and sad, although sometimes also optimistic, resilient, positive and purposeful – in other words, recognisably human. In the best cases, this will elicit respect and compassion, finding expression in their work and making a difference to the experience of being punished.

## Notes

1. Motivations are often complex, multi-faceted and obscure even to those who act on them (Nisbett and Wilson 1977). And we usually have an interest in the ways in which we report on our reasons for actions (Haidt 2012).
2. Matza, perhaps, elides correctionalism (the aim to reduce offending) with the different and wider social reaction to denounce and repudiate, irrespective of any attempts to bring about change.
3. There are parallels here with crimes. Specific harms – physical and psychological injury or loss of property – may heal over time and can often be repaired. But the victim is also being used, diminished as a person, treated of no more than a means to the offender's ends. Personal dominion is reduced by the invasion of graver crime – a 'psychological subversion'. (Braithwaite and Pettit 1992: 67). This seems close to Sexton's distinction about punishment.
4. Notably, Sykes (1958), Morris and Morris (1963), Carlen (1983), Liebling (2004), Crewe (2012), Schenwar (2014), Dreisinger (2016), Fassin (2017) and Skarbek (2020).
5. In England and Wales, the costs of phone calls far exceed the prices people enjoy outside (Cattermole 2019).
6. There have been recent attempts to enquire more systematically. Early findings from one instrument of evaluation, incidentally, reveal marked differences in probationers' experience in different countries (Durnescu 2019), even though there is a need for a careful interpretation of these data.
7. Inferences about behaviour or even intentions may be drawn from that information. For example, *we know you were in the pub/near the school/in the park and how long you were there for.*

8. Not all these insights can be assumed to apply to staff in other countries, where variations in resourcing, staff-prisoner ratios and conceptions of role will affect staff's attitude to their work (Skarbek 2020). Different prisons pose different problems for staff, and there are likely to be variations even within a single institution. This fact alone complicates the notion of a 'prison culture' (Crewe 2012).

9. Petersilia was writing here about parole officers. In USA, this is a different role from that of probation officer, while in many other countries the same personnel supervise both probation and parole. Even so, her remarks are likely to apply to probation staff as well.

10 This terminology designates staff who try to engage in a supportive manner; in some countries, including England and Wales, personnel do not work for the probation service.

# 5

# THE ENDS OF PUNISHMENT

The chapter's title plays on different meanings of the word 'end': an end is a conclusion, but also an aim or purpose. A punishment might be thought to be over once purposes set for it had been achieved. For example, if the aim is deserved punishment, serving the term of imprisonment or completing a community sanction should conclude the matter; interventions should cease when rehabilitation had been accomplished; confinement to guard against risks of reoffending should end when the risk was sufficiently reduced. But the matter turns out to be more complicated: complex judgements are involved and normative as well as evidential questions arise. Does completion of the sentence end the matter? What would it take to show that an individual had been rehabilitated? How can it be ascertained that risk has been reduced, or is now at a level that could be managed in other ways (perhaps by vigilant community supervision)?

Leaving prison will first be discussed. The massive material, social and emotional challenges of returning to the community are considered. The involvement of the formal agencies of the state will then be discussed, before attention turns to the concept of reconciliation – a term associated with the ideas of rehabilitation and desistance considered in Chapter 3, but which bears the implication that the community, and not only the (ex-)offender, has to work towards resolution. For, as Linda Radzik insists, '[W]e need some way of talking about the end

DOI: 10.4324/9780429055829-6

state of cases of wrongdoing – some point at which we can describe the wrongful act as having been successfully resolved' (Radzik 2009: 112). Making connections with the emotions of punishment reviewed in Chapter 2, there will be consideration of those emotions that might support or frustrate the achievement of an end state.

## Leaving prison

> Some guys in prison, they climb up on chairs and tables in the cells and look out through the bars at what they can see of the outside world. And they talk of it, and talk of it, but it's never anything else but fantasies and dreams. 'When I get out, when I get out …'
>
> *(Parker 1991: 110)*

Imagining return is a perennial motif in tales about voyagers, soldiers and exiles. Yet yearnings of return, from danger and hostility to familiar places and to relationships of love and comfort, are often overshadowed, at least in the dark hours, by anxieties and fears. Many prisoners have no (or no recent) experiences of anything like comfort and even those with better memories to draw upon may be uncertain about their future. Fantasies and realities collide from the very first days of release and people are often beset by anxiety, fear and despondency (Western 2018; Durnescu 2019).

Leaving prison, especially after longer sentences, is for many an acute existential shock. There is a surfeit of new sensations; daily habits and routines are starkly changed; the world has to be negotiated altogether differently; the very possibility of independent action, reasons to behave in particular ways, the costs and benefits of courses of action are radically altered. Carl Cattermole captures this precisely:

> The major aspects of reintegration are often much harder to identify because no one explains explicitly what you've had taken away – privacy, dignity, trust, choice, being your true self. … choice underpins every element of the free world so when you are thrown back, at a time when making the right choices is more crucial than ever, you are at your least practised.
>
> *(Cattermole 2019: 170)*

Technologies may have changed. Someone just released from a long sentence remarked: 'I'm 65, but I'm a baby out here now. It's a different world' (Ferretti 2019). He went on to speak of the hazards of adjusting to traffic, while travelling in a car made him anxious, as did choosing a meal off a restaurant menu.[1] The transactions and etiquette of the street and the shop are very different from those of the landing or the wing. In prison, chance interactions may be over-interpreted, perhaps as threats or challenges; relationships have to be carefully managed and there is often mutual wariness, at least until people come to know one another. That attitude is likely to complicate relations on release. 'Socialising is like a muscle and prison is like breaking your leg: once you get the cast removed, the muscle is atrophied and you can barely walk. I know from my own experience that it can take years to become healthy and open again ...' (Cattermole 2019: 51; see also Schenwar 2014: ch. 4).

Among the hardest challenges can be re-establishing intimate relationships, disrupted and sometimes wrecked by imprisonment. This seems a priority for women especially (Western 2018: ch. 9). Mothers may have relied upon women in their families to look after their children and resuming a day-to-day relationship of motherhood will never be straightforward for anyone. Where family bonds are fragile, there may be anxieties about attempting to repair them; even where relationships are more secure, high expectations may be frustrated, bringing feelings of disillusionment and despair. No doubt prisoners' own release fantasies are matched by those of their loved ones, where a happy anticipation of return is mixed with forebodings about the future, concern about continuing financial and emotional burdens – and maybe a degree of resentment on that account.

Bare subsistence, housing and income are immediate challenges. In almost all countries, financial support on release is woefully insufficient and it can be difficult to access welfare provision. This is all the harder when prisoners are released at the end of the week or before public holidays when offices are closing or closed. Some have families to bring support, although this brings further financial burdens to hard-pressed households. The material challenges can be overwhelming, often aggravated by poor physical and mental health or problems of substance use.

The inadequacy of state provision may open opportunities for those who see the precarious position of people released from prison as a chance for commercial profit. With affordable accommodation so hard to find, some squalid and miserable places claim to offer 'programs', while making no such provision. They receive referrals from a range of organisations under government contract, but there is no formal regulation or oversight. While the worst abuses are the responsibility of unscrupulous owners and operators, structural incentives allow and even encourage these practices: funding arrangements make overcrowding practically inevitable. (John Jay College 2013). Dreisinger found landlords who receive kickbacks from programs, writing of someone who lost 'several job opportunities ... because he had to attend drug treatment at his halfway house, lest he be evicted – even though he has never had a drug problem' (Dreisinger 2016: 262).

Danielle Allen's powerful memoir (Allen 2017) shows how even those with their own talents and legitimate ambitions, with loving, resourceful and reasonably well-off families, can find it almost impossible to make a future. The many problems people face interact viciously and welfare support is not up to the challenge. Distressing outcomes include reoffending, recall and even death (Binswanger et al. 2007). In England and Wales, there has been an alarming (six-fold) increase in rates of suicide by those under post-release supervision.[2] The neglect of such a vulnerable group has been denounced as 'state abandonment' (Phillips and Roberts 2019).

In the United Kingdom, the report *Reducing re-offending by ex-prisoners* (Social Exclusion Unit 2002) foregrounded disadvantage and social exclusion, noting the strong association between indices of deprivation and the likelihood of reoffending. Yet the report also recognises this is a matter of social injustice. Censuses of prison populations, always and everywhere, disclose enormous social and economic disadvantage and this should be redressed, irrespective of any contingent effects on reconviction. The neediest of people, often reliant for their subsistence on over-burdened and impoverished families, are routinely failed by welfare systems.

The formidable problems of establishing adequate material security are compounded by the suspicions of many in mainstream society. Homelessness is a common problem (HM Inspectorate of Probation

2020): nearly six out of every ten women leaving prison in England have nowhere safe to go (Prison Reform Trust 2020). While struggling with such limited resources, former prisoners find accommodation providers to be wary of them. Work will be hard to find, especially if jobs are scarce. In some states of USA, some people with convictions are ineligible for welfare payments (Hoskins 2019). Insurance will be difficult to obtain with premiums prohibitively high, and claims can be refused if the criminal record of members of the household had not been disclosed. Credit will only be obtainable at exorbitant rates of interest. Even opening a bank account – close to an essential in UK and many other countries – can prove impossible because someone with a criminal record, a poor or non-existent credit history and lack of settled accommodation will fail to meet most banks' eligibility criteria. Social exclusion is marked in many other ways besides. In 2016 in USA it was estimated that just over 6 million people had lost the right to vote because of their criminal record (Sentencing Project 2016). More generally, in many countries, there is a broader denial of civic participation, including prohibitions on running for political office, acting as a trustee or sitting on a jury. A record may preclude any claim for compensation for criminal injury– as if being an offender (even an ex-offender) makes someone unworthy to be a victim (Henley 2018, 2019).

Sometimes obstacles are legally required (for example, there may be legal restrictions on the kinds of work that ex-prisoners may undertake), but at the least they are legally *countenanced* and tolerated (Henley 2019). Some countries try to protect people with criminal convictions from grosser injustices, allowing that convictions may become 'spent' and disregarded. Yet there are usually many exceptions and disclosure is often required: protection against discrimination is generally weak. In many countries, these exclusions and disadvantages follow the depressingly familiar contours of discrimination on racial grounds (Pager 2003). In one (UK) study, more than one-fifth of respondents reported on the 'double discrimination' of racism and suspicions of criminality, even when the most recent conviction was ten or more years ago (Stacey 2019). Released prisoners, then, are disadvantaged legally, economically, and socially (Visher and Travis 2003). Especially after long periods of imprisonment, the resources of civil society can be exceptionally hard for people to access. Attempts to remedy this can stumble over 'less eligibility' objections: when many people are in hardship and struggling to find adequate accommodation or to gain or keep employment, initiatives to support ex-offenders are always vulnerable to criticism that they are being unjustly favoured.

Ioan Durnescu (2019) highlights that while some of the 'pains of re-entry' are universal, some are more specific to nations and cultures. He discovered differences, for example, between the experiences of Romanian and Roma families. Socially excluded in most countries, Roma people were 'more inclusive and supporting, providing practical help, moral support, and emotional support' to members of their community returning from prison (Durnescu 2019: 1494). Western (2018) similarly found local and subcultural differences. There are, then, personal, social, cultural and structural variations in re-entry experiences (Visher and Travis 2003). Similarly, there are differences associated with age, gender, social class and other dimensions of diversity, and while statisticians might try to disentangle these variables, it is precisely the intersections and interactions between them that compound social injustice (Durnescu 2019).

## Resettlement, aftercare, supervision – and recall

The innumerable difficulties that confront people leaving prison have prompted initiatives to lend practical support and encouragement. In many countries, charitable organisations have offered material assistance and general guidance, practices which, with their avowed concerns for the ex-prisoner's well-being, used commonly to be known as aftercare. In England and Wales in the mid-1960s, these tasks were assigned to the Probation Service. For most adults, aftercare was voluntary: ex-prisoners had choice about availing themselves of this, although it remained a statutory responsibility for probation to provide it. At the same time, many people were released under various forms of statutory licence – parole and, for younger offenders, borstal, detention centre and young offender institution licences. Minimally these involved a requirement to report to a probation officer and to notify (and sometimes seek prior approval for) a change of address. Recall to custody was a possible response to non-compliance, although not common.

Aftercare, however, was gradually pushed to the margin by other conceptions of the purpose of contact. Post-release supervision now rested not on a decent acknowledgement of the difficulties that confront individuals leaving prison and returning to the earlier circumstances of disadvantage, typically made worse by the effects of incarceration; rather, the priority was to manage and reduce any risks of reoffending. A second consideration, however, related but conceptually distinct, was that parole and early release mechanisms brought with them a political obligation to show that the sentence was still being served, only now in the community. The term *aftercare* was replaced by *resettlement* or *re-entry*.

Although this looked like a new conception, a sentence carrying on after the time spent in custody had been part of the original vision for the semi-indeterminate sentence of Borstal Training for young offenders. There was a recognised need for continuity between the detention and post-custodial periods, although the emphasis had been on continuity of treatment rather than of punishment. Aftercare was not, as it were, an afterthought, but at the heart of the rationale – 'an essential element in the experiment' (Radzinowicz and Hood 1990: 384). Perhaps this was always over-ambitious or even fanciful. Not only did the institution fall short of its own aspirations, but the outside community, even when later professionalised by the involvement of probation staff, never had the skills or resources to provide anything like the treatment that the pioneers of Borstal envisaged. The aspiration of continuity of treatment nevertheless finds modern expression in the idea of 'through the gate' services. The more prison emphasises its rehabilitative purposes, the more insistent the demand that treatment should be sustained and built upon after release – a 'seamless' transition (Home Office 2001). Whether this is a realistic aspiration is debatable. As we have seen, there is a sharp ontological fracture between prison and the community: daily routines, priorities and motivations are altogether different. Any idea of continuity will always struggle against this reality.

As with those subject to CSM, the requirements of post-release supervision must be seen to be rigorously enforced. Indeed the political imperative is even more pressing because both the original offence and the perceived risks are likely to be more serious. Supervision must be demanding and tightly enforced; but the more the demands and the more assiduously they are supervised, the greater the scope for non-compliance. And for those released from prison under supervision, the options are few: recall[3] to prison is a common and even a first resort. Supervising staff are often so pressed for time and with such demanding caseloads that they lack the time to nurture compliance.

In many parts of the USA and (more arguably) in England and Wales, parole has moved away from a social work ethos towards control through monitoring and surveillance (Western 2018). Bruce Western found that staff in Boston (Massachusetts) administer drug tests, carry guns, monitor curfews, and collect fees. Those under supervision make brief and formal visits to offices where they may be tested for drug use and instructed to submit proofs of residence and employment. They may be required to pay towards the cost of their supervision, while non-payment could result in a violation and possible recall. Some supervisory practices are vexatious and unfair. Western (2018) came across cases where the reporting instructions of probation and parole agents could not possibly be fulfilled simultaneously, while release conditions substantially interfered with family life or with searches for employment – factors known to support desistance (Shapland and Bottoms 2017). Those with long criminal histories were well-known to the police, frequently stopped on the street and checked for warrants and supervision status. Some were caught up in incidents of crime or disorder with which they were no more than loosely associated and where any wrongdoing was never put to legal test, but even suspicions can be enough to trigger a recall to prison. Remarkably, those on supervision had a much lower self-reported crime rate than those unsupervised, but were reincarcerated twice as often (Western 2018: 127). This study found that being supervised was one of the strongest predictors of a return to custody (second only to relapse into substance misuse.) Practices like these, as well as a professional mind-set that regards individuals in terms of their risks and needs rather than cultivating strengths and potential (Maruna and LeBel 2010) can make criminal justice intervention more the hole in the boat than the fuel in the tank on the voyage to desistance (McNeill 2016b).

The US Council of State Governments Justice Center (2019) found that one in four admissions to state prisons nationwide is for a technical violation – for example, missing an appointment or failing a drug test –

and in thirteen states on any given day one-third of prisoners are
for a breach of supervision. In England and Wales, the number of
recalls rose by more than a quarter over four years, following the
extension of formal supervision to those serving shorter (under 12
month) sentences (Bulman 2019). The impact on women has been
especially marked (see also Holtfreter and Wattanaporn 2014). Imprisoned for shorter sentences and for much less serious offences, many
more women are now under supervision and liable to recall (Prison
Reform Trust 2018). At HM Prison Bronzefield, the largest female
prison in Europe, the number of recalls increased by nearly 40 per cent
in a year (Independent Monitoring Board 2018). The shift from aftercare to the priorities of resettlement has led to short-term but enor-
mously disruptive returns to prison.

Many have lost confidence and trust in their supervisors because of
this shift (Prison Reform Trust 2018). Their paramount needs – settled
accommodation, safety from violence and assistance with problems of
substance misuse and/or mental health – are beyond the capacity and
skills of criminal justice staff. But in addition people become wary of
confiding their difficulties to their supervisors, who may interpret
overwhelming needs as risk factors and invoke recall procedures. Drug
use, for example, is notoriously a lapsing condition and being open
with a supervisor about a lapse ought to lead to supportive interventions, but the prominent threat of enforcement and recall can make
people very wary of disclosure. Risk management becomes self-defeat-
ing. As Adrian Grounds argued:

> Supervision is not primarily a surveillance and crime control pro-
> cess, but a framework of support. Monitoring depends centrally on
> the maintenance of a relationship ... with every effort being made
> to achieve co-operation, openness and trust. Surveillance that is
> onerous and outside a framework of support may reduce the co-
> operation and disclosure on which effective continuing risk assess-
> ment depends.
>
> *(Grounds 1995: 56)*

In an atmosphere of mutual mistrust, misunderstandings are all the
more likely to occur. Kate Parsons (2019) found that both the grounds

and the processes of recall were poorly understood by those under supervision so that when recall did take place, unsurprisingly, it was often felt as unfair punishment rather than legitimate risk management (see also Digard 2010; Padfield 2012). Procedures experienced as unfair detract from legitimacy and may prejudice future dealings with probation.

Not only the process of recall, but also the scope for representation against such decisions and the question of what the prisoner must now accomplish to be released again are complex and unclear (Padfield 2012). Risk is supposed to be the determining factor in England and Wales, but its assessment is an uncertain exercise. As we saw in Chapter 4, Crewe (2011) showed that indeterminacy and what was seen as the arbitrariness of psychological assessment added depth, weight and tightness to the pains of imprisonment. But these insights, as Crewe notes, may have application also to people subject to community supervision. Especially in the case of more serious offenders, those under supervision may experience a constant anxiety about the threat of recall and uncertainty about how they are to show that their risks of reoffending are not increasing. Sometimes expectations are very clear, but interpretation of indices of risk, just as in prison, is contentious, amplifying the pains of re-entry. Digard's (2010) study group is of particular interest. He looked at people convicted of sex offences, where fears of reoffending may well lead to risk aversion and where procedures in place to guard against this can impose not only heavy burdens, but involve such 'tightness' (Hudson and Henley 2015). Violations like missed appointments may be taken as more than mere technicalities and as signs of increasing risk. Colin reflects 'I feel like I'm living on a knife edge with Probation, I feel under threat every day' (Hardwick 2017: 228).

Recall can bring benefits. Crimes may be averted (although maybe just postponed); relapse into self-destructive behaviour like serious drug misuse may be prevented by return to custody. Alice Goffman found examples of people actively seeking out prison 'as a safe haven when the streets get too dangerous' (Goffman 2015: 200). It seems as if returning to prison can be used *strategically*, by parolees as well as by their supervisors. Even so, it is sad to reflect that there has to be recourse to imprisonment when things are going badly wrong. Here, as in many other circumstances, prison is made to be the (far from last) resort when welfare provision fails. Most commonly, even when recall leads to just a short period of imprisonment, it can be quite enough time to disrupt resettlement. Any system that holds numbers of people in prison not because of their offences or as a deterrent or even as a means of managing risk, but often just because of formal or sometimes trivial failures to comply is losing its way. This is more recycling than resettlement (Maruna 2004).

Post-release supervision could find a rationale as a recognition of the needs of people leaving prison and society's duty to lend support (especially those needs associated with the damage occasioned by prison); as a means of providing rehabilitative continuity of treatment; as a continuation of the punishment; as a means of reducing risk. As so often in punishment, these several objectives do not always fit comfortably together. Notably, attempts to respond to need or to accomplish an effective continuity of care are subverted by the political imperative to be seen to monitor assiduously and to respond robustly to any violations – which, in effect, too often means going back to prison.

## Reoffending, reconviction and desistance

If technical breaches of licence requirements can lead to recall, reoffending is even more likely to bring about a return to prison. Indeed reoffending during the period of licence is considered to be the ultimate failure, the litmus test of the wisdom of the decision to release someone before full term. Yet the matter is more complex than this. If offences subsequent to release are less serious or less frequent than earlier patterns of offending, or with longer intervals between, this looks like progress. It is also necessary to keep in mind here distinctions between reoffending, re-arrest and reconviction. Arrest and conviction are artefacts of a criminal justice process – not just straightforward consequences of criminal conduct. Former prisoners, especially those subject to statutory supervision, are highly 'visible' and consequently more likely than others to have their behaviour closely scrutinised. Further offences are more likely to be detected and prosecuted.

Most studies propose that desistance should be seen as a sustained process – one that may involve 'drifts' in and out of offending (Matza

1964), an indirect pathway marked by lapses and relapses (Farrall and Calverley 2006). But if further offences are characteristic, reconviction is an inept measure of progress; recall procedures are poorly aligned to what evidence suggests about how desistance is accomplished. Recall to prison, moreover, is likely to cause disruption and delay to movements away from crime. Post-release supervision, then, is a clear example of the difficulties of understanding short-term interventions in the context of complex and uneven processes of desistance (Farrall, Mawby and Worrall 2007). The task might better be seen as an endeavour to respect people's dignity and their efforts to establish the lives that they would aspire to lead – matters of intrinsic value, irrespective of contingent effects upon reoffending and however elusive to measure statistically (Western 2018).

There is an extensive literature on how people come to make lives for themselves in which offending has no place (see, for example, Farrall and Calverley 2006; McNeill, Farrall, Lightowler and Maruna 2012; Shapland and Bottoms 2017; Graham and McNeill 2017). Scholars dispute the relative importance of personal motivation and agency or of more or less propitious social circumstances. Perhaps a sharp distinction is unhelpful: agency and structure, interacting continuously and mutually influential, are fully operative for everyone all the time. Personal relationships, opportunities for employment, accommodation and social resources are recognised to be especially supportive of desistance. At the same time, these 'hooks for change' (Giordano, Cernkovich and Rudolph 2002) have to be recognised *as* opportunities, appreciated for their worth and significance, and here the meaning that people make in events in their lives and the purposes they set for themselves are fundamentally important. It is here, perhaps, that criminal justice personnel can make their most valuable contributions, helping people to recognise 'hooks', building professional relationships that are truly valued, offering encouragement and hope (Rex 1999; Farrall and Calverley 2006).

Maruna (2001) emphasised the importance of personal narrative as the core of a new identity, a way of understanding oneself and the place of offending in this autobiography. Primary desistance (stopping offending) is accompanied by a secondary process (coming to regard oneself as someone who does not commit crimes). But identity cannot easily be formed or sustained without acknowledgement and endorse-ment from others and McNeill (2016a) has accordingly written of a tertiary desistance in which that new identity is fully respected and reinforced by other people. Nugent and Schinkel adopt a different terminology – 'act-desistance' for non-offending, 'identity desistance' for the internalisation of a non-offending identity and 'relational desis-tance' for recognition of change by others – which 'does not suggest sequencing in time or importance' (Nugent and Schinkel 2016: 570). Indeed changes in behaviour, in identity and in relationship are likely to be concurrent and mutually influential. Perhaps the restoration of rights is better seen as a precondition of successful rehabilitation rather than a reward for it (Henley 2019).

Desistance may be frustrated or obstructed where others are reluctant to accept this new identity, to allow that change is taking place. Many people with a criminal record encounter suspicion and mistrust: finding employment is a notorious challenge. Direct discrimination is not the only factor at work here: many offenders have few formal qualifications and structural changes in the employment market may compound their disadvantage (Farrall, Bottoms and Shapland 2010; Farrall, Gray and Jones 2020). Still, mistrust and even disdain of people with a criminal record persist, with imprisonment especially casting a long and deep moral shadow. This poses daunting obstacles to secondary desistance; an identity that is sought or even claimed while denied by others is hard to sustain. And since this new identity seems to be of such importance in the process overall, primary desistance may falter with an increased likelihood of further offending.

These burdens are all the heavier for people who encounter sexism, racism, homophobia and transphobia – doubly (or more) discriminated against, especially at the intersections where aversion and even hostility can increase exponentially. Some reactions from others may be inter-nalised, people coming to regard themselves as unworthy or even des-picable. Many convicted people feel too much guilt and remorse even when it may be hard for them to profess it. Lucy Baldwin writes mov-ingly of mothers leaving prison, who had anticipated a return to the comfort of familiar relationships but found instead that they were for-ever 'tainted' by prison – they felt themselves failures as mothers, with damaging consequences for their relationships with their children and families and their own self-esteem (Baldwin 2017).

The punishment continues, then, even when the sentence of the court has been completed. Continuing impositions may not be legally defined as punishment, but are often experienced in this way none-theless (Hudson and Henley 2015). Criminal records formalise this unfairness. In the United Kingdom the Rehabilitation of Offenders Act 1974 set a rehabilitation period after which convictions are regarded as 'spent', protections somewhat enhanced by the Legal Aid, Sentencing and Punishment of Offenders Act 2012. Yet the time periods them-selves (based on the punishment originally assigned, presumably as a proxy for the seriousness of the offence) have no basis in evidence of risk of reoffending. Indeed 'the ability of criminal records to predict future offending declines over time with reported rates of offending becoming similar to (or even lower than) those for previously un-con-victed people after approximately seven years' (Henley 2018: 293). Andrew Henley argues persuasively that legislation should be much bolder in its attempts to reclaim people from the 'civic purgatory' in which they are confined (see also Weaver 2018).

At various times and places, clipping the ear, slitting the nose, tattoos and brandings have been inflicted to mark the body, a token of bad character. The Greek word for such a mark is stigma. Anyone so stig-matised will probably be looked at askance and shunned, although there may be more confrontational and aggressive reactions. There is a sense in which a criminal record, widely accessible and too often accessed, performs this same function. Meanwhile, the accumulation and deployment of enormous amounts of personal criminal justice data have become commercialised in a financially profitable enterprise, drawing a number of organisations in civil society into the continuation of punishment in a haphazard and unreliable manner. This 'disorganised punishment … is characterized by a shift of *control* of criminal record information from government to private interests, which in turn shapes the form, content and reach of criminal records' (Corda and Lageson 2020: 260; their emphasis). New technologies have expanded the reach and public accessibility of criminal record data. Sarah Lageson (2020) suggests 'We've reached a point where the American public not only uses criminal records to make important decisions about who we employ or rent to, but also as fodder for entertainment, voyeurism, and public shaming' – a form of digital pursuit and persecution. Labels have become increasingly sticky (Uggen and Blahnik 2016). In a context of structural disadvantage, it is not surprising that many of those struggling to move away from offending experience 'real pain inherent in the maintenance of desistance' (Nugent and Schinkel 2016: 570), including isolation, loneliness and a miserable liminal state between being 'an offender' and an uncertain future self.

## The end state of wrongdoing and the conclusion of punishment

While jurists and philosophers have paid a great deal of attention to the allocation of punishment, to matters of desert, proportion and reductive effectiveness, much less consideration has been given to 'the end state of cases of wrongdoing' (Radzik 2009: 112). This state cannot be said to have been achieved while punishment persists and, as we have seen, the matter is not ended by the completion of the court's sentence. What, then, might this end state be like and how can it be accomplished? These are questions that arise not only for former prisoners, but for anyone who has been subject to punishment and indeed anyone with a criminal record, which may cover more than convictions.

A natural way of investigating this topic would be to focus on the position of the offender (or 'ex-offender' – or better still a person no longer regarded in terms of their past and worst behaviour). The concepts of rehabilitation and desistance have at their centre the individual's behaviour, and sometimes their associated attitudes, thoughts and emotions. But changes in these respects are just one way of understanding rehabilitation. Also to be considered are legal rehabilitation (the restoration of the individual to full civil rights once a punishment has been duly served) and social rehabilitation (a fair and effective opportunity to have access to the resources of civil society) (McNeill 2012).

McNeill writes also of 'moral rehabilitation', a fundamental if rather elusive idea. McNeill's own discussion of this centres on the individual and what is expected of them if they are to regain their status before the offence. First and least, what may be expected from them is a commitment to strive for better behaviour. It is hard to see how membership of a moral community can be regained unless the wrongdoer acknowledges and 'owns' the wrong, affirming shared values by promising to try to do better. Reparation or amends may be required, although it is not always easy to see how this could be achieved, especially where the offender has been sent to prison. Even when reparation is beyond the ability or resources of the offender, apology and remorse may be expected. In her perceptive analysis of remorse, Maslen writes of an unfolding, internal process, 'a complex syndrome involving affect, beliefs, desires, intentions and, often, action' (Maslen 2015: 6). Yet remorse can be difficult to express and its sincerity hard to gauge. Apology, a public avowal of remorse, seems valuable, if perhaps too easy, and can be powerful (Lazare 2004). While an apology ritual (Bennett 2008) may be the most that can be expected, in our usual associations with one another a good apology ought to be sincere, a genuine expression of true remorse.

Reform, apology and remorse still centre on the wrongdoer and thus fail to capture the relational aspect of achieving the end state. There is a need for more attention to the responses, acceptance and sometimes the active participation of victims, the community and the state. Crime itself can be understood as a disturbance of relationships: 'Whether or not they ever meet, offenders and their victims are locked into a relationship. Without knowing each other in reality, they know one another intimately in their imagination' (Marshall and Merry 1990: 1). The offence also damages the relationship between the wrongdoer and her community, a community bound together by commitment to the values her crime has violated. Raynor and Robinson (2009: 160) refer accordingly to a 'relational reintegration' into a moral community. Perhaps an end to punishment can be said to take place when these damaged relationships are repaired, 'the relational' implying responsibilities on all sides (Bazemore 1998).

Perhaps forgiveness could achieve a resolution of the wrongful act, bringing an end to punishment. If apology seems too easy, similarly forgiveness may call for more than words, more too than passive forbearance. Forgiveness, like remorse, seems to involve feelings, beliefs and actions: for example, where emotions and actions still evince resentment, forgiveness has not been achieved. If crimes are offences against the state and the community as well as against victims, however, it is not clear where the right to forgive rests. Forgiveness seems personal, implying the wrong kind of relationship between the state and the citizen. There may still be a place for this in seeking to mend the relationship between offender and victim. Restorative justice is a process that may attempt this mending, although it is instructive to discover that the words 'forgive' and 'forgiveness' are not often heard in these encounters (Shapland 2016; for general accounts of restorative justice, see Johnstone 2002; Cornwell, Blad and Wright 2013.)

Nussbaum (2016) expresses other misgivings about forgiveness. Where it is conditional on expressions of remorse, it may involve abasement and humiliation so that some forms of conditional forgiveness in themselves come close to punishment. Even unconditional forgiveness risks claiming a moral superiority and an undue focus on the past, which could disfigure a relationship. Forgiveness can also be self-serving (with insufficient regard to the other) if the purpose is simply to set aside one's own destructive anger without regard to the intrinsic moral worth of words or acts of forgiveness. Forgiveness bespeaks generosity and grace, but maybe also condescension: 'if we are the ones doing the forgiving, we are proud of our generous behavior in forgiving the offending party' (Lazare 2004: 228).

The US 'Second Chance Act' similarly proclaims the (religiously inspired) generosity of those bestowing this opportunity (Green 2013). But the conclusion of the lawfully assigned punishment should not depend on any such graciousness, with an implication that it might be withheld, but is a matter of justice. (And given the massive disadvantages and trauma in the lives of so many people with convictions, it is fair to wonder when they had their first chance.) And isn't forgiveness supposed to be *instead of* punishment – not as well as or after?

If rehabilitation is too centred on the offender and forgiveness problematic, a better term might be *reconciliation* which implies responsibilities on all sides. Testimony of remorse and expressions of a determination to do better must be met by reciprocal commitments from the community and the state. McNeill's (2012) forms of rehabilitation, here reframed as forms of reconciliation, once more constitute a useful framework for exploring what this might amount to. The state's most obvious contribution might be to attend to legal reconciliation so that the formalised and legal obstructions of an end to punishment can be removed, by forbidding improper discrimination on the grounds of a criminal record. The record will sometimes remain relevant but disclosure should be targeted so that opportunities are not denied merely on the basis of vague intimations of bad character (Henley 2019).

Social reconciliation should involve active and considered attempts to enable fair access to opportunities and resources to match individuals' efforts to desist. This would be a fitting recognition of the positive rights of offenders, entitlements that derive not only from their membership of the community, but also from the damage that has been done to them collaterally by the imposition of the punishment. Two caveats should be noted. First, fair access will not be a privileged access, but will take full account of the (typically disadvantaged) position of so many. Resources must be genuinely accessible and this will sometimes call for special arrangements accordingly. Second, opportunities should not depend upon individuals' efforts at desistance or, more precisely, on somebody's judgements about this: doors, as it were, should always remain open.

## Moral reconciliation and associated emotions

What then of moral reconciliation? Chapter 1 discussed the *relegation* that marked punishment and posed the question what it would take to restore someone to their moral standing.[4] The rituals of arrest, prosecution and conviction need somehow to be reversed before the end state could be said to have been achieved. Some cultures practise 'reintegration ceremonies', although these take place in the immediate aftermath of wrongdoing and are the means to determine the fitting response, rather than taking place after (often protracted) punishment by the state (Braithwaite and Mugford 1994). They are perhaps better described as *repentance rituals* (Braithwaite 2000). Examples may also be found in the western European tradition. In sixteenth-century Calvinist kirks in Scotland, for instance, a 'stool of repentance' could be found on which penitent wrongdoers were seated throughout the service, facing the congregation. At the end of the service, penitents were welcomed and restored. The stool bespeaks the humiliation of punishment, but also the certainty of restoration (Todd 2002). The stool was often the last in a sequence of rites on successive Sundays: 'a cliff-hanger serial in several episodes. ... the penitent might move in a series of stages from the kirk prison to the burgh market-place to the kirk door to the stool in the centre of the kirk before finally hearing forgiveness pronounced' (MacCulloch 2004: 598).

Shadd Maruna (2011) has mounted a strong argument for modern rituals of reintegration, involving public participation as well as witnessing, offering examples of where these already take place and how they might be elaborated. There are practices now that attempt to acknowledge efforts towards desistance – certificates of programmes completed, letters of commendation, early discharge from licence obligations or court orders – although these are all private and can do nothing to sway the emotions of the public. Maruna argues that rituals can 'play a particularly powerful role in the shaping of human sensibility and imagination. *They create mental states, not simply express them*' (ibid.: 9; emphasis added). This latter point is significant. It may be the rituals in the kirk succeeded just because they went with the grain of community sentiment, expressing precisely how community members did and should regard one another. Similarly, rituals of downgrading of the offender chime with the sentiments that such crimes typically arouse. But here Maruna is insisting on the possibility that rituals may inspire and lead, not merely express existing feelings. As Mary Douglas puts it, '[But] in fact ritual does not play this secondary role, it can come first in formulating experience. ... It does not merely externalise experience, bringing it out into the light of day, but it modifies experience in so expressing it' (Douglas 2003 [1966]: 65).

A ritual of reintegration might afford an opportunity to focus on the achievements and other dimensions of character to resist any reduction of an individual to their worst behaviour, constituting a formally endorsed and certificated 'de-labelling'. One concern, however, is that, notoriously, rituals can fail or misfire (Maruna 2011; see also Chapter 1 above): what might have been intended as a formal declaration of regained status could be construed differently by others and appropriated for other purposes. In particular, such a ritual, in order to achieve its aims, would inevitably call to mind the very wrongs that the ritual is now trying to expunge, risking a rekindling of the anger that the crime originally evoked. The familiar problem arises of meanings intended and meanings received.

One of the most conspicuous strengths of Maruna's analysis lies in its recognition that such rituals should be 'symbolic and emotive' (Maruna 2011: 14). It is emotions that lie behind a reluctance to adopt the legal and social measures required for reconciliation and it is in and through actions more than words that other emotions may be engaged. Nils Christie (1977) similarly emphasised the importance of *participation* in processes of responding to wrongs, while Ian Loader (2011) argues that changes in attitudes towards punishment are more likely to be achieved when people are involved in these processes, rather than being insulated from them by experts or 'persuaded' by evidence. Mike Nellis (2009) urges reformers to make greater use of the emotive power of stories in films and novels of wrongdoers returning, redeemed and welcomed.

There have been such optimistic anticipations of the end of punishment. In 1787, Benjamin Rush, extolling the spirit and ambitions of the new penitentiary, waxed lyrical:

> Methinks I already hear the inhabitants of our villages and townships counting the years that shall complete the reformation of one of their citizens. I behold them running to meet him on the day of his deliverance. His friends and family bathe his cheeks with tears of joy; and the universal shout of the neighbourhood is, 'This our brother was lost as is found – was dead, and is alive.'
>
> *(Rush 1787: 7; quoted in Goodman, Page and Phelps 2017: 24)*

Rather more than a century later and on another continent, Oscar Wilde's reflections make a stark contrast: 'prison makes a man a pariah. I, and such as I am, have hardly any right to air and sun. Our presence taints the pleasures of others. We are unwelcome when we reappear. To revisit the glimpses of the moon is not for us' (Wilde 1999 [1897]: 54).

The emotions that lie behind the attitudes that Wilde encountered and which block moral reconciliation may be the same as those associated with the original will to punish. Anger at the original offence may, as time passes, be dormant, but it may not take much for it to awaken: to bring a grave offence to memory may be to relive it. Fear of future bad behaviour is often put forward – notably when early release is under consideration for someone who has committed the gravest of crimes. Yet sometimes these responses make much more sense when they are understood as an aversion closer to disgust, masquerading as (though sometimes no doubt mingled with) fear. The unspoken sentiment is that people who have committed such appalling crimes are unfit to live among us. Since disgust is an uncomfortable emotion to avow, these reactions may be rationalised as fear. Meanwhile the emotionally sterile language of risk assessment and management may be put to use to lend a specious scientific respectability to decisions that are grounded in these concealed emotions.[5] It is as if the bad character which found expression in dreadful crimes is inherent and ineradicable – intrinsic wickedness in moral language, intractable psychopathy (or other personality disorder) in the terminology of psychiatry. *He's the man who did* becomes *he's the kind of man who does* and hence *he will*. Grave crime is taken as a manifestation of the essence of the person – their inherent and irremediable evil. This countenances extreme punishments leaving efforts at rehabilitation futile (Cusac 2009). Wilde's choice of words like *pariah* and *taints* is revealing: these terms evoke disgust and anxieties about contamination (Miller 1997; Kahan 1998). And in the absence of accepted rituals of cleansing, distancing – specifically, the distancing achieved by prolonged incarceration – can seem the only alternative.

Disgust may be the most plausible emotional characterisation of reactions to the most serious crimes, although it seems too strong for less serious offences. Even so, the persistence of aversive attitudes towards people who steal, for example, or who do violence to others cannot be accounted for by fear and certainly not by fear alone. There are other emotions at work here as well – whether disgust, contempt, disdain, suspicion or mistrust – and the assuaging of fear (itself hard to achieve) would not necessarily lead to a change in attitude or behaviour towards them. It may be that the vehement resistance to making improvements in processes towards legal and social reconciliation is animated by these darker and deeper emotions, harder to identify and harder still to acknowledge.

What might it be like for those striving towards desistance (or even those who have yet to make such attempts) to be so regarded? As one of Tony Parker's respondents said:

> I do feel prison's where I belong. There are good days and bad days, but even on the good days that feeling doesn't change … if the truth's to be said, I'm beyond the pale of ordinary society and couldn't ever get back inside it again. I don't think I'm properly living in society and never could because I'm not a fit member of it, I only belong to it in theory, I'd like to put it like that. I'm outside humanity, both in humanity's eyes and mine.
>
> *(Parker 1991: 167)*

It is hard to imagine a more crushing way of being regarded. Sometimes those encountering such attitudes will react with anger or aggression; more usually, they will respond by retreating with mixed feelings of shame and resentment. These are not feelings that are likely to bring out the best in people or encourage them in desistance.

## Conclusions

This chapter began by discussing the enormous adversities that people released from prison usually encounter. 'More than just poor and out of work, these men and women embody vulnerability, struggling with mental illness, drug addiction, and physical disability. Poor mental and physical health are markers of human frailty that add decisively to the insults of poverty' (Western 2018: 46). Yet the dominant status of offender (even ex-offender) can obscure recognition of vulnerability, constraining any inclination to respond to their needs. Since the actions of the state in imposing its punishments have led to the worsening of so many difficulties, it might be supposed that the state has incurred a corresponding duty to redress this (Rotman 1986). This is a matter of justice: however deserved the punishment, the incidental detrimental consequences are beyond desert. Yet the predicament is exacerbated by formal supervision and arrangements for resettlement, which, so far from lending the required support, are often experienced as burdensome and discouraging.

Exploring the 'end state', the word *reconciliation* was preferred to the more common terms of *rehabilitation* or *desistance* which put the principal focus on the individual. Reconciliation may capture the inherently *relational* character of the end state and the corresponding obligations on all sides to contribute: as Erving Goffman (1963) insisted, stigma is better understood as a function of relationships, rather than a personal attribute. Oscar Wilde pondered:

> When the man's punishment is over, it leaves him to himself; that is to say, it abandons him at the very moment when its highest duty towards him begins. It is really ashamed of its own actions, and shuns those whom it has punished, as people shun a creditor whose debt they cannot pay, or one on whom they have inflicted an irreparable, an irremediable wrong. I can claim on my side that if I realise what I have suffered, society should realise what it has inflicted on me; and that there should be no bitterness or hate on either side.
>
> *(Wilde 1999 [1897]: 61)*

In so many ways, society shows its disdain and rejection towards those it claims to want to rehabilitate and, as well as riding roughshod over their rights, puts itself at greater risk of their reoffending. Bad characters are thought likely to commit crimes, any further offences vindicating these suspicions. Yet these very attitudes contribute to recidivism: continuing discrimination, marginalisation and unwillingness to countenance full reconciliation make offending more likely. When the formal punishment has concluded, many people are stuck in a liminal state, trapped between hope and despondency, between society's claims to support them in their efforts towards desistance and the reality of the circumstances and attitudes that confront them. No longer prisoners, but by no means free, they often engage with agencies who should be helping but often speak the language of threat in a relationship marked by imbalances of power. Mary Douglas, recognising that liminal states in themselves attract confusion and suspicion, remarked

> The man who has spent any time 'inside' is put permanently 'outside' the ordinary social system. With no right of aggregation which can definitively assign him to a new position he remains in

the margins, with other people who are similarly credited with unreliability, unteachability, and all the wrong social attitudes.

*(Douglas 2003 [1966]: 97)*

Radzik (2009: 8) ponders 'how might wrongdoers come to merit a better evaluation?', but the question has been raised here whether they will get it, even if merited. To answer this question it is necessary to reflect on the emotions that enable society to accept and sometimes even to celebrate an unwillingness to call an end to punishment. In their different ways, several scholars have recognised the need to engage with these emotions and appreciated that this is much more likely to be accomplished by ritual (Maruna 2011), participation (Christie 1977; Loader 2011) or by the empathy invoked by film and literature (Nellis 2009).

The chapter opened with the supposition that once a punishment had achieved its ends (purposes) it would conclude. The multiplicity of purposes set for punishment, not all mutually compatible or even achievable, complicate that idea. The criminal justice system often supposes that the end state is desistance, but it has been argued that this risks losing the relational aspects and the corresponding duties on all sides. That a society has duties towards people with convictions and not just rights against them is a politically unfashionable notion, but is therefore all the more in need of affirmation. Without a fuller understanding of the obstacles to reconciliation, the legal, social and moral burdens that persist long after the court sentence has been fulfilled, there is unlikely to be a change from the experience voiced by one of Hardwick's respondents: 'The punishment never stops' (Rebecca, quoted in Hardwick 2017: 197).

## Notes

1. For some other vivid examples, see https://content-static.detroitnews.com/projects/second-chance-granted/index.htm.
2. The suicide rate for the general population is about 14 per 100,000; for prisoners it is around 83; the rate among people leaving prison in 2018–2019 was 212 (Phillips and Roberts 2019).
3. The word *recall* reveals the conditionality of their status. People are not being 'sent' to prison, but called back on the basis of a failure to respect the conditions of release.

4. Among the reservations sometimes expressed about rehabilitation/restoration is its implication that people should be returned to their state before the offence – often a state of disadvantage and hardship (for example, Carlen 2012). In the terms of this account, however, this objection relates to social rather than moral rehabilitation.
5. Assessment instruments are said to be at their most reliable when based on unchangeable indicators like previous record (Howard, Francis, Soothill and Humphreys 2009), making change much harder to demonstrate.

# CONCLUSION

## Punishment and the good society

This chapter attempts to draw out some of the implications for policy and practice of the ideas set out throughout the book. Understanding punishment involves much more than attention to its material forms or the purposes set for it. Like any other human institution, punishment can only be appreciated by trying to grasp the meanings found and made in its practices – by politicians, by the general public, by staff involved in its implementation and, especially, by those subject to it. Emotions are irreducibly involved in these determinations of meaning. The concept of hegemony was adduced in Chapter 2 to explain how dominant patterns of thinking about crime and punishment suppress other interpretations, embedding some ideas so deeply that to question them seems not only foolish, an affront to common sense, but disloyal and vicious. Hegemony also shapes feelings about fitting responses to crimes, evoking especially anger, fear and disgust, directing these sentiments towards actions and people.

While most of this book has tried to understand punishment, attention here turns to normative theories as well. In truth, those who study this subject with a view to enhancing justice need to engage with both types of theory: an explanatory theory – to gauge the scope for reform, trying to identify opportunities, obstacles and resistance to change; a normative account to guide direction. Discussion begins with the ethics of punishment, reviewing the familiar attempts at justification. Many accounts suppose that punishment brings benefits, but the argument here is that punishment rarely achieves the goals set for it and makes many of the problems it purports to resolve much worse. Abolitionism will be considered as a strategy, but especially as 'a way of seeing' (Ruggiero 2014: 3464) – one that is starkly opposed to any project of

DOI: 10.4324/9780429055829-7

governing through crime and punishment (Simon 2007). Reliance on punishment to pursue social goods is both inept and corrupting. Many common modes of punishment should be regarded as unworthy of a good society.

## Ethics of punishment

Moral philosophers and theologians have attended to punishment, their discussions interwoven with inquiries into good and evil, free will and responsibility, causality and determinism, eschatology and theodicy (Bean 1981). Consequentialist arguments (the moral value of actions to be assessed their effects) are countered by deontic approaches (grounded in obligations and duties), with the topic of punishment constituting a fertile ground for exploring and exposing the merits and shortcomings of these respective approaches to ethics (Canton 2017).

Much of this extensive literature approaches the topic as an inquiry into *the justification of punishment*. A usual beginning is to try to establish why punishment requires justification and, at its simplest, this is held to arise because punishment involves the state's imposing harms, pains, deprivations and indignities, which is not something that the state is normally expected or entitled to do. Rights are at their most vulnerable during processes of arrest, prosecution and punishment and the state must be seen to act with probity in these matters. A nation's moral standing internationally is at least partly determined by its respect for human rights and treatment of people who have broken its laws. Almost all writers are eager to explain that their attempts at justification do not amount to a defence of any existing practices: their project is to specify what a morally defensible form of punishment would have to be like.

Those who attempt justification typically make it on one or more of three grounds: (i) punishment makes a community safer by reducing crime; or (ii) it vindicates the suffering of victims; or (iii) it is something due to the offender as a matter of desert or even as of right.[1] Each of these attempts at justification rests on an important social good: people should be safe from the abuse or exploitation of others; those who have been harmed are entitled to compassionate regard and support;

wrongdoers should be treated in a manner that is fitting, deserved and respects their standing as responsible agents.

i The empirical case for believing that punishment is the way to reduce crimes is unpersuasive (Bottoms and von Hirsch 2012; Tonry 2020). Incapacitation and rehabilitation may sometimes contribute to reduced reoffending, but the stock of offenders is constantly replenished. It is for this reason that particular weight is often put upon deterrence, though also on the educative force of the affirmation of shared values. These address everyone, not only people who have been convicted. Yet the weight of evidence is that the chances of detection are a much more compelling deterrent than the prospect of the punishment (Nagin 2013). Again, there is merit in a society declaring and clarifying its values and punishment may be one way to do this, contributing to the education of its citizens (Hampton 1984). But the weight of punishment must not obscure the message it is intended to impart. If undue emphasis is placed upon prudential, self-interested reasons to refrain from crime, this risks suppressing the proper normative considerations. Punishment, after all, provides a reason not to get caught, rather than grounds for refraining from offending.

ii The claim that punishment alone or best honours the victim is also prominent in political debate. The decent compassion that people feel for victims of crime appears to be frustrated when punishment is found inadequate. The association between the weight of the punishment and the gravity of crime can be so culturally embedded that a failure to punish sufficiently is taken as an indication that the crime is not being taken seriously enough, the victim denied due respect. Yet punishment is not all that victims may need. There may, for instance, be a place for material recompense, for counselling or other forms of support. While compassion and solidarity are common motives for punishment, where this leads to nothing but a demand for imposing pains these sentiments look more like anger. Moreover, preoccupation with retribution can lock victims into a destructive cycle of bitterness and resentment. As with bereavement, anger may be a step – perhaps a necessary step – but it must not become a destination.

iii There is a compelling intuition that punishment is something that is deserved and it is this, not its consequences, that constitutes its justification. Giving a robust and morally defensible account of this intuition and its implications turns out to be complex, however (Canton 2017: ch. 4; Brooks 2021). How much punishment is deserved is a function of harm (not always easy to assess), but also of responsibility which is even more difficult to work out: the criminal law can struggle to accommodate the many ways in which full responsibility might be compromised by (for example) constraint, poverty, distress or confusion (Kelly 2021). Assigning a just punishment is further complicated when its impact can be so different on different people.

Still, to respect the agency of the wrongdoer and their standing as a morally responsible member of a community there must be an expression of censure (see Chapter 1). The wrongdoer must be addressed explicitly and called to account; society should not be indifferent towards the flouting of its values, victims assured their distress evokes a response of solidarity. The pains of punishment constitute a communication and this is taken to justify hard treatment. It is a further question, however, what forms of punishment might accomplish the appropriate communication. Heavy punishment may suppress the moral message, shifting the individual's attention away from repentant recognition of their wrongs towards self-pity and resentment. If censure is to be more than mere scolding and include an appeal to moral responsibility, some forms of punishment undermine the message, as does any reluctance to countenance reconciliation (Chapters 4 and 5).

Defences of punishment, then, invoke three undoubted social goods, but the extent to which they could be advanced in these ways is much less certain. A better beginning is to recognise there are three endeavours that call for distinct responses rather than simple reliance on punishment. Instead of enquiring about 'the justification of punishment' questions might be reframed to ask:

- *What interventions and changes would make for a safer society?*
- *How best might the experience of victims be vindicated?*
- *What response to wrongdoing would best respect the wrongdoer?*

These questions should be addressed both in terms of moral propriety and effectiveness, which punishment largely fails on both counts (Canton 2017). So far from advancing social goods, established modes of punishment may undermine them – by making crimes more rather than less likely to occur, by ignoring victims or compounding their distress, by suppressing opportunities for individual wrongdoers to understand and so to take full responsibility for what they have done.

Two of the purposes set for punishment – doing right by victims and by offenders – might be advanced by restorative approaches, recognising that dialogue and the active participation of all most directly affected by crime are not only central to resolution, but also to strengthening community bonds. Restorative justice also appreciates the importance of context: wrongdoer and victim are not reduced to those roles, but recognised holistically with regard to other dimensions of their lives, their relationships with one another and with the rest of the community. Others have urged the value of transformative justice (for example Schenwar 2014): a crime should be an occasion for learning in order to minimise the possibility of recurrence – and often for discovering other things besides. Punishment's singular focus on wrongdoers distracts from these enquiries, forfeiting opportunities to understand.

The powerful emotions of fear, anger and disgust, driving the will to punish, suppress more measured, principled and effective responses. It will not be enough to apply ethical principles to guide practices. There must also be regard to what takes place when such attempts are made, to what the world tells us back when punishments are put into effect. Aspirations are constantly thwarted with undesirable consequences, perhaps because both the application of principle and the implementation of policy are always refracted through these emotional impulses.

## The wrongs and harms of punishment

An ethical appraisal of punishment should also foreground its impact on the undeserving and the most vulnerable. The children of imprisoned parents may be profoundly harmed (see Chapter 4). The pains visited upon these children can be seriously detrimental and long-lasting, damaging not only intimate relationships at formative times, but also implanting in their minds the notion that the state is hostile, its institutions not worthy of trust (Condry and Minson 2020). The effect of this on the social order is underestimated, considerable and long-term (Wakefield and Wildeman 2013). Relationships with partners (a common pathway to desistance) are likely to be disturbed and sometimes brought to an end, even though many show extraordinary levels of commitment and resilience (Comfort 2009). The parents of people in prison are also subject to sadness and stress (Gueta 2018). These 'drifts' are recognised for their injustices and there are possibilities to mitigate them (Lippke 2017), but it is disquieting and instructive to see how little these efforts achieve and indeed how rarely and feebly attempts are made.

Damage extends to neighbourhoods and communities. All countries have their 'high crime' zones, typically coinciding with districts whose residents experience high levels of punishment. In parts of USA, for example, these areas, already ravaged by poverty and multiple disadvantage, are further devastated by the mass incarceration of men (especially young black men), distorting both the economy and the local demography (Clear, Rose, Waring and Scully 2003; Clear 2007, 2008). Moreover, 'the heavy reliance on incarceration as a formal control may weaken the social ties and community structures that support informal social control' (Morenoff and Harding 2014: 421), leading to further crime. These are communities that are over-policed in pursuit of offenders, while under-policed in the protection of victims (Goffman 2015).

In many Western societies, punishment is concentrated, weighing most heavily on the poorest and most disadvantaged. It is also commonly racialised, fomenting racism and resentment with disastrous consequences for the social fabric (Western 2007; Alexander 2011). Poorer people have sorely limited access to resources that might help with problems of addiction and/or mental health. When the welfare safety net fails (not unusual), those in poverty lack the resources to seek out supports and remedies, and the manifestation of these problems can lead to crimes, arrest and punishment. Living or working on the streets, gang associations, and drug use make people more likely to be prosecuted, convicted, and sentenced more heavily. The deprivations and disadvantages so overrepresented in prison populations are sometimes regarded as criminogenic factors. But they 'predict' punishment more reliably than offending. In this way, 'punishment plays a central role in constructing and reinforcing social inequalities' (McNeill 2018: 54). The emotional responses which drive punishment neutralise misgivings about punishing the least advantaged and most damaged members of society. Their plight is taken to be their own fault and contempt may block compassion. These are dimensions of the ethics of punishment that are rarely scrutinised in philosophical debate. Yet a penal system that compounds social inequalities and disadvantages forfeits any entitlement to the name of justice.

The harms that punishment inflicts go beyond personal pains imposed upon wrongdoers, their families and communities. It has a direct effect on the character of society itself: punishment 'creeps'.

> [A] nation's attitudes towards the methods it adopts have a tendency to pervade its culture. They move into and through society, affecting (and shaped by) sometimes surprising things – our jokes, popular culture, political attitudes, and influential religious practices. As we punish, so we are.
>
> *(Cusac 2009: 74)*

It is not always easy to assess whether this is an insidious creep or a strategic extension. Jonathan Simon (2007) argued that the US government, confronted with intractable problems of poverty and disadvantage arising from or aggravated by market capitalism, increasingly began to reframe many of these problems *as crimes*. While the consequences of deprivation and poverty cannot be resolved – not, at least, without a radical change to social structures – people can be threatened, arrested and sent to prison, demonstrating the authority of the state and enhancing its legitimacy. Mentalities and technologies considered appropriate to crimes began to infiltrate other institutions of civil society so that any number of kinds of unwanted actions were either criminalised or treated as crime-like, calling for threats to avert them and punitive responses when they did occur.

The hegemonic stipulation of what counts as a social problem and how to respond is further buttressed by the emotional: governments have encouraged particular kinds of feeling about crime and what counts as a fitting response. Instructively, Simon begins his account by arguing that one origin of 'governing through crime' was the state's recognition of *fear* – a fear which, however well-grounded, is sometimes conjured and directed for political gain. Governing through crime includes reliance on and early resort to punishment. Among the effects of this are an overwhelming demand on the agencies of criminal justice that expand (more prisons for instance) or, where resource constraints preclude this, target their diminishing resources on the most vulnerable, most catchable and most punishable. For example, all the apparatus of criminalisation and enforcement are commonly brought to bear against substance misuse (and even use), bringing further pains and frustrations to users with no social benefit. Crimes that are precipitated by trauma, abuse, neglect and poverty are also behaviours that call for a more considered response, for both practical and ethical reasons. And it is crimes with such origins that are most found within the criminal justice systems of many countries. Understanding these as manifestations of social problems, rather than resting content with the denunciation of wrongdoing, would conduce to safer and more peaceful societies.

The framing of some problems as crimes is not only inept but cruel. A conspicuous example is the response of some countries towards migration (Bosworth 2017). The reasons for the mass movement of peoples are economic and geopolitical, while the consequent difficulties are complex and can seem intractable. Yet criminalisation – walls, patrol boats, detentions and punishments supposed to be deterrent – brings further misery to people in acute distress. The term *crimmigration* has been coined to refer to this melding of penal practice and the management of immigration which has often entailed a hostile response to people who can so readily be represented as 'other'. Decent responses are warped by fear, while disdain or contempt can countenance cruelties that might otherwise be considered intolerable (for example, conditions in some immigration camps or centres, the forcible separation of parents and children). Crimmigration reinforces and is reinforced by racism in those (common) circumstances in which migrants are or are believed to be of an ethnic group minoritised in the country in which they are seeking refuge (Franko 2020). In this regard, punitivism and racism form ready alliance. Michael Ignatieff writes (Ignatieff 2017: 133): 'The debates that matter most in any society are always about who belongs. Everyone ... turns this from a question of fact to a question of value – in other words, into a question of who deserves to be counted as one of "us".'

## Abolitionism[2]

The strategy most starkly opposed to governing through crime and punishment might be called abolitionism. The cause of abolishing prisons has a long history, associated with political positions recognising the dangers of an over-mighty state (Ruggiero 2014). Abolitionism tends to be favoured by those with faith in human goodness and mutual aid which the state and its coercive institutions are believed to corrupt. The case usually begins with an indictment of punishment, and in particular of the prison, its limitations, outright failures and aggravations of the problems that it is supposed to solve. Crime is better reduced by changes to the political and social order and by ensuring effective access to adequate services and resources, especially in education, housing, healthcare and other welfare provision. Prison cannot and should not attempt to substitute for these. Enhancing equality and social justice would almost certainly have marked effects on the levels of many crimes and are in any case morally imperative undertakings. Although many people find a way of protecting themselves from recognising the inherent cruelties of prison, its miseries, heaped upon the most vulnerable, provide another push towards abolition. In response to those who urge prison reform, some have concluded that the prison is so fundamentally corrupted and toxic an institution that it needs to be done away with (Davis 2003; Scott 2018).

To ask what might take its place is an unpromising start. Angela Davis (2003: 106) urges the need 'to let go of the desire to discover one single alternative system of punishment that would occupy the same footprint as the prison system.' Rather than proposing a specific set of institutions or practices, abolitionism is 'an approach, a perspective, a methodology, and most of all a way of seeing' (Ruggiero 2014: 3464).

It has already been argued that there are three distinct challenges to be separated out. First, the aspiration to make society safer. This might begin with social rather than criminal justice. Just as governing through crime conceptualises any number of regulatory infractions as crimes, abolitionism should seek opportunities to conceptualise bad behaviours that are now treated as crimes in different ways – as manifestations of trauma, for example, distress, addiction or poverty. So regarded, other responses – both more principled and more effective – might begin to suggest themselves. Secondly, the vindication of the distress of victims should keep its focus on the needs of victims rather than on the infliction of pains on the wrongdoer. Third, the legitimate censure of wrongdoing should attend how that communication can be meaningfully conveyed, rather than relying on a communicatively inept hard treatment that is likely to result in resentment and self-pity more than engaging the individual's sense of moral responsibility. Unless censure leaves a place for attending to the individual's perspective and encourages change, it amounts only to denunciation.

An illuminating way of exploring abolitionism might be to note correspondences with the concept of desistance. First, both abolition and desistance refer to the absence or elimination of something and, in the first instance, have less to say about what follows. Many people with criminal convictions see their prospects as limited and bleak, daunted by doubts about what desistance might involve (Nugent and Schinkel 2016). Similarly, prison is so taken for granted that proposals to abolish it meet with puzzlement and scepticism. Indeed, 'Decarceration comes with a heavy share of unpredictability' (Schenwar 2014: 134). Yet just as efforts to desist should not be abandoned, so uncertainties about what may follow should not discourage the cause of doing away with harmful penal institutions.

Second, both desistance and abolition are better considered as a process than an event. Desistance should be understood in this way – as a continuing endeavour, an ongoing accomplishment, rather than a specific goal or end state (for example, Bushway et al. 2001; McNeill and Weaver 2010). Similarly, the abolitionist project may be regarded as a process, one which is always 'unfinished' but in which progress can always be imagined (Mathiesen 2014). Third and relatedly, the process of desistance is rarely straightforward, characteristically marked by relapses into offending – a zigzag path as it is commonly called. Even so, there are possibilities to identify direction, steps or way-markers of desistance (Bottoms and Shapland 2011), including reductions in rates, frequency or seriousness of any further offending. Instructively,

Schenwar uses the metaphor of a 'jagged' path in discussing abolition (Schenwar 2014: 122) and this too will suffer its setbacks. A political climate of anxiety (not necessarily crime-related) or some dreadful event may induce people to revert to the reassuringly familiar mechanisms of punishment. Progress towards abolition may nevertheless be discerned by decriminalisation, by diversion from prosecution, by decreases in the numbers in prison and subject to community supervision, by reduction in the reach and grip of the criminal justice system, and perhaps by 'defunding' the organisations of criminal justice or other financial strategies to shift incentives away from imprisonment (Ball 2014; Bierschbach and Bibas 2017). These approaches are all likely to raise anxiety because of the hegemonic belief that criminal justice is the way to check bad behaviour. Yet the only certain consequence of criminalisation and punishment is to create crimes and criminals, its effect on incidence usually speculative (Christie 2004).

Fourth, the path to desistance is often not a direct reversal of the path into crime. Rather than addressing the 'criminogenic needs' that assessment attempts to uncover, strengths may be nurtured and developed, new ways of living found to supersede old habits (Shapland and Bottoms 2017). In the same way, a commitment to abolitionism should seek to strengthen trustworthiness and trust, compassion, decency and other virtues inimical to punitive instincts. To the extent those ambitions prosper, the emotional impulses to punish will recede and punishment's institutions progressively be seen as unnecessary and unworthy.

Fifth, different dimensions of desistance have been usefully distinguished (Maruna and Farrall 2004; Nugent and Schinkel 2016), as discussed in Chapter 5, and abolition may be conceptualised in just this manner (see Table 1).

A sixth parallel is an awareness of the resistance and obstacles to achieving desistance and abolition. For example, financial hardship and excitement may be inducements to renewed offending (Shapland and Bottoms 2011); former associates may encourage offending; those who attempt to put their past behind them often find their efforts frustrated by others who doubt their motivation or capacity to change, limiting their social inclusion and their opportunities to find ways of living without offending. Abolitionists too will certainly be challenged and

**TABLE 1** Parallels between desistance and abolition

| *Desistance* | | *Abolition* |
|---|---|---|
| No (or progressively less) offending | **Primary** | Decreases in the reach of criminal justice and in weights of punishment. Reduction of prison population (fewer admissions, shorter sentences). Reductions in numbers of people subject to CSM, with emphasis on securing compliance (by establishing legitimacy and providing reasons to comply) rather than threat of enforcement action. |
| Coming to see oneself as a person who doesn't offend | **Secondary** | Recognition of the limitations of punishment (especially prison) in achieving the purposes conventionally set for it. Changes in public attitudes, in the tone and substance of political discourse and media representation. Social measures and the enhancement of justice to reduce crimes and dependence on penal responses. |
| Being recognised as someone who doesn't offend | **Tertiary** | Acknowledgement of the value of membership of an international community in supporting progress towards abolition – for example, through a common commitment to human rights. Accountability to that community. Taking pride in demonstrating less recourse to punishment. |

blocked. Principled concerns about safety and justice may militate against abolition. As well as the overpowering momentum of established processes and institutions, there are strong political, organisational, professional and commercial interests in resisting the radical transformation envisaged by abolitionism.

Abolitionism, no less than punishment itself, is riven with dilemmas and contradictions. Perverse consequences beset not only the institutions of criminal justice, but also initiatives to dismantle them. Pressures on a prison system can lead to the building of new establishments which, however much they may improve living conditions, enlarge the system's capacity overall. The amelioration of immediate pains – for instance the replacement of a rundown and squalid establishment with more salubrious living conditions – could lead to complacency. Closing a prison can aggravate overcrowding elsewhere or make it harder for people to visit. Schenwar (2014) warns of lobbying to take money saved from penal institutions to invest in stricter surveillance and security, unsurprisingly still targeted at black people and poor people – a corruption of what might be meant by 'justice reinvestment'. Among her conclusions is that the dangers of abolition may lie less in terror scenarios like *what shall we do with the rapists?* than in the substitution of one form of oppression for another – another which may be just as insidious and corrosive to civil society. How anger, fear and disgust might be managed and the risk they may find expression in other institutions and practices will be a persistent concern for abolitionists.[3]

The conception of abolitionism advanced here is, at least in the short term, close to penal reductionism or minimalism (Hayes 2019). Even if prison is flawed beyond redemption, moreover, abolitionists can find common cause with reformists in campaigning for prisoners' rights and improved prison conditions. The litmus test for any reform proposal should be its effect on the system's capacity overall: any proposal which is likely to extend the reach or intensity of punishment will fail this test. The history of 'alternatives to custody' (see Chapter 3) suggests that many sanctions of this type, at least as understood and implemented at present, fail this test. And since it is the job of business to expand, to develop new technologies and extend their markets,[4] the involvement of commerce through privatisation should be opposed on these (among other) grounds.

Sceptics about abolitionism should bear in mind that communities have always responded to wrongdoings, including many serious ones, without recourse to criminal justice. Not all such responses – for example, feuding, vigilantism and other forms of violence – are ones to emulate, although state punishment itself can also be violent and coercive. Yet processes like apology, compensation, reparation, mediation – with parties working things out for themselves or with the assistance of associates and communities – are altogether familiar, tested and effective. Spontaneous attempts at healing are blocked by the formal processes of criminal justice, as the state asserts its monopoly on dealing with certain kinds of misconduct, prolonging unhappiness and delaying 'closure'. Punishment neither heals the past (as restorative justice attempts) nor protects for the future (as transformative justice promises).

Writers within the abolitionist tradition often consider relatively small communities where informal resolutions thrive. These approaches succeed because the community members know one another through regular and frequent associations, enabling people to 'develop social feelings and, particularly, a collective sense of justice that grows until it becomes a habit' (Ruggiero 2014: 3473). The appropriation of disputes by professions and a central state undermines community, denying people opportunities to learn from their conflicts (Christie 1977, 1998). Here, perhaps, is one further correspondence between abolitionism and desistance. Maruna (2017) envisages desistance as a 'social movement', urging an emphasis on recovery and mutual support in the communities where desistance is achieved – a shift away from academic and professional dominance towards a movement led by those who are themselves in the process of desistance. In the same way, abolitionism, understood as a rejection of punishment in its most common forms and a repudiation of anger, fear and disgust as fitting reactions to wrongdoing, might be led (as it has often been) by prisoners, former prisoners, their families and allies. In the end, the social movements of desistance and abolition may turn out to be one and the same.

## Punishment and the good society

Anne-Marie Cusac's proposition – as we punish, so we are – not only provokes reflections about the ethics of punishment, but unavoidably raises questions of what we aspire to be, of what a good society would be like and the place that punishment should have within it. If any sense is to be made of the idea of a good society, it is a society founded on reciprocity, trust, inclusion, goodwill, a recognition of the ways in which people are all alike and all different, and of the value such diversity brings. These are the characteristics to be nurtured to bring about social justice, peace and safety (Bregman 2021). Reliance on punishment by contrast rests on mistrust, exclusion, persecution of those who are different, ill temper and coercion – all of which erode the values of a good society.

The vectors through which punishment 'creeps' include technologies and mentalities, but perhaps especially emotions. The central thesis of this book has been that the will to punish is a product of anger, fear and disgust or disdain. These are emotions that of their nature are inclined to spread and to spill over in unpredictable ways, going well beyond original targets and agitating other people into sharing them. They are emotions, not coincidentally, associated with some of the worst behaviour in any community. Violence is often the outcome of anger and fear; the aggressive 'othering' which can countenance cruelties in punishment is a source of a great deal of hate crime, provoked by fear, with contempt and disdain overcoming any moral inhibitions. A punitive mentality can infiltrate intimate relationships. Punitivism urges that punishment is permissible or even obligatory in response to wrongdoing. Many a self-righteous man (usually a man) has accounted for his bullying and violent coercion as something his victims deserved, as 'asked for', as punishment. This is manifestly self-serving, but a punitive mentality provides a culturally authorised pretext for deplorable behaviour. This may be a direct consequence of conjuring punitivism, unleashing anger and a disdain which suppresses concern for the abused victim. Where punishing practices express these emotions, then, as Nietzsche didn't quite say, we may become the monsters we have conjured into being.

Aristotle knew that behaviour cultivates and expresses virtues and vices: acting bravely, loyally or with generosity makes us brave, loyal or generous; acting meanly, dishonestly or selfish makes us mean, dishonest and selfish. As with individuals, so with societies: enraged, fearful and contemptuous attitudes and practices make for a society defaced by anger, fear and disdain. Whenever politicians talk up punishment, they are inciting ugly emotions that soon spill over, escape any control and poison our associations with one another. Getting angry makes people angrier; fears and attitudes of disdain and disgust are not assuaged by unreflective indulgence. As these sentiments burgeon, they encourage attitudes and practices that are wholly counter-productive in achieving the social goods that punishment promises.

Bryan Stevenson (2012) reflected:

> I represent people on death row. It's interesting, this question of the death penalty. In many ways, we've been taught to think that

the real question is, do people deserve to die for the crimes they've committed? And that's a very sensible question. But there's another way of thinking about where we are in our identity. The other way of thinking about it is not, do people deserve to die for the crimes they commit, but do we deserve to kill?

This question has a wider application. It might, for instance, be asked not only if people deserve to be sent to prison, but whether a society deserves to impose pain and misery on some of its most abused and troubled members. The imprisonment of children, of people with mental illnesses or disabilities, the forced separation of children from their parents, the reluctance to allow even the possibility of change much less to act in support of it – these are cruelties to shame a society. Doing better should be a matter of national self-respect and honour (Appiah 2010).

## Last remarks

The meaning(s) of punishment[5] has been a principal concern throughout this book. The messages of punishment always call for interpretation and, notoriously, what politicians and sentencers attempt to convey may not be what is received. Within these limitations, penal policies and practices must bespeak justice. While punishment persists, it should be marked by proportion, clemency, parsimony, decency and solidarity (Hayes 2019). These are principles that politicians and sentencers should invoke as they explain their decisions, avoiding outrage and intemperate expressions that incite the public and mislead them into pretending that punishment can achieve the social goods claimed for it.

The meanings found by those subject to punishment are often strikingly different from the censure that theorists expect to be imparted. The moral responsibility that censure should evoke is largely suppressed by the pains that most forms of punishment entail. These pains are not always what they are imagined to be and retributive justice requires a much deeper understanding of these matters, with respectful attention to the accounts individuals give of their own experiences. As punishments are put into effect, those charged with fulfilling these responsibilities must look to reinforce messages of justice, optimism and a commitment to a different future. Practitioners need to find worth in what they do, convinced that their job is to cultivate the strengths and meet the needs of the individuals in their charge or care – not to relate to them just in terms of the wrongs they have done or the risks they pose. The censure should be confined to the pronouncement of sentence, while probation and prison staff must undertake their work with encouragement and, where they can, affording opportunities for individuals to live law-abiding lives. Society must do much more to play its part in this reconciliation instead of adding to the burdens of people whose plights have typically been made harder by their punishment. Continuing suspicions and hostilities bring about exclusions that lead to further offending, as well as being intrinsically unjust.

Cognitive behavioural psychology recognises mutual influences among behaviour, thoughts and feelings. There exists a parallel relationship in the hegemonic thoughts and feelings about punishment and in penal practices and institutions. Practices and the rationales for them are mutually sustaining and both support and are supported by the associated emotions. Campaigns for change must therefore challenge all these influences on attitudes and practices. The progressive dismantling of damaging procedures and institutions must be accompanied by a critical scrutiny of the reasoning adduced in support of penal policies, questioning pretensions to being 'evidence-led'. At the same time, the attempt must be made to understand and engage with the emotions of punishment. Compassion and solidarity should be brought to bear against the main emotional drivers of punishment, but a beginning is to recognise the influence of these emotions – an emotional literacy that enables an awareness of feelings and a recognition that while anger, fear and disgust can sound necessary alarms, they make for very poor counsellors. Crimes, then, should first elicit concern for its direct victims, then be seen as opportunities for considered thinking about how such offences might be reduced. Wrongdoers should be held to account and censured, not denounced and spurned. Punishment promises to advance all these social goods and, in its most usual forms in Western societies, accomplishes none of them.

## Notes

1. For discussion, see Canton (2017) and Focquaert, Shaw and Waller (2021).
2. The account here would not be recognised by everyone as 'abolitionist'. It could as well be characterised as penal minimalism (Hayes 2019), although this would be a minimalism that continues to strive for ever further reductions.
3. There is a parallel, perhaps, with the abolition of slavery. Because of relationships of power, encouraged by emotions of disdain, even after the formal abolition of slavery, many of its practices persisted or mutated into other unconscionable attitudes and behaviour (Alexander 2011; Goodman, Page and Phelps 2017).
4. New technologies often have a 'mission creep', with deployment and consequences that are hard to anticipate. For instance, monitoring of whereabouts may be used as a cheaper alternative to adequate personal care for vulnerable people at risk of wandering unsafely.
5. The salience of meaning is prominent among the reasons to oppose the involvement of commerce in the institutions and administration of punishment. The involvement of the market in some human institutions perverts meaning (Sandel 2012). Punishment is a plain example: justice is not for sale; honouring victims is not an opportunity to make profit; peace and safety are not commodities. It is this effect on meaning, quite as much as the expansionism that commercialisation entails, that is a principal objection to the involvement of the private sector (Zedner 2018; Worrall 2020; Burke and Collett 2020).

# REFERENCES

All Internet sites were accessed in August 2021 unless otherwise indicated.
Aebi, M. and Hashimoto, Y. (2018) *Persons under the Supervision of Probation Agencies*, Strasbourg: Council of Europe, retrieved from https://tinyurl.com/3n2efj7f.

Aebi, M., Delgrande, N. and Marguet, Y. (2015) 'Have community sanctions and measures widened the net of the European criminal justice systems?', *Punishment & Society*, 17 (5): 575–597.

Aebi, M., Hashimoto, Y. and Tiago, M. (2019) *Probation and Prisons in Europe 2018: Key Findings of the SPACE Reports*, Strasbourg: Council of Europe, retrieved from https://wp.unil.ch/space/files/2019/05/Key-Findings_SPACE-II_190520-1.pdf.

Ainslie, S. (2021) 'Seeing and believing: Observing desistance-focused practice and enduring values in the National Probation Service', *Probation Journal*, 68 (2): 146–165.

Alexander, M. (2011) *The New Jim Crow: Mass Incarceration in the Age of Colorblindness*, New York: New Press.

Allen, D. (2017) *Cuz: The Life and Times of Michael A.*, London: Penguin.

Allen, R. (2016) 'What is the impact of probation on satisfying the public's desire for justice or punishment?' in F. McNeill, I. Durnescu and R. Butter (eds) *Probation: 12 Essential Questions*, London: Palgrave Macmillan.

Amatrudo, A. (ed.) (2017) *Social Censure and Critical Criminology: After Sumner*, London: Palgrave Macmillan.

Anderson, C. (ed.) (2018). *A Global History of Convicts and Penal Colonies*. London: Bloomsbury Academic.

Anderson, S. (2016) 'The value of "bearing witness" to desistance', *Probation Journal*, 63 (4): 408–424.

Andrews, D. and Bonta, J. (2010) 'Rehabilitating criminal justice policy and practice', *Psychology, Public Policy, and Law*, 16 (1): 39–55.

Annison, H. (2021) 'The role of storylines in penal policy change', *Punishment & Society*, online ahead of print.

Annison, J., Eadie, T. and Knight, C (2008) 'People first: Probation officer perspectives on probation work', *Probation Journal*, 55 (3): 259–272.

Appiah, A.K. (2010) *The Honor Code: How Moral Revolutions Happen*, New York: W. W. Norton.

Applebaum, A. (2003) *Gulag: A History*, London: Allen Lane.

Armstrong, S. and Weaver, B. (2010) *What Do the Punished Think of Punishment?*Glasgow: Scottish Centre for Crime and Justice, Research Report No. 04/2010.

Armstrong, S. and Weaver, B. (2013) 'Persistent punishment: User views of short prison sentences', *The Howard Journal of Criminal Justice*, 52 (3): 285–305.

Arnold, H. (2016) 'The prison officer', in Y. Jewkes, J. Bennett and B. Crewe (eds) *Handbook on Prisons*, Abingdon: Routledge.

Ashworth, A. and Zedner, L. (2008) 'Defending the criminal law: Reflections on the changing character of crime, procedure, and sanctions', *Criminal Law and Philosophy*, 2 (1): 21–51.

Ashworth, A., Zedner, L. and Tomlin, P. (eds) (2013) *Prevention and the Limits of the Criminal Law*, Oxford: Oxford University Press.

Atwood, M. (2008) *Payback: Debt and the Shadow Side of Wealth*, London: Bloomsbury.

Bagaric, M. (2001) *Punishment and Sentencing: A Rational Approach*, London: Cavendish.

Baldwin, L. (ed.) (2015) *Mothering Justice: Working with Mothers in Criminal and Social Justice Settings*, Winchester: Waterside Press.

Baldwin, L. (2017) 'Tainted love: The impact of prison on maternal identity', *Prison Service Journal*, 233: 28–34.

Baldwin, L. (2021) 'Motherhood challenged', PhD thesis, De Montfort University, Leicester.

Ball, W. (2014) 'Defunding state prisons', *Criminal Law Bulletin*, 50 (5): 1060–1090.

Bandes, S. (ed.) (1999) *The Passions of Law*, New York: New York University Press.

Barbalet, J. (2001) *Emotion, Social Theory and Social Structure: A Macrosociological Approach and Sociology*, Cambridge: Cambridge University Press.

Barker, P. (1996) *The Ghost Road*, London: Penguin.

Barry, M. (2007) 'Listening and learning: The reciprocal relationship between worker and client', *Probation Journal*, 54 (4): 407–422.

Barry, M. (2016) 'On the cusp of recognition: Using critical theory to promote desistance among young offenders', *Theoretical Criminology*, 20 (1): 91–106.

Barton, C. (1999) *Getting Even: Revenge as a Form of Justice*, Chicago, IL: Open Court.

Bastian, B., Denson, T. and Haslam, N. (2013) 'The roles of dehumanization and moral outrage in retributive justice', *PloS ONE*, 8 (4): 61842.

Bateman, T. (2012) *Criminalising Children for No Good Purpose: The Age of Criminal Responsibility in England and Wales*, London: National Association for Youth Justice, retrieved from http://thenayj.org.uk/wp-content/files_mf/criminalisingchildrennov12.pdf.

Bazemore, G. (1998) 'Restorative justice and earned redemption: Communities, victims, and offender reintegration', *American Behavioral Scientist*, 41 (6): 768–813.

Bean, P. (1981) *Punishment: A Philosophical and Criminological Inquiry*, Oxford: Martin Robertson.

Bean, P. (ed.) (2020) *Criminal Justice and Privatisation: Key Issues and Debates*, Abingdon: Routledge.

Beccaria, C. (1963 [1763]) *On Crimes and Punishments*, translated by H. Paolucci, Upper Saddle River, NJ: Prentice Hall.

Beckett, K. and Harris, A. (2011) 'On cash and conviction: Monetary sanctions as misguided policy', *Criminology & Public Policy*, 10 (3): 505–507.

Belur, J., Thornton, A., Tompson, L., Manning, M., Sidebottom, A. and Bowers, K. (2020) 'A systematic review of the effectiveness of the electronic monitoring of offenders', *Journal of Criminal Justice*, 68: 101686.

Bennett, C. (2008) *The Apology Ritual: A Philosophical Theory of Punishment*, Cambridge: Cambridge University Press.

Bhui, H.S. and Fossi, J. (2008) 'The experiences of black and minority ethnic prison staff' in J. Bennett, B. Crewe, A. Wahidin (eds) *Understanding Prison Staff*, Cullompton: Willan.

Bierschbach, R. and Bibas, S. (2017) 'Rationing criminal justice', *Michigan Law Review*, 116: 187–246.

Binswanger, I., Stern, M., Deyo, R., Heagerty, P., Cheadle, A., Elmore, J. and Koepsell, T. (2007) 'Release from prison: A high risk of death for former inmates', *New England Journal of Medicine*, 356 (2): 157–165.

Bloom, P. (2016) *Against Empathy: The Case for Rational Compassion*, London: Bodley Head.

Bloom, P. (2017) 'The root of all cruelty', *The New Yorker* (27 November): 74–77, retrieved from www.newyorker.com/magazine/2017/11/27/the-root-of-all-cruelty.

Bochel, D. (1976) *Probation and After-Care: Its Development in England and Wales*, Edinburgh: Scottish Academic Press.

Bögelein, N. (2018) '"Money rules": Exploring offenders' perceptions of the fine as punishment', *British Journal of Criminology*, 58 (4): 805–823.

Bonta, J. and Andrews, D. (2007) 'Risk-need-responsivity model for offender assessment and rehabilitation', retrieved from www.publicsafety.gc.ca/cnt/rsrcs/pblctns/rsk-nd-rspnsvty/index-en.aspx.

Book, A. (1998) 'Shame on you: An analysis of modern shame punishment as an alternative to incarceration', *William & Mary Law Review*, 40: 653–686.

Boonin, D. (2008) *The Problem of Punishment*, Cambridge: Cambridge University Press.

Booth, N. (2018) 'Family matters: A critical examination of family visits for imprisoned mothers and their children', *Prison Service Journal*, 238: 10–15.

Booth, N. (2020a) 'Disconnected: Exploring provisions for mother–child telephone contact in female prisons serving England and Wales', *Criminology & Criminal Justice*, 20 (2): 150–168.

Booth, N. (2020b) *Maternal Imprisonment and Family Life: From the Caregiver's Perspective*, Bristol: Policy Press.

Bosworth, M. (2012) 'Subjectivity and identity in detention: Punishment and society in a global age', *Theoretical Criminology*, 16 (2): 123–140.

Bosworth, M. (2017) 'Border criminology and the changing nature of penal power', in A. Liebling, S. Maruna and L. McAra (eds) *The Oxford Handbook of Criminology* (6th edition), Oxford: Oxford University Press.

Bottoms, A. (1983) 'Neglected features of contemporary penal systems', in D. Garland and P. Young (eds) *The Power to Punish*, London: Heinemann.

Bottoms, A. (1995) 'The philosophy and politics of punishment and sentencing', in C. Clarkson and R. Morgan (eds) *The Politics of Sentencing Reform*, Oxford: Oxford University Press.

Bottoms, A. (2001) 'Compliance and community penalties', in A. Bottoms, L. Gelsthorpe and S. Rex (eds), *Community Penalties: Change and Challenges*, Cullompton: Willan.

Bottoms, A. and Shapland, J. (2011) 'Steps towards desistance among male young adult recidivists', in S. Farrall, M. Hough, S. Maruna and R. Sparks (eds) *Escape routes: Contemporary Perspectives on Life after Punishment*, Abingdon: Routledge.

Bottoms, A. and von Hirsch, A. (2012) 'The crime-preventive impact of penal sanctions', in P. Cane and H. Kritzer (eds) *The Oxford Handbook of Empirical Legal Research*, Oxford: Oxford University Press.

Bottoms, A., Shapland, J., Costello, A., Holmes, D., and Muir, G. (2004) 'Towards desistance: Theoretical underpinnings for an empirical study', *The Howard Journal of Criminal Justice*, 43 (4): 368–389.

Bourke, J. (2005) *Fear: A Cultural History*, London: Virago.

Box, S. (1977) *Recession, Crime and Punishment*, Basingstoke: Macmillan.

Box, S. (1983) *Power, Crime and Mystification*, London: Tavistock.

Bradley, R. and Davino, K. (2002) 'Women's perceptions of the prison environment: When prison is "the safest place I've ever been"', *Psychology of Women Quarterly*, 26 (4): 351–359.

Braithwaite, J. (1989) *Crime, Shame and Reintegration*, Cambridge: Cambridge University Press.

Braithwaite, J. (2000) 'Repentance rituals and restorative justice', *Journal of Political Philosophy*, 8 (1): 115–131.

Braithwaite, J. and Mugford, S. (1994) 'Conditions of successful reintegration ceremonies: Dealing with juvenile offenders', *British Journal of Criminology*, 34 (2): 139–171.

Braithwaite, J. and Pettit, P. (1992) *Not Just Deserts: A Republican Theory of Criminal Justice*, Oxford: Oxford University Press.

Brangan, L. (2019) 'Civilizing imprisonment: The limits of Scottish penal exceptionalism', *British Journal of Criminology*, 59 (4): 780–799.

Brangan, L. (2020) 'Exceptional states: The political geography of comparative penology', *Punishment & Society*, 22 (5): 596–616.

Bregman, R. (2021) *Humankind: A Hopeful History*, London: Bloomsbury.

Bronson, J. and Carson, E. (2019) 'Prisoners in 2017', retrieved from www.bjs.gov/content/pub/pdf/p17.pdf.

Brooks, T. (2012) *Punishment*, Abingdon: Routledge.

Brooks, T. (2021) 'Retribution', in F. Focquaert, E. Shaw and B. Waller (eds) *The Routledge Handbook of the Philosophy and Science of Punishment*, Abingdon: Routledge.

Brown, M. (2009) *The Culture of Punishment: Prison, Society, and Spectacle*, New York: New York University Press.

Brownlee, I. (1998) *Community Punishment: A critical introduction*, Harlow: Longman.

Bucerius, S., Haggerty, K. and Dunford, D. (2021) 'Prison as temporary refuge: Amplifying the voices of women detained in prison', *British Journal of Criminology*, 61 (2): 519–537.

Bulman, M. (2019) 'Number of offenders recalled to prison surges following "disastrous" probation reforms', *The Independent* (17 January), retrieved from www.independent.co.uk/news/uk/home-news/prison-probation-reform-recalls-women-chris-grayling-jail-overcrowding-stewart-ministry-justice-a8732486.html?amp&.

Bülow, W. (2014) 'The harms beyond imprisonment: Do we have special moral obligations towards the families and children of prisoners?', *Ethical Theory and Moral Practice*, 17 (4): 775–789.

Burke, L. and Collett, S. (2015) *Delivering Rehabilitation: The Politics, Governance and Control of Probation*, Abingdon: Routledge.

Burke, L. and Collett, S. (2020) 'The gift relationship: What we lose when rehabilitation is privatised', in P. Bean (ed.) *Criminal Justice and Privatisation: Key Issues and Debates*, Abingdon: Routledge.

Burke, L., Millings, M. and Robinson, G. (2017) 'Probation migration(s): Examining occupational culture in a turbulent field', *Criminology & Criminal Justice*, 17 (2): 192–208.

Burnett, R. and McNeill, F. (2005) 'The place of the officer–offender relationship in assisting offenders to desist from crime', *Probation Journal*, 52 (3): 247–268.

Burrell, W. and Gable, R.S. (2008) 'From BF Skinner to Spiderman to Martha Stewart: The past, present and future of electronic monitoring of offenders', *Journal of Offender Rehabilitation*, 46 (3–4): 101–118.

Bushway, S., Piquero, A., Broidy, L., Cauffman, E. and Mazerolle, P. (2001) 'An empirical framework for studying desistance as a process', *Criminology*, 39 (2): 491–516.

Campbell, J. (2013) *Crime and Punishment in African American History*, Basingstoke: Palgrave Macmillan.

Canton, R. (2006) 'Penal policy transfer: A case study from Ukraine', *Howard Journal of Criminal Justice*, 45 (5): 502–520.

Canton, R. (2009) 'Taking probation abroad', *European Probation Journal*, 1 (1): 66–78.

Canton, R. (2010) 'Not another medical model: Using metaphor and analogy to explore crime and criminal justice', *British Journal of Community Justice*, 8 (1): 40–57.

Canton, R. (2014a) 'Reason, evidence and emotion in the dynamics of penal change', in R. Franks and J. Robertson (eds) *The Letter of the Law: Contemporary Debates on Language, Dignity and the Punished Body*, Oxford: Inter-Disciplinary Press.

Canton, R. (2014b) 'Transfer of policies and practices to other countries', in G. Bruinsma and D. Weisburd (eds) *Encyclopedia of Criminology and Criminal Justice*, New York: Springer.

Canton, R. (2014c) 'Yes, no, possibly, maybe: Community sanctions, consent and cooperation', *European Journal of Probation*, 6 (3): 209–224.

Canton, R. (2015) 'Crime, punishment and the moral emotions: Righteous minds and their attitudes towards punishment', *Punishment & Society*, 17 (1): 54–72.

Canton, R. (2017) *Why Punish? An Introduction to the Philosophy of Punishment*, London: Palgrave Macmillan.

Canton, R. and Dominey, J. (2017) *Probation* (2nd edition), Abingdon: Routledge.

Canton, R. and Dominey, J. (2020) 'Punishment and care reappraised', in L. Gelsthorpe, P. Mody and B. Sloan (eds) *Spaces of Care*, Oxford: Hart.

Carlen, P. (1982) 'Papa's discipline: An analysis of disciplinary modes in the Scottish women's prison', *The Sociological Review*, 30 (1): 97–124.

Carlen, P. (1983) *Women's Imprisonment: A Study in Social Control*, London: Routledge & Kegan Paul.

Carlen, P. (2012) 'Against rehabilitation: For reparative justice', 22nd Eve Saville Memorial Lecture, retrieved from www.crimeandjustice.org.uk/resources/against-rehabilitation-reparative-justice.

Carlsmith, K., Wilson, T. and Gilbert, D. (2008) 'The paradoxical consequences of revenge', *Journal of Personality and Social Psychology*, 95 (6): 1316–1324.

Carlsmith, K., Darley, J. and Robinson, P. (2002) 'Why do we punish? Deterrence and just deserts as motives for punishment', *Journal of Personality and Social Psychology*, 83 (2): 284–299.

Carrabine, E., Cox, P., Lee, M., Plummer, K. and South, N. (2014) *Criminology: A Sociological Introduction*, London: Routledge.

Carvalho, H. and Chamberlen, A. (2018) 'Why punishment pleases: Punitive feelings in a world of hostile solidarity', *Punishment & Society*, 20 (2): 217–234.

Cattermole, C. (2019) *Prison: A Survival Guide*, London: Ebury.

Cavadino, M. and Dignan, J. (2006a) 'Penal policy and political economy', *Criminology and Criminal Justice*, 6 (4): 435–456.

Cavadino, M. and Dignan, J. (2006b) *Penal Systems: A Comparative Approach*, London: Sage.

Cavadino, M., Crow, I. and Dignan, J. (1999) *Criminal Justice 2000: Strategies for a New Century*, Winchester: Waterside Press.

Cavadino, M., Dignan, J. and Mair, G. (2013) *The Penal System: An Introduction* (5th edition), London: Sage.

Cavendish, R. (2003) 'Daniel Defoe put in the pillory', *History Today*, 53 (7), retrieved from www.historytoday.com/archive/daniel-defoe-put-pillory.

Cheliotis, L. (2006) 'How iron is the iron cage of new penology? The role of human agency in the implementation of criminal justice policy', *Punishment & Society*, 8 (3): 313–340.

Christie, N. (1977) 'Conflicts as property', *British Journal of Criminology*, 17 (1): 1–15.

Christie, N. (1981) *Limits to Pain*, Oxford: Martin Robertson.

Christie, N. (1998) 'Between civility and state', in V. Ruggiero, N. South and I. Taylor (eds) *The New European Criminology: Crime and Social Order in Europe*, London: Routledge.

Christie, N. (2000) *Crime Control as Industry: Towards Gulags, Western Style* (3rd edition), London: Routledge.

Christie, N. (2004) *A Suitable Amount of Crime*, London: Routledge.

Clear, T. (2007) *Imprisoning Communities: How Mass Incarceration Makes Disadvantaged Neighborhoods Worse*, New York: Oxford University Press.

Clear, T. (2008) 'The effects of high imprisonment rates on communities', *Crime and Justice: A Review of Research*, 37: 97–132.

Clear, T., Rose, D., Waring, E. and Scully, K. (2003) 'Coercive mobility and crime: A preliminary examination of concentrated incarceration and social disorganization', *Justice Quarterly*, 20 (1): 33–64.

Cohen, S. (1985) *Visions of Social Control*, Cambridge: Polity Press.

Colgan, B. (2018) 'The excessive fines clause: Challenging the modern debtors' prison', *UCLA Law Review*, 65 (1): 2–77.

Comfort, M. (2007) 'Punishment beyond the legal offender', *Annual Review of Law and Social Science*, 3: 271–296.

Comfort, M. (2008) '"The best seven years I could'a done": the reconstruction of imprisonment as rehabilitation', in P. Carlen (ed.) *Imaginary Penalities*, Cullompton: Willan.

Comfort, M. (2009) *Doing Time Together*, Chicago, IL: University of Chicago Press.

Condry, R. (2007) *Families Shamed: The Consequences of Crime for Relatives of Serious Offenders*, Cullompton: Willan.

Condry, R. and Minson, S. (2020) 'Conceptualizing the effects of imprisonment on families: Collateral consequences, secondary punishment, or symbiotic harms?', *Theoretical Criminology*, 25 (4): 540–558.

Condry, R. and Smith, P. (eds) (2018) *Prisons, Punishment, and the Family: Towards a New Sociology of Punishment?*, Oxford: Oxford University Press.

Condry, R., Kotova, A. and Minson, S. (2016) 'Social injustice and collateral damage: The families and children of prisoners', in Y. Jewkes, J. Bennett and B. Crewe (eds) *Handbook on Prisons*, Abingdon: Routledge.

Corda, A. and Lageson, S. (2020) 'Disordered punishment: Workaround technologies of criminal records disclosure and the rise of a new penal entrepreneurialism', *British Journal of Criminology*, 60 (2): 245–264.

Cornwell, D., Blad, J. and Wright, M. (eds) (2013) *Civilising Criminal Justice: An International Restorative Agenda for Penal Reform*, Hook: Waterside Press.

Corston, J., Prentis, V. and Green, K. (2018) 'The UK penal system is designed by men, for men', *The Guardian* (13 March), retrieved from www.theguardia n.com/public-leaders-network/2018/mar/13/penal-system-men-wom en-new-strategy-inquiry.

Costelloe, M., Chiricos, T. and Gertz, M. (2009) 'Punitive attitudes toward criminals: Exploring the relevance of crime salience and economic insecurity', *Punishment & Society*, 11 (1): 25–49.

Council of Europe (2014) 'Recommendation CM/Rec (2014)4 on electronic monitoring', retrieved from www.cep-probation.org/wp-content/uploads/ 2018/10/Recommendation-CM-Rec-2014-of-the-Committee-of-Minis ters-to-member-States-on-electronic-monitoring.pdf.

Council of State Governments Justice Center (2019) 'Confined and costly: How supervision violations are filling prisons and burdening budgets', retrieved from https://csgjusticecenter.org/confinedandcostly.

Coyle, A., Fair, H., Jacobson, J. and Walmsley, R. (2016) *Imprisonment Worldwide: The Current Situation and an Alternative Future*, Bristol: Policy Press.

Coyle, M. (2013) *Talking Criminal Justice*, Abingdon: Routledge.

CPT (2017) 'Remand detention (extract from the 26th General Report of the CPT)', retrieved from https://rm.coe.int/168070d0c8.

Crawley, E. (2004) *Doing Prison Work: The Public and Private Lives of Prison Officers*, Cullompton: Willan.

Crewe, B. (2011) 'Depth, weight, tightness: Revisiting the pains of imprisonment', *Punishment & Society*, 13 (5): 509–529.

Crewe, B. (2012) 'Prison culture and the prisoner society', in B. Crewe and J. Bennett (eds) *The Prisoner*, Abingdon: Routledge.

Crewe, B. (2012) *The Prisoner Society: Power, Adaptation and Social Life in an English Prison*, Oxford: Oxford University Press.

Crewe, B. (2016) 'The sociology of imprisonment', in Y. Jewkes, J. Bennett and B. Crewe (eds) *Handbook on Prisons*, Abingdon: Routledge.

Crewe, B. and Ievins, A. (2020) 'The prison as a reinventive institution', *Theoretical Criminology*, 24 (4): 568–589.

Crockett Thomas, P., McNeill, F., Cathcart Fröden, L., Collinson Scott, J., Escobar, O. and Urie, A. (2021) 'Re-writing punishment? Songs and narrative problem-solving', *Incarceration*, 2 (1), online ahead of print.

Cunha, M. (2014) 'The ethnography of prisons and penal confinement', *Annual Review of Anthropology*, 43: 217–233.

Cusac, A. (2009) *Cruel and Unusual: The Culture of Punishment in America*, New Haven, CT: Yale University Press.

Damasio, A. (2006) *Descartes' Error: Emotion, Reason, and the Human Brain*, London: Vintage.

Darley, J. (2009) 'Morality in the law: The psychological foundations of citizens' desires to punish transgressions', *Annual Review of Law and Social Science*, 5: 1–23.

Darley, J. and Latané, B. (1968) 'Bystander intervention in emergencies: Diffusion of responsibility', *Journal of Personality and Social Psychology*, 8 (4): 377–383.

Darwin, C. (1872) *The Expression of the Emotions in Man and Animals*. London: John Murray.

Davis, A. (2003) *Are Prisons Obsolete?*, New York: Seven Stories Press.

Deering, J. (2010) 'Attitudes and beliefs of trainee probation officers: a "new breed"?', *Probation Journal*, 57 (1): 9–26.

Deering, J. and Feilzer, M. (2019) 'Hollowing out probation? The roots of transforming rehabilitation', *Probation Journal*, 66 (1): 8–24.

Digard, L. (2010) 'When legitimacy is denied: Offender perceptions of the prison recall system', *Probation Journal*, 57 (1): 43–61.

Dominey, J. (2016) 'Fragmenting probation? A qualitative study of voluntary, public and private sectors' interactions in supervision', PhD thesis, University of Cambridge, retrieved from https://aspace.repository.cam.ac.uk/bitstream/handle/1810/254960/Dominey_2015_PhD.pdf?sequence=1&isAllowed=y.

Dominey, J. (2019) 'Probation supervision as a network of relationships: Aiming to be thick, not thin', *Probation Journal*, 66 (3): 283–302.

Dorling, D. (2010) *Injustice: Why Social Inequality Persists*, Bristol: Policy Press.

Dorling, D., Gordon, D., Hillyard, P., Pantazis, C., Pemberton, S. and Tombs, S. (2008) *Criminal Obsessions: Why Harm Matters More than Crime* (2nd edition), London: Centre for Crime and Justice Studies, retrieved from www.crimea ndjustice.org.uk/publications/criminal-obsessions-why-harm-matters-more-crim e-2nd-edition.

Douglas, M. (2003 [1966]) *Purity and Danger: An Analysis of the Concerns of Pollution and Taboo*, London: Routledge.

Dowden, C. and Andrews, D. (2004) 'The importance of staff practice in delivering effective correctional treatment: A meta-analytic review of core correctional practice', *International Journal of Offender Therapy and Comparative Criminology*, 48 (2): 203–214.

Drake, D., Earle, R. and Sloan, J. (eds) (2016) *The Palgrave Handbook of Prison Ethnography*, London: Springer.

Dreisinger, B. (2016) *Incarceration Nations*, New York: Other Press.

du Bois-Pedain, A. and Bottoms, A. (eds) (2019) *Penal Censure: Engagements Within and Beyond Desert Theory*, Oxford: Hart.

Duff, A. (2003) 'Restoration and retribution', in A. von Hirsch, J. Roberts, A. Bottoms, K. Roach and M. Scheff (eds) *Restorative Justice and Criminal Justice: Competing or Reconcilable Paradigms*, Oxford: Hart.

Duff, R. A. (2001) *Punishment, Communication and Community*, Oxford: Oxford University Press.

Dunbar, I. and Langdon, A. (1998) *Tough Justice: Sentencing and Penal Policies in the 1990s*, Oxford: Oxford University Press.

Duncan, M.G. (1996) *Romantic Outlaws, Beloved Prisons*, New York: New York University Press.

Durnescu, I. (2011) 'Pains of probation: Effective practice and human rights', *International Journal of Offender Therapy and Comparative Criminology*, 55 (4): 530–545.

Durnescu, I. (2019) 'Innovation in probation: The Eurobarometer on experiencing supervision', retrieved from www.justiceinspectorates.gov.uk/hmiproba tion/wp-content/uploads/sites/5/2019/10/Academic-Insights-Durnescu.pdf.

Durnescu, I. (2019) 'Pains of reentry revisited', *International Journal of Offender Therapy and Comparative Criminology*, 63 (8):1482–1498.

Easton, S. and Piper, C. (2016) *Sentencing and Punishment: The Quest for Justice* (4th edition), Oxford: Oxford University Press.

Elias, N. (2000 [1939]) *The Civilizing Process: Sociogenetic and Psychogenetic Investigations*, Oxford: Blackwell.

European Court of Human Rights (2007) *Case of Dickson v. The United Kingdom* (application no. 44362/04).

Evans, D. (2001) *Emotion: A Very Short Introduction*, Oxford: Oxford University Press.

Evans, R. (1982) *The Fabrication of Virtue: English Prison Architecture, 1750–1840*, Cambridge: Cambridge University Press.

Fabricant, M. (2010) 'War crimes and misdemeanors: Understanding zero-tolerance policing as a form of collective punishment and human rights violation', *Drexel Law Review*, 3: 373–414.

Farrall, S. (2002) *Rethinking What Works with Offenders: Probation, Social Context and Desistance from Crime*, Cullompton: Willan.

Farrall, S. and Calverley, A. (2006) *Understanding Desistance from Crime: Theoretical Directions in Resettlement and Rehabilitation*, Maidenhead: Open University Press.

Farrall, S., Bottoms, A. and Shapland, J. (2010) 'Social structures and desistance from crime', *European Journal of Criminology*, 7 (6): 546–570.

Farrall, S., Gray, E. and Jones, P. (2020) 'Politics, social and economic change, and crime: Exploring the impact of contextual effects on offending trajectories', *Politics & Society*, 48 (3): 357–388.

Farrall, S., Mawby, R. and Worrall, A. (2007) 'Prolific/persistent offenders and desistance', in L. Gelsthorpe and R. Morgan (eds) *Handbook of Probation*, Cullompton: Willan.

Farrington, D. (2007) 'Childhood risk factors and risk-focused prevention', in M. Maguire, R. Morgan and R. Reiner (eds) *The Oxford Handbook of Criminology* (4th edition), Oxford: Oxford University Press.

Fassin, D. (2017) *Prison worlds: An Ethnography of the Carceral Condition*, London: John Wiley & Sons.

Fassin, D. (2018) *The Will to Punish: The Berkeley Tanner Lectures*, New York: Oxford University Press.

Feeley, M. (1992) *The Process Is the Punishment: Handling Cases in a Lower Criminal Court*, New York: Russell Sage.

Feeley, M. and Simon, J. (1992) 'The new penology: Notes on the emerging strategy of corrections and its implications', *Criminology*, 30 (4): 449–474.

Fehr, E. and Gächter, S. (2002) 'Altruistic punishment in humans', *Nature*, 415 (6868): 137–140.

Feinberg, J. (1965) 'The expressive function of punishment', *The Monist*, 49 (3): 397–423.

Ferguson, R. (2014) *Inferno: An Anatomy of American Punishment*, Cambridge, MA: Harvard University Press.

Ferretti, C. (2019) 'Second chance granted', *Detroit News* (23 August), retrieved from https://eu.detroitnews.com/story/news/local/michigan/2019/08/22/second-chance-granted-abner-hines/1922319001.

Fischer, A. and Roseman, I. (2007) 'Beat them or ban them: The characteristics and social functions of anger and contempt', *Journal of Personality and Social Psychology*, 93 (1): 103–115.

Fitzgibbon, W. and Healy, D. (2019) 'Lives and spaces: Photovoice and offender supervision in Ireland and England', *Criminology & Criminal Justice*, 19 (1): 3–25.

Flanders, C. (2006) 'Shame and the meaning of punishment', *Cleveland State Law Review*, 54: 609–635.

Flegg, D. (1976) *Community Service: consumer survey 1973–1976*, Nottingham: Nottinghamshire Probation and After-Care Service.

Flew, A. (1954) 'The justification of punishment', *Philosophy*, 29 (111): 291–307.

Focquaert, F., Shaw, E. and Waller, B. (eds) (2021) *The Routledge Handbook of the Philosophy and Science of Punishment*, Abingdon: Routledge.

Forgacs, D. (1988) *A Gramsci Reader*, London: Lawrence and Wishart.

Foucault, M. (1977) *Discipline and Punish: The Birth of the Prison*, Harmondsworth: Penguin.

Franko, K. (2020) *The Crimmigrant Other: Migration and Penal Power*, London: Routledge.

Freiberg, A. (2001) 'Affective versus effective justice: Instrumentalism and emotionalism in criminal justice', *Punishment & Society*, 3 (2): 265–278.

Fricker, M. (2007) *Epistemic Injustice: Power and the Ethics of Knowing*, New York: Oxford University Press.

Gacek, J. (2019) 'Stuck in the carceral web: Prisoners' experiences of electronic monitoring', *Criminological Encounters*, 2 (1): 35–52.

Garfinkel, H. (1956) 'Conditions of successful degradation ceremonies', *American Journal of Sociology*, 61: 420–424.

Garland, D. (1985) *Punishment and Welfare: A History of Penal Strategies*, Aldershot: Gower.

Garland, D. (1990) *Punishment and Modern Society: A Study in Social Theory*, Oxford: Oxford University Press.

Garland, D. (2001) *The Culture of Control: Crime and Social Order in Contemporary Society*, Oxford: Oxford University Press.

Garland, D. (2002) 'Of crimes and criminals: the development of criminology in Britain', in M. Maguire, R. Morgan and R. Reiner (eds) *The Oxford Handbook of Criminology* (3rd edition), Oxford: Oxford University Press.

Garland, D. (2018) 'The rule of law, representational struggles and the will to punish', in D. Fassin, *The Will to Punish*, New York: Oxford University Press.

Garland, D. (2020) 'Penal controls and social controls: Toward a theory of American penal exceptionalism', *Punishment & Society*, 22 (3): 321–352.

Garland, D. and Young, P. (eds) (1983) *The Power to Punish: Contemporary Penality and Social Analysis*, London: Heinemann.

Gelsthorpe, L. (2007) 'Probation values and human rights', in L. Gelsthorpe and R. Morgan (eds) *Handbook of Probation*, Cullompton: Willan.

Gelsthorpe, L. and Canton, R. (2020) 'Paradoxes of care: Women in the criminal justice system in England and Wales', in L. Gelsthorpe, P. Mody and B. Sloan (eds) *Spaces of Care*, Oxford: Hart.

Gibbs, A. and King, D. (2003) 'The electronic ball and chain? The operation and impact of home detention with electronic monitoring in New Zealand', *Australian & New Zealand Journal of Criminology*, 36 (1): 1–17.

Gilligan, J. (2003) 'Shame, guilt and violence', *Social Research*, 70 (4): 1149–1180.

Giordano, P., Cernkovich, S. and Rudolph, J. (2002) 'Gender, crime, and desistance: Toward a theory of cognitive transformation', *American Journal of Sociology*, 107 (4): 990–1064.

Glover, J. (1999) *Humanity: A Moral History of the Twentieth Century*, London: Jonathan Cape.

Goffman, A. (2015) *On the Run: Fugitive Life in an American City*, New York: Picador.

Goffman, E. (1961) *Asylums: Essays on the Condition of the Social Situation of Mental Patients and Other Inmates*, New York: Anchor Books.

Goffman, E. (1963) *Stigma: Notes on the Management of Spoiled Identity*, Upper Saddle River, NJ: Prentice Hall.

Goodman, P., Page, J. and Phelps, M. (2017) *Breaking the Pendulum: The Long Struggle over Criminal Justice*, New York: Oxford University Press.

Gorman, T. (1997) 'Back on the chain gang: Why the Eighth Amendment and the history of slavery proscribe the resurgence of chain gangs', *California Law Review*, 85 (2): 441–478.

Gov.uk (2020) 'MQPL decency audit', retrieved from https://data.justice.gov.uk/prisons/prison-reform/mqpl-decency.

Graeber, D. (2011) *Debt: The First 5000 Years*, New York: Melville House.

Graham, H. and McIvor, G. (2015) *Scottish and International Review of the Uses of Electronic Monitoring*, Report 8/2015, Glasgow: Scottish Centre for Crime and Justice Research.

Graham, H. and McNeill, F. (2017) 'Desistance: Envisioning futures' in P. Carlen and F. Ayres (eds) *Alternative Criminologies*, London: Routledge.

Green, D. (2007) 'Comparing penal cultures: Child-on-child homicide in England and Norway', *Crime and Justice*, 36 (1): 591–643.

Green, D. (2013) 'Penal optimism and second chances: The legacies of American Protestantism and the prospects for penal reform', *Punishment & Society*, 15 (2): 123–146.

Greene, J. (2014) *Moral Tribes: Emotion, Reason, and the Gap Between Us and Them*, New York: Penguin.

Gregory, M. (2011) 'Practical wisdom and the ethic of care in probation practice', *European Journal of Probation*, 3 (3): 60–77.

Griffin, J. (2008) *On Human Rights*, Oxford: Oxford University Press.

Grounds, A (1995) 'Risk assessment and management in clinical context', in J. Crichton (ed.) *Psychiatric Patient Violence: Risk and Relapse*, London: Duckworth.

Guardian (2009) 'Blaze of criminality', retrieved from www.theguardian.com/ society/joepublic/2009/jan/12/community-payback-vests.

Guardian (2018) 'Britain's immigration detention: how many people are locked up?', retrieved from www.theguardian.com/uk-news/2018/oct/11/brita ins-immigration-detention-how-many-people-are-locked-up.

Gueta, K. (2018) 'The experience of prisoners' parents: A meta-synthesis of qualitative studies', *Family Process*, 57 (3): 767–782.

Hacking, I. (1999) *Mad Travellers: Reflections on the Reality of Transient Mental Illnesses*, London: Free Association Books.

Haggerty, K. and Bucerius, S. (2020) 'The proliferating pains of imprisonment', *Incarceration*, 1 (1): online ahead of print.

Haidt, J. (2001) 'The emotional dog and its rational tail: A social intuitionist approach to moral judgment', *Psychological Review*, 108 (4): 814–834.

Haidt, J. (2003) 'The moral emotions', in R. Davidson, K. Scherer and H. Goldsmith (eds) *Handbook of Affective Sciences*, Oxford: Oxford University Press.

Haidt, J. (2012) *The Righteous Mind: Why Good People are Divided by Politics and Religion*, London: Allen Lane.

Hamilton, M. (2021) 'The effectiveness of sentencing options: A review of key research findings', retrieved from https://sentencingacademy.org.uk/2021/01/ the-effectiveness-of-sentencing-options-a-review-of-key-research-findings.

Hampton, J. (1984) 'The moral education theory of punishment', *Philosophy & Public Affairs*, 13 (3): 208–238.

Haney, C. (2003) 'Mental health issues in long-term solitary and "supermax" confinement', *Crime & Delinquency*, 49 (1): 124–156.

Haney, C. (2008) 'A culture of harm: Taming the dynamics of cruelty in supermax prisons', *Criminal Justice and Behavior*, 35 (8): 956–984.

Hardwick, R. (2017) *The Truth about Prison: Prisoners, Professionals and Families speak out*, Northumberland: Lapwing.

Harris, R. (1995) 'Reflections on comparative probation', in K. Hamai, R. Villé, R. Harris, M. Hough and U. Zvekic (eds), *Probation Round the World*, Abingdon: Routledge.

Harris, A., Evans, H. and Beckett, K. (2010) 'Drawing blood from stones: Legal debt and social inequality in the contemporary United States', *American Journal of Sociology*, 115 (6): 1753–1799.

Hartnagel, T. and Templeton, L. (2012) 'Emotions about crime and attitudes to punishment', *Punishment & Society*, 14 (4): 452–474.

Hay, D. (1975) 'Property, authority and the criminal law', in D. Hay, P. Linebaugh, J. Rule, E. P. Thompson and C. Winlow (eds) *Albion's Fatal Tree: Crime and Society in Eighteenth Century England*, London: Allen Lane.

Hayes, D. (2015) 'The impact of supervision on the pains of community penalties in England and Wales: An exploratory study', *European Journal of Probation*, 7 (2): 85–102.

Hayes, D. (2016) 'Penal impact: Towards a more intersubjective measurement of penal severity', *Oxford Journal of Legal Studies*, 36 (4): 724–750.

Hayes, D. (2018) 'Proximity, pain, and state punishment', *Punishment & Society*, 20 (2): 235–254.

Hayes, D. (2019) *Confronting Penal Excess: Retribution and the Politics of Penal Minimalism*, Oxford: Hart.

Henley, A. (2018) 'Mind the gap: sentencing, rehabilitation and civic purgatory', *Probation Journal*, 65 (3): 285–301.

Henley, A. (2019) 'Alternative approaches to criminal records: how can we achieve justice as fairness?', in P. Carlen and L. Ayres França (eds), *Justice Alternatives*, London: Routledge.

Herrity, K., Schmidt, B. and Warr, J. (eds) (2021) *Sensory Penalities: Exploring the Senses in Spaces of Punishment and Social Control*, Bingley: Emerald Publishing.

Hill, A. (2017) 'Prisons taking role of care homes and hospices as older population soars', retrieved from www.theguardian.com/society/2017/jun/20/prisons-taking-role-of-care-homes-and-hospices-as-older-population-soars.

Hillyard, P., Pantazis, C., Tombs, S. and Gordon, D. (eds) (2004) *Beyond Criminology: Taking Harm Seriously*, London: Pluto Press.

Hillyard, P. and Tombs, S. (2017) 'Social harm and zemiology', in A. Liebling, S. Maruna and L. McAra (eds) *The Oxford Handbook of Criminology* (6th edition), Oxford: Oxford University Press.

HM Inspectorate of Prisons (2018) 'Social care in prisons in England and Wales: A thematic report', retrieved from www.justiceinspectorates.gov.uk/hmiprisons/wp-content/uploads/sites/4/2018/10/Social-care-thematic-2018-web.pdf.

HM Inspectorate of Probation (2020) 'Accommodation and support for adult offenders in the community and on release from prison in England', retrieved from www.justiceinspectorates.gov.uk/hmiprobation/wp-content/uploads/sites/5/2020/07/FINAL-Accomodation-Thematic-inspection-report-v1.0.pdf.

HM Inspectorate of Probation (2021a) 'Caseloads, workloads and staffing levels in probation services', retrieved from www.justiceinspectorates.gov.uk/hmiprobation/wp-content/uploads/sites/5/2021/03/Caseloads-and-Workloads-RAB-v.3.pdf.

HM Inspectorate of Probation (2021b) 'Race equality in probation: the experiences of black, Asian and minority ethnic probation service users and staff', retrieved from www.justiceinspectorates.gov.uk/hmiprobation/inspections/race-equality-in-probation.

Holtfreter, K. and Wattanaporn, K. (2014) 'The transition from prison to community initiative: An examination of gender responsiveness for female offender reentry', *Criminal Justice and Behavior*, 41 (1): 41–57.

Home Office (2001) 'Making punishments work: The report of a review of the Sentencing Framework for England and Wales (Halliday Report) I', retrieved from https://webarchive.nationalarchives.gov.uk/+/http:/www. homeoffice.gov.uk/documents/halliday-report-sppu/chap-1-2-halliday2835. pdf?view=Binary.

Hood, R. and Hoyle, C. (2015) *The Death Penalty: A Worldwide Perspective* (5th edition), Oxford: Oxford University Press.

Hoskins, Z. (2019) *Beyond Punishment?: A Normative Account of the Collateral Legal Consequences of Conviction*, New York: Oxford University Press.

Howard, J. (1929 [1777]) *The State of the Prisons* (Everyman edition), London: Dent.

Howard, P., Francis, B., Soothill, K. and Humphreys, L. (2009) 'OGRS 3: the revised Offender Group Reconviction Scale', Ministry of Justice Research Summary 7/09, retrieved from https://eprints.lancs.ac.uk/id/eprint/49988/1/ogrs3.pdf.

Howard League (2014) 'Coercive sex in prison, evidence to the Commission on Sex in Prison', retrieved from http://howardleague.org/wp-content/up loads/2016/03/Coercive-sex-in-prison.pdf.

Howard League (2015) 'Deaths, assaults and self-injury in prisons reach highest levels for a decade', retrieved from http://howardleague.org/news/deathsassa ultsselfinjury.

Hucklesby, A. (2008) 'Vehicles of desistance? The impact of electronically monitored curfew orders', *Criminology and Criminal Justice*, 8 (1): 51–71.

Hucklesby, A. (2011) 'The working life of electronic monitoring officers', *Criminology & Criminal Justice*, 11 (1): 1–18.

Hucklesby, A. (2013) 'Insiders' views: Offenders and staffs experiences of electronically monitored curfews' in M. Nellis, K. Beyens and D. Kaminski (eds) *Electronically Monitored Punishment: International and Critical Perspectives*, Cullompton: Willan.

Hucklesby, A. and Holdsworth, E. (2016) 'Electronic monitoring in England and Wales', retrieved from www.antoniocasella.eu/nume/Hucklesby_Holds worth_2016.pdf.

Hucklesby, A. and Holdsworth, E. (2020) 'Electronic monitoring in probation practice', retrieved from www.justiceinspectorates.gov.uk/hmiprobation/wp -content/uploads/sites/5/2020/12/Academic-Insights-Hucklesby-and-Holds worth-FINAL.pdf.

Hucklesby, A., Beyens, K. and Boone, M. (2021) 'Comparing electronic monitoring regimes: Length, breadth, depth and weight equals tightness', *Punishment & Society*, 23 (1): 88–106.

Hucklesby, A., Beyens, K., Boone, M., Dunkel, F., McIvor, G. and Graham, H. (2016) 'Creativity and effectiveness in the use of electronic monitoring: A case study of five jurisdictions', retrieved from https://dspace.stir.ac.uk/bit stream/1893/23603/1/Electronic%20Monitoring%20Comparative%20Synth esis%20Report.pdf.

Hudson, K. and Henley, A. (2015) 'Disparities in public protection measures against sexual offending in England and Wales: An example of preventative injustice?', *Criminology & Criminal Justice*, 15 (5): 561–577.

Hughes, E. (1961) 'Letter to Erving Goffman', retrieved from http://cdclv.unlv.edu/ega/documents/eg_hughes.pdf.

Hulley, S., Crewe, B. and Wright, S. (2016) 'Re-examining the problems of long-term imprisonment', *British Journal of Criminology*, 56 (4): 769–792.

Hume, D. (1967 [1739]) *A Treatise of Human Nature*, edited by L. Selby-Bigge, Oxford: Oxford University Press.

Hummelsheim, D., Hirtenlehner, H., Jackson, J. and Oberwittler, D. (2010) 'Social insecurities and fear of crime: A cross-national study on the impact of welfare state policies on crime-related anxieties', *European Sociological Review*, 27 (3): 327–345.

Hunter, L. (2017) 'The US is still forcibly sterilizing prisoners', retrieved from https://talkpoverty.org/2017/08/23/u-s-still-forcibly-sterilizing-prisoners.

Hyatt, J. and Barnes, G. (2017) 'An experimental evaluation of the impact of intensive supervision on the recidivism of high-risk probationers', *Crime & Delinquency*, 63 (1): 3–38.

Ibarra, P., Gur, O. and Erez, E. (2014) 'Surveillance as casework: Supervising domestic violence defendants with GPS technology', *Crime, Law and Social Change*, 62 (4): 417–444.

Ignatieff, M. (1978) *A Just Measure of Pain: The Penitentiary in the Industrial Revolution 1750–1850*, Harmondsworth: Penguin.

Ignatieff, M. (2017) *The Ordinary Virtues*, Cambridge MA: Harvard University Press.

Independent Monitoring Board (2018) 'Annual report of the Independent Monitoring Board at HMP and YOI Bronzefield', retrieved from www.imb.org.uk/report/bronzefield-2017-18-annual-report.

Inquest (2020) 'Deaths in prison: A national scandal', retrieved from www.inquest.org.uk/deaths-in-prison-a-national-scandal.

Jackson, J., Bradford, B., Hough, M., Myhill, A., Quinton, P. and Tyler, T. (2012) 'Why do people comply with the law? Legitimacy and the influence of legal institutions', *British Journal of Criminology*, 52 (6): 1051–1071.

Jacobson, J. and Hough, M. (2010) *Unjust Deserts: Imprisonment for Public Protection*, London: Prison Reform Trust', retrieved from www.prisonreform trust.org.uk/uploads/documents/unjustdesertsfinal.pdf.

Jewkes, Y. and Moran, D. (2017) 'Prison architecture and design', in A. Liebling, S. Maruna and L. McAra (eds) *The Oxford Handbook of Criminology* (6th edition), Oxford: Oxford University Press.

John Jay College (2013) *Three Quarter Houses: The View from the Inside*, New York: Prisoner Reentry Institute John Jay College of Criminal Justice City University of New York', retrieved from https://justiceandopportunity.org/research/three-quarter-houses.

Johnson, D. (2009) 'Anger about crime and support for punitive criminal justice policies', *Punishment & Society*, 11 (1): 51–66.

Johnson, K. (2018) 'Prison labor is modern slavery. I've been sent to solitary for speaking out', *The Guardian* (23 August), retrieved from www.theguardian.com/commentisfree/2018/aug/23/prisoner-speak-out-american-slave-labor-strike.

Johnson, N. (2000) *Forms of Constraint: A History of Prison Architecture*, Chicago, IL: University of Illinois Press.

Johnstone, G. (2002) *Restorative Justice: Ideas, Values, Debates*, Cullompton: Willan.

Johnstone, G. and Ward, T. (2010) *Law and Crime*, London: Sage.

Jones, T. and Newburn, T. (2007) *Policy Transfer and Criminal Justice: Exploring US Influence over British Crime Control Policy*, Maidenhead: Open University Press.

Kahan, D. (1998) '"The anatomy of disgust" in criminal law', *Michigan Law Review*, 96 (6): 1621–1657.

Kahan, D. (1999) 'The progressive appropriation of disgust', in S. Bandes (ed.) *The Passions of Law*, New York: New York University Press.

Kahan, D. (2010) 'Fixing the communications failure', *Nature*, 463 (21 January): 296–297.

Kahneman, D. (2011) *Thinking, Fast and Slow*, Harmondsworth: Penguin.

Karstedt, S. (2002) 'Emotions and criminal justice', *Theoretical Criminology*, 6 (3) 299–317.

Karstedt, S. and Farrall, S. (2007) 'Law-abiding majority? The everyday crimes of the middle classes', retrieved from www.crimeandjustice.org.uk/publications/law-abiding-majority-everyday-crimes-middle-classes.

Karstedt, S., Loader, I. and Strang, H. (eds) (2013) *Emotions, Crime and Justice*, Oxford: Hart.

Kass, L. (1997) 'The wisdom of repugnance', *New Republic* (June), retrieved from https://web.stanford.edu/~mvr2j/sfsu09/extra/Kass2.pdf.

Kelly, E. (2021) 'The retributive sentiments', in F. Focquaert, E. Shaw and B. Waller (eds) *The Routledge Handbook of the Philosophy and Science of Punishment*, Abingdon: Routledge.

King, A. and Maruna, S. (2009) 'Is a conservative just a liberal who has been mugged? Exploring the origins of punitive views', *Punishment & Society*, 11 (2): 147–169.

King, S. (2013) 'Assisted desistance and experiences of probation supervision', *Probation Journal*, 60 (2): 136–151.

Knight, C. (2014) *Emotional Literacy in Criminal Justice: Professional Practice with Offenders*, Basingstoke: Palgrave Macmillan.

Knudsen, W. (2018) 'The systemic invisibility of children of prisoners', in R. Condry and P. Smith (eds) *Prisons, Punishment, and the Family: Towards a New Sociology of Punishment?*, Oxford: Oxford University Press.

Kohm, S. (2009) 'Naming, shaming and criminal justice: Mass-mediated humiliation as entertainment and punishment', *Crime, Media, Culture*, 5 (2): 188–205.

Kübler-Ross, E. and Kessler, D. (2005) *On Grief and Grieving: Finding the Meaning of Grief through the Five Stages of Loss*, London: Simon and Schuster.

Lacey, N. (2008) *The Prisoners' Dilemma: Political Economy and Punishment in Contemporary Democracies*, Cambridge: Cambridge University Press.

Lacey, N. and Pickard, H. (2015) 'The chimera of proportionality: Institutionalising limits on punishment in contemporary social and political systems', *The Modern Law Review*, 78 (2): 216–240.

Lacey, N. and Soskice, D. (2019) *American Exceptionalism in Inequality and Poverty: A (Tentative) Historical Explanation*, working paper 32, London: London School of Economics.

Lacey, N. and Zedner, L. (1995) 'Discourses of community in criminal justice', *Journal of Law and Society*, 22 (3): 301–325.

Lacey, N., Soskice, D. and Hope, D. (2018) 'Understanding the determinants of penal policy: Crime, culture, and comparative political economy', *Annual Review of Criminology*, 1: 195–217.

Lageson, S. (2020) 'The criminal justice system's big data problem', retrieved from https://blog.oup.com/2020/06/the-criminal-justice-systems-big-data-problem/?utm_campaign=oupac-campaign:793583&utm_source.

Laqueur, T. (1989) 'Crowds, carnival, and the state in English executions, 1604–1868', in A. Beier, D. Cannadine and J. Rosenheim (eds) *The First Modern Society*, Cambridge: Cambridge University Press.

Lazare, A. (2004) *On Apology*, New York: Oxford University Press.

Liebling, A. (2004) *Prisons and their Moral Performance: A Study of Values, Quality, and Prison Life*, assisted by H. Arnold, Oxford: Oxford University Press.

Liebling, A., Hulley, S. and Crewe, B. (2011), 'Conceptualising and measuring the quality of prison life', in D. Gadd, S. Karstedt and S. Messner (eds) *The Sage Handbook of Criminological Research Methods*. London: Sage.

Liebling, A., Price, D. and Elliott, C. (1999) 'Appreciative inquiry and relationships in prison', *Punishment & Society*, 1 (1): 71–98.

Liebling, A., Price, D. and Shefer, G. (2011) *The Prison Officer* (2nd edition), Cullompton: Willan.

Lilly, J.R. and Deflem, M. (1996) 'Profit and penality: An analysis of the corrections-commercial complex', *Crime & Delinquency*, 42 (1): 3–20.

Lippke, R. (2004) 'Against supermax', *Journal of Applied Philosophy*, 21 (2): 109–124.

Lippke, R. (2017) 'Punishment drift: The spread of penal harm and what we should do about it', *Criminal Law and Philosophy*, 11 (4): 645–659.

Little, R. (2018) 'Congratulations, you're ten! Now you can be arrested', retrieved from https://theconversation.com/congratulations-youre-ten-now-you-can-be-arrested-106115.

Loader, I. (2006) 'Fall of the "platonic guardians": liberalism, criminology and political responses to crime in England and Wales', *British Journal of Criminology*, 46 (4): 561–586.

Loader, I. (2010) 'For penal moderation: Notes towards a public philosophy of punishment', *Theoretical Criminology*, 14 (3): 349–367.

Loader, I. (2011) 'Playing with fire? Democracy and the emotions of crime and punishment', in S. Karstedt, I. Loader and H. Strang (eds) *Emotions, Crime and Justice*, Oxford: Hart.

Lösel, F. (2012) 'Offender treatment and rehabilitation: What works?', in M. Maguire, R. Morgan and R. Reiner (eds) *The Oxford Handbook of Criminology* (5th edition), Oxford: Oxford University Press.

Ludlow, A. (2017) 'Marketizing criminal justice', in A. Liebling, S. Maruna and L. McAra (eds) *The Oxford Handbook of Criminology* (6th edition), Oxford: Oxford University Press.

Lukes, S. (2005) *Power: A Radical View* (2nd edition), Basingstoke: Palgrave Macmillan.

Lukes, S. (2008) *Moral Relativism*, London: Profile Books.

Lukes, S. and Scull, A. (eds) (2013) *Durkheim and the Law*, Basingstoke: Palgrave Macmillan.

Lynch, M. (2000) 'On-line executions: The symbolic use of the electric chair in cyberspace', *Political and Legal Anthropology Review*, 23 (2): 1–20.

Lynch, M. (2004) 'Punishing images: Jail Cam and the changing penal enterprise', *Punishment & Society*, 6 (3): 255–270.

MacCulloch, D. (2004) *Reformation: Europe's House Divided 1490–1700*, London: Penguin.

Maguire, M. and Raynor, P. (2006) 'How the resettlement of prisoners promotes desistance from crime: Or does it?', *Criminology & Criminal Justice*, 6 (1): 19–38.

Markel, D. (2001) 'Are shaming punishments beautifully retributive: Retributivism and the implications for the alternative sanctions debate', *Vanderbilt Law Review*, 54: 2157–2242.

Marshall, T. F. and Merry, S. (1990) *Crime and Accountability: Victim/Offender Mediation in Practice*, London: HM Stationery Office.

Mars-Jones, A. (1981) 'Bathpool Park', in A. Mars-Jones, *Lantern Lecture*, London: Picador.

Martin, K. D., Sykes, B. L., Shannon, S., Edwards, F. and Harris, A. (2018) 'Monetary sanctions: Legal financial obligations in US systems of justice', *Annual Review of Criminology*, 1: 471–495.

Maruna, S. (2001) *Making Good*, Washington, DC: American Psychological Association.

Maruna, S. (2004) 'California dreamin': are we heading toward a national offender "waste management" service?', *Criminal Justice Matters*, 56 (1): 6–7.

Maruna, S. (2011) 'Reentry as a rite of passage', *Punishment & Society*, 13 (1): 3–28.

Maruna, S. (2017) 'Desistance as a social movement', *Irish Probation Journal*, 14: 5–20.

Maruna, S. and Farrall, S. (2004) 'Desistance from crime: A theoretical reformulation', *Kolner Zeitschrift fur Soziologie und Sozialpsychologie*, 43: 171–194.

Maruna, S. and King, A. (2004) 'Public opinion and community penalties', in A. Bottoms, S. Rex and G. Robinson (eds), *Alternatives to Imprisonment: Options for an Insecure Society*, Cullompton: Willan.

Maruna, S. and LeBel, T. (2010) 'The desistance paradigm in correctional practice: From programmes to lives', in F. McNeill, P. Raynor and C. Trotter (eds) *Offender Supervision: New Directions in Theory, Research and Practice*, Cullompton: Willan.

Maruna, S. and Mann, R. (2019) 'Reconciling "desistance" and "what works"', retrieved from www.justiceinspectorates.gov.uk/hmiprobation/wp-content/uploads/sites/5/2019/02/Academic-Insights-Maruna-and-Mann-Feb-19-final.pdf.

Maslen, H. (2015) *Remorse, Penal Theory and Sentencing*, Oxford: Hart.

Mathiesen, T. (2006) *Prison on Trial*, Winchester: Waterside Press.

Mathiesen, T. (2014) *The Politics of Abolition Revisited*, London: Routledge.

Matthews, R. (2005) 'The myth of punitiveness', *Theoretical Criminology*, 9 (2): 175–201.

Matza, D. (1964) *Delinquency and Drift*, New York: Wiley.

Matza, D. (1969) *Becoming Deviant*, Upper Saddle River, NJ: Prentice Hall.

Matza, D. and Sykes, G. (1961) 'Juvenile delinquency and subterranean values', *American Sociological Review*, 26 (5): 712–719.

Mawby, R. and Worrall, A. (2013) *Doing Probation Work: Identity in a Criminal Justice Occupation*, Abingdon: Routledge.

McAra, L. and McVie, S. (2017) 'Developmental and life course-criminology: Innovations, impacts, and applications', in A. Liebling, S. Maruna and L. McAra (eds) *The Oxford Handbook of Criminology* (6th edition), Oxford: Oxford University Press.

McCulloch, T. (2005) 'Probation, social context and desistance: Retracing the relationship', *Probation Journal*, 52 (1): 8–22.

McCullough, M. (2008) *Beyond Revenge: The Evolution of the Forgiveness Instinct*, San Francisco, CA: John Wiley.

McGowen, R. (1995) 'The well-ordered prison: England 1780–1865', in N. Morris and D. Rothman (eds) *The Oxford History of the Prison*, New York: Oxford University Press.

McGuire, J. (2001) 'Cognitive-behavioural approaches', retrieved from http://webarchive.nationalarchives.gov.uk/20130206163808/www.justice.gov.uk/downloads/publications/inspectorate-reports/hmiprobation/other-reports/cogbeh1-rps.pdf.

McIvor, G. (2007) 'Paying back: Unpaid work by offenders', in G. McIvor and P. Raynor (eds), *Developments in Social Work with Offenders*, London: Jessica Kingsley.

McIvor, G. (1992) *Sentenced to Serve*, Aldershot: Avebury.

McIvor, G. (2016) 'What is the impact of community service?', in F. McNeill, I. Durnescu and R. Butter (eds) *Probation: 12 Essential Questions*, London: Palgrave Macmillan.

McIvor, G., Beyens, K., Blay, E. and Boone, M. (2010) 'Community service in Belgium, the Netherlands, Scotland and Spain: a comparative perspective', *European Journal of Probation*, 2 (1): 82–98.

McLennan, R. (2018) 'Ideal History and Historical Complexity', in D. Fassin (ed.), *The Will to Punish: The Berkeley Tanner Lectures*, New York: Oxford University Press.

McNeill, F. (2006) 'A desistance paradigm for offender management', *Criminology & Criminal Justice*, 6 (1): 39–62.

McNeill, F. (2012) 'Four forms of "offender" rehabilitation: Towards an interdisciplinary perspective', *Legal and Criminological Psychology*, 17 (1) 18–36.

McNeill, F. (2014) 'Punishment as rehabilitation', in G. Bruinsma and D. Weisburd (eds) *Encyclopedia of Criminology and Criminal Justice*, 4195–4206. New York: Springer Reference.

McNeill, F. (2014) 'Three aspects of desistance?', retrieved from https://discoveringdesistance.home.blog/2014/05/23/three-aspects-of-desistance.

McNeill, F. (2016a) 'Desistance and criminal justice in Scotland', in H. Croall, G. Mooney and R. Munro (eds) *Crime, Justice and Society in Scotland*, London: Routledge.

McNeill, F. (2016b) 'The fuel in the tank or the hole in the boat? Can sanctions support desistance?', in J. Shapland, S. Farrall and A. Bottoms (eds) *Global Perspectives on Desistance*, London: Routledge.

McNeill, F. (2018) *Pervasive Punishment: Making Sense of Mass Supervision*, Bingley: Emerald Publishing.

McNeill, F. and Weaver, B., (2010) *Changing Lives? Desistance Research and Offender Management*, Research Report No. 3/2010, Glasgow: Scottish Centre for Crime and Justice, retrieved from www.sccjr.ac.uk/publications/changing-lives-desistance-research-and-offender-management.

McNeill, F., Farrall, S., Lightowler, C. and Maruna. S. (2012) 'How and why people stop offending: Discovering desistance', retrieved from www.iriss.org.uk/resources/insights/how-why-people-stop-offending-discovering-desistance.

McPherson, T. (1967) 'Punishment: Definition and justification', *Analysis*, 28 (1): 21–27.

Melossi, D. and Pavarini, M. (1981) *The Prison and the Factory: Origins of the Penitentiary System*, Basingstoke: Macmillan.

Miethe, T. and Lu, H. (2005) *Punishment: A Comparative Historical Perspective*, Cambridge: Cambridge University Press.

Miles, H. and Raynor, P. (2014) *Reintegrative Justice in Practice: The Informal Management of Crime in an Island Community*, Farnham: Ashgate.

Miller, D. (2001) 'Disrespect and the experience of injustice', *Annual Review of Psychology*, 52 (1): 527–553.

Miller, J. (2015) 'Contemporary modes of probation officer supervision: The triumph of the "synthetic" officer?', *Justice Quarterly*, 32 (2): 314–336.

Miller, W. (1997) *The Anatomy of Disgust*, Cambridge, MA: Harvard University Press.

Milmo, C. (2020) 'Prisons chief admits hi-tech security available to only handful of jails amid "chronic" levels of inmate crime', retrieved from https://inews.co.uk/news/uk/prisons-chief-hi-tech-security-crime-drugs-whatsapp-805679.

Ministry of Justice (2020) 'Criminal justice statistics quarterly, England and Wales, July 2019 to June 2020', retrieved from https://assets.publishing.service.gov.uk/government/uploads/system/uploads/attachment_data/file/934391/criminal-justice-statistics-quarterly-june-2020.pdf.

Minson, S. (2018) 'The sins and traumas of fathers and mothers should not be visited on their children', in R. Condry and P. Smith (eds) *Prisons, Punishment, and the Family: Towards a New Sociology of Punishment?*, Oxford: Oxford University Press.

Minson, S. (2019) 'Direct harms and social consequences: An analysis of the impact of maternal imprisonment on dependent children in England and Wales', *Criminology & Criminal Justice*, 19 (5): 519–536.

Moran, D. (2013) 'Between outside and inside? Prison visiting rooms as liminal carceral spaces', *GeoJournal*, 78 (2): 339–351.

Morenoff, J. and Harding, D. (2014) 'Incarceration, prisoner reentry, and communities', *Annual Review of Sociology*, 40: 411–429.

Morgan, R. (1992) 'Following Woolf: The prospects for prisons policy', *Journal of Law and Society*, 19 (2): 231–250.

Morgan, R. and Liebling, A. (2007) 'Imprisonment: An expanding scene', in M. Maguire, R. Morgan and R. Reiner (eds) *The Oxford Handbook of Criminology* (4th edition), Oxford: Oxford University Press.

Morgan, S. (1999) 'Prison lives: Critical issues in reading prisoner autobiography', *The Howard Journal of Criminal Justice*, 38 (3): 328–340.

Morris, H. (1971) 'Guilt and suffering', *Philosophy East and West*, 21 (4): 419–434.

Morris, N. and Rothman, D. (eds) (1995) *The Oxford History of the Prison: The Practice of Punishment in Western Society*, Oxford: Oxford University Press.

Morris, T. and Morris, P. (1963) *Pentonville: A Sociological Study of an English Prison*, London: Routledge & Kegan Paul.

Morrison, T. (1993) 'Interview with Toni Morrison', retrieved from www.esquire.com/entertainment/books/a28621535/toni-morrison-white-supremacy-charlie-rose-interview-racism.

Murphy, J. (1973) 'Marxism and retribution', *Philosophy & Public Affairs*, 2 (3): 217–243.

Murphy, J. (2012) *Punishment and the Moral Emotions: Essays in Law, Morality, and Religion*, New York: Oxford University Press.

Murray, J., Farrington, D. and Sekol, I. (2012) 'Children's antisocial behavior, mental health, drug use, and educational performance after parental incarceration: a systematic review and meta-analysis', *Psychological Bulletin*, 138 (2): 175.

Nagin, D. (2013) 'Deterrence in the twenty-first century', *Crime and Justice*, 42 (1): 199–263.

Natapoff, A. (2018) *Punishment without Crime: How our Massive Misdemeanour System Traps the Innocent and Makes America More Unequal*, New York: Basic Books.

National Audit Office (2012) *Comparing International Criminal Justice Systems*, Briefing for the House of Commons Justice Committee, London: National Audit Office.

Nelken, D (1994) 'Community involvement in crime control', in N. Lacey (ed.) *A Reader on Criminal Justice*, Oxford: Oxford University Press.

Nelken, D. (2000) *Contrasting Criminal Justice: Getting from Here to There*, Aldershot: Ashgate.

Nellis, M. (2012) 'Prose and cons: Autobiographical writing by British prisoners', in L. Cheliotis (ed.) *The Arts of Imprisonment: Control, Resistance and Empowerment*, Farnham: Ashgate.

Nellis, M. (2000) 'Creating community justice', in S. Ballintyne, K. Pease and V. McLaren (eds) *Secure Foundations: Key Issues in Crime Prevention, Crime Reduction and Community Safety*, London: Institute for Public Policy Research.

Nellis, M. (2002) 'Prose and cons: Offender auto/biographies, penal reform and probation training', *The Howard Journal of Criminal Justice*, 41 (5): 434–468.

Nellis, M. (2009) 'Surveillance and confinement: Explaining and understanding the experience of electronically monitored curfews', *European Journal of Probation*, 1 (1): 41–65.

Nellis, M. (2009) 'The aesthetics of redemption: Released prisoners in American film and literature', *Theoretical Criminology*, 13 (1): 129–146.

Nellis, M. (2010) 'Eternal vigilance Inc.: The satellite tracking of offenders in "real time"', *Journal of Technology in Human Services*, 28 (1–2): 23–43.

Nellis, M. (2015) *Standards and Ethics in Electronic Monitoring*, Strasbourg: Council of Europe, retrieved from https://rm.coe.int/handbook-standards-e thics-in-electronic-monitoring-eng/16806ab9b0.

Nellis, M. (2016) 'Electronic monitoring and probation practice', in F. McNeill, I. Durnescu and R. Butter (eds) *Probation: 12 Essential Questions*, London: Palgrave Macmillan.

Nellis, M., Beyens, K. and Kaminski, D. (eds) (2013) *Electronically Monitored Punishment: International and Critical Perspectives*, Cullompton: Willan.

Newburn, T. (2017) *Criminology* (3rd edition), Abingdon: Routledge.

Newman, G. (2008) *The Punishment Response* (2nd edition), New Brunswick, NJ: Transaction.

Nietzsche, F. (1996 [1887]) *On the Genealogy of Morality*, translated by D. Smith, Oxford: Oxford University Press.

Nisbett, R. and Wilson, T. (1977) 'Telling more than we can know: Verbal reports on mental processes', *Psychological Review*, 84 (3): 231–259.

NOMS (2015) 'Offender equalities annual report 2014/2015', retrieved from www.gov.uk/government/statistics/noms-annual-offender-equalities-report-2014-to-2015.

Nozick, R. (1981) *Philosophical Explanations*, Oxford: Oxford University Press.

Nugent, B. and Schinkel, M. (2016) 'The pains of desistance', *Criminology & Criminal Justice*, 16 (5): 568–584.

Nussbaum, M. (1999) '"Secret sewers of vice": Disgust, bodies and the law', in S. Bandes (ed.) *The Passions of Law*, New York: New York University Press.

Nussbaum, M. (2004) *Hiding from Humanity: Disgust, Shame and the Law*, Princeton, NJ: Princeton University Press.

Nussbaum, M. (2016) *Anger and Forgiveness: Resentment, Generosity, Justice*, New York: Oxford University Press.

Nussbaum, M. (2017) 'Powerlessness and the politics of blame', The Jefferson Lecture in the Humanities, May, retrieved from www.law.uchicago.edu/news/martha-c-nussbaums-jefferson-lecture-powerlessness-and-politics-blame.

Ocen, P. (2012) 'Punishing pregnancy: Race, incarceration, and the shackling of pregnant prisoners', *California Law Review*, 100: 1239–1311.

Ocen, P. (2019) 'Awakening to a mass-supervision crisis', *The Atlantic* (26 December), retrieved from www.theatlantic.com/politics/archive/2019/12/parole-mass-supervision-crisis/604108.

O'Donnell, I. and Edgar, K. (1998) 'Routine victimisation in prisons', *Howard Journal of Criminal Justice*, 37 (3): 266–279.

O'Malley, P. (2009) 'Theorizing fines', *Punishment & Society*, 11 (1): 67–83.

O'Malley, P. (2010) *Crime and Risk*, London: Sage.

O'Malley, P. (2013) 'Monetized justice: Money and punishment in consumer societies', in J. Simon and R. Sparks (eds), *The Sage Handbook of Punishment and Society*, London: Sage.

Padfield, N. (2012) 'Recalling conditionally released prisoners in England and Wales', *European Journal of Probation*, 4 (1): 34–44.

Page, J. (2011) *The Toughest Beat: Politics, Punishment, and the Prison Officers Union in California*, New York: Oxford University Press.

Pager, D. (2003) 'The mark of a criminal record', *American Journal of Sociology*, 108 (5): 937–975.

Pakes, F. and Gunnlaugsson, H. (2018) 'A more Nordic Norway? Examining prisons in 21st century Iceland', *The Howard Journal of Crime and Justice*, 57 (2): 137–151.

Panzarella, R. (2002) 'Theory and practice of probation on bail in the report of John Augustus', *Federal Probation*, 66 (3): 38–42.

Parker, T. (1991) *Life after Life: Interviews with Twelve Murderers*, London: Pan.

Parsons, K. (2019) 'The process of recall: What do those on licence expect?', *Probation Quarterly*, 12: 20–22, retrieved from http://probation-institute.org/magazine.

Paterson, C. (2007) '"Street-level surveillance": Human agency and the electronic monitoring of offenders', *Surveillance & Society*, 4 (4): 314–328.

Paterson, C. (2007) 'Commercial crime control and the electronic monitoring of offenders in England and Wales', *Social Justice*, 34 (3–4): 98–110.

Patterson, O. (1982) *Slavery and Social Death: A Comparative Study*, Cambridge MA: Harvard University Press.

Payne, B. and Gainey, R. (1998) 'A qualitative assessment of the pains experienced on electronic monitoring', *International Journal of Offender Therapy and Comparative Criminology*, 42 (2): 149–163.

Payne, B. and Gainey, R. (2002) 'The influence of demographic factors on the experience of house arrest', *Federal Probation*, 66 (3): 64–70.

Petersilia, J. (2003) *When Prisoners Come Home: Parole and Prisoner Reentry*, New York: Oxford University Press.

Peterson, D. (1982) *A Mad People's History of Madness*, Pittsburgh, PA: University of Pittsburgh Press.

Phelps M., and Curry, C., (2017) 'Supervision in the community: Probation and parole', in H. Pontell (ed.) *Oxford Research Encyclopaedia of Criminology and Criminal Justice*, New York: Oxford University Press.

Phelps, M. (2013) 'The paradox of probation: Community supervision in the age of mass incarceration', *Law & Policy*, 35 (1–2): 51–80.

Phelps, M. (2018) 'Ending mass probation', *The Future of Children*, 28 (1): 125–146.

Phillips, J. (2014) 'The architecture of a probation office: A reflection of policy and an impact on practice', *Probation Journal*, 61 (2): 117–131.

Phillips, C. and Bowling, B. (2017) 'Ethnicities, racism, crime and criminal justice', in A. Liebling, S. Maruna and L. McAra (eds) *The Oxford Handbook of Criminology* (6th edition), Oxford: Oxford University Press.

Phillips, J. and Roberts, R. (2019) 'Deaths of people following release from prison', retrieved from www.inquest.org.uk/deaths-following-release-from-prison-report (accessed November 2021).

Phillips, J., Albertson, K., Collinson, B. and Fowler, A. (2020) 'Delivering desistance-focused probation in community hubs: Five key ingredients', *Probation Journal*, 67 (3): 264–282.

Piacentini, L. (2004) *Surviving Russian Prisons: Punishment, Economy and Politics in Transition*, Cullompton: Willan.

Pinker, S. (2011) *The Better Angels of Our Nature: The Decline of Violence in History and Its Causes*, New York: Penguin.

Polaschek, D (2012) 'An appraisal of the risk–need–responsivity (RNR) model of offender rehabilitation and its application in correctional treatment', *Legal and Criminological Psychology*, 17 (1): 1–17.

Porporino, F. (2010) 'Bringing sense and sensitivity to corrections', in J. Brayford, F. Cowe and J. Deering (eds) *What Else Works? Creative Work with Offenders*, Cullompton: Willan.

Porter, R. (2002) *Madness: A Brief History*, Oxford: Oxford University Press.

Pratt, J. (2000) 'The return of the wheelbarrow men; or, the arrival of postmodern penality?', *British Journal of Criminology*, 40 (1): 127–145.

Pratt, J. (2008a) 'Scandinavian exceptionalism in an era of penal excess. Part I: The nature and roots of Scandinavian exceptionalism', *British Journal of Criminology*, 48 (3): 119–137.

Pratt, J. (2008b) 'Scandinavian exceptionalism in an era of penal excess. Part II: Does Scandinavian exceptionalism have a future?', *British Journal of Criminology*, 48 (3): 275–292.

Pratt, J., Brown, D., Brown, M., Hallsworth, S. and Morrison, W. (eds) (2005) *The New Punitiveness: Trends, Theories, Perspectives*, Cullompton: Willan.

Presser, L. (2009) 'The narratives of offenders', *Theoretical Criminology*, 13 (2): 177–200.

Prison Commission (1932) *The Principles of the Borstal System*, London: Home Office.

Prison Reform Trust (1991) 'The Woolf report: A summary of the main findings and recommendations of the inquiry into prison disturbances', retrieved from www.prisonreformtrust.org.uk/Portals/0/Documents/Woolf%20report.pdf.

Prison Reform Trust (2018) 'Broken trust: The rising numbers of women recalled to prison', retrieved from www.prisonreformtrust.org.uk/Portals/0/Documents/Women/Broken_Trust_printlo.pdf.

Prison Reform Trust (2020) 'Safe homes for women leaving prison', retrieved from www.prisonreformtrust.org.uk/Portals/0/FINAL%20Safe%20Homes%20Initiative%20briefing.pdf.

Radzik, L. (2009) *Making Amends: Atonement in Morality, Law and Politics*, New York: Oxford University Press.

Radzinowicz, L. and Hood, R. (1990) *The Emergence of Penal Policy in Victorian and Edwardian England*, Oxford: Oxford University Press.

Raynor, P. (2019) 'Supervision skills for probation practitioners', retrieved from www.justiceinspectorates.gov.uk/hmiprobation/wp-content/uploads/sites/5/2019/08/Academic-Insights-Raynor.pdf.

Raynor, P. and Robinson, G. (2009) *Rehabilitation, Crime and Justice*, Basingstoke: Palgrave Macmillan.

Raynor, P. and Vanstone, M. (2002) *Understanding Community Penalties: Probation, Policy and Social Change*, Buckingham: Open University Press.

Raynor, P. and Vanstone, M. (2018) 'What matters is what you do: The rediscovery of skills in probation practice', *European Journal of Probation*, 10 (3): 199–214.

Reiman, J. and Leighton, P. (2013) *The Rich Get Richer and the Poor Get Prison: Ideology, Class and Criminal Justice* (10th edition), New York: Pearson.

Reitz, K. (ed.) (2017) *American Exceptionalism in Crime and Punishment*, New York: Oxford University Press.

Renteln, A. (1990) *International Human Rights: Universalism versus Relativism*, Newbury Park CA: Sage.

Rex, S. (1999) 'Desistance from offending: Experiences of probation', *Howard Journal*, 38 (4): 366–383.

Rex, S. (2004) 'Punishment as communication', in A. Bottoms, S. Rex and G. Robinson (eds) *Alternatives to Prison: Options for an Insecure Society*, Cullompton: Willan.

Rex, S. (2005) *Reforming Community Penalties*, Cullompton: Willan.

Rex, S. and Hosking, N. (2013) 'A collaborative approach to developing probation practice: Skills for effective engagement, development and supervision (SEEDS)', *Probation Journal*, 60 (3): 332–338.

Roberts, J. and Von Hirsch, A. (eds) (2010) *Previous Convictions at Sentencing: Theoretical and Applied Perspectives*, Oxford: Hart.

Roberts, S. (1979) *Order and Dispute: An Introduction to Legal Anthropology*, Harmondsworth: Penguin.

Robinson, G. (2008) 'Late-modern rehabilitation: The evolution of a penal strategy', *Punishment & Society*, 10 (4): 429–445.

Robinson, G. (2016) 'The Cinderella complex: Punishment, society and community sanctions', *Punishment & Society*, 18 (1): 95–112.

Robinson, G. and McNeill, F. (2008) 'Exploring the dynamics of compliance with community penalties', *Theoretical Criminology*, 12 (4): 431–449.

Robinson, G. and McNeill, F. (2017) 'Punishment in the community: Evolution, moderation, and expansion', in A. Liebling, S. Maruna and L. McAra (eds) *The Oxford Handbook of Criminology* (6th edition), Oxford: Oxford University Press.

Robinson, G. and McNeill, F. (eds) (2016) *Community Punishment: European Perspectives*, Abingdon: Routledge.

Robinson, G., Burke, L. and Millings, M. (2016) 'Criminal justice identities in transition: The case of devolved probation services in England and Wales', *British Journal of Criminology*, 56 (1): 161–178.

Robinson, G., McNeill, F. and Maruna, S. (2013) 'Punishment in society: The improbable persistence of probation and other community sanctions and measures', in J. Simon and R. Sparks (eds) *The Sage Handbook of Punishment and Society*, London: Sage.

Robinson, G., Priede, C., Farrall, S., Shapland, J. and McNeill, F. (2014) 'Understanding "quality" in probation practice: Frontline perspectives in England & Wales', *Criminology & Criminal Justice*, 14 (2): 123–142.

Roche, D. (2013) 'Retribution and restorative justice', in G. Johnstone and D. Van Ness (eds) *Handbook of Restorative Justice*, London: Routledge.

Roscoe, K. (2018) 'A natural hulk: Australia's carceral islands in the colonial period, 1788–1901', *International Review of Social History*, 63 (26): 45–63.

Rossner, M. (2011) 'Emotions and interaction ritual: A micro analysis of restorative justice', *British Journal of Criminology*, 51 (1): 95–119.

Roth, M. (2014) *An Eye for an Eye: A Global History of Crime and Punishment*, London: Reaktion Books.

Rothman, D. (1980) *Conscience and Convenience: The Asylum and its Alternatives in Progressive America*, Boston MA: Little, Brown.

Rotman, E. (1986) 'Do criminal offenders have a constitutional right to rehabilitation?', *The Journal of Criminal Law and Criminology* (1973–), 77 (4): 1023–1068.

Rubin, A. and Phelps, M. (2017) 'Fracturing the penal state: State actors and the role of conflict in penal change', *Theoretical Criminology*, 21 (4): 422–440.

Ruggiero, V. (2014) 'Penal abolitionism', in G. Bruinsma and D. Weisburd (eds) *Encyclopedia of Criminology and Criminal Justice*, pp. 3463–3473, New York: Springer.

Ruggiero, V. and Ryan, M. (eds) (2013) *Punishment in Europe: A Critical Anatomy of Penal Systems*, Basingstoke: Palgrave.

Rusche, G. and Kirchheimer, O. (2003 [1939]) *Punishment and Social Structure*, Hillsdale, NJ: Transaction.

Rush, B. (1787) 'An enquiry into the effects of public punishments upon criminals, and upon society', retrieved from https://quod.lib.umich.edu/e/evans/N16141.0001.001?rgn=main;view=fulltext.

Russo, J., Woods, D., Shaffer, J. and Jackson, B. (2019) 'Caring for those in custody', *Corrections Today* (July–August): 16–21.

Rutherford, A. (1993) *Criminal Justice and the Pursuit of Decency*, Oxford: Oxford University Press.

Rutherford, A. (1997) 'Criminal policy and the eliminative ideal', *Social Policy & Administration*, 31 (5): 116–135.

Sainato, M. (2019) 'Why are so many people dying in US prisons and jails?', *The Guardian* (26 May), retrieved from https://amp.theguardian.com/us-news/2019/may/26/us-prisons-jails-inmate-deaths.

Sandel, M. (2009) *Justice: What's the Right Thing to Do?*, London: Allen Lane.

Sandel, M. (2012) *What Money Can't Buy: The Moral Limits of Markets*, London: Allen Lane.

Sarang, A., Platt, L., Vyshemirskaya, I. and Rhodes, T. (2016) 'Prisons as a source of tuberculosis in Russia', *International Journal of Prisoner Health*, 12 (1): 45–56.

Scheingold, S. (1995) 'Politics, public policy, and street crime', *The Annals of the American Academy of Political and Social Science*, 539 (1): 155–168.

Schenwar, M. (2014) *Locked Down, Locked Out: Why Prison Doesn't Work and How We Can Do Better*, San Francisco, CA: Berrett-Koehler.

Schinkel, M. (2014) *Being Imprisoned: Punishment, Adaptation and Desistance*, London: Palgrave Macmillan.

Schinkel, M. and Lives Sentenced Participants (2021) 'Persistent short-term imprisonment: Belonging as a lens to understand its shifting meanings over the life course', *Incarceration*, 2 (1): online ahead of print.

Schlanger, M. (2013) 'Plata v. Brown and realignment: Jails, prisons, courts, and politics', *Harvard Civil Rights-Civil Liberties Law Review*, 48: 165–215.

Schlosser, E. (1998) 'The prison-industrial complex', *The Atlantic Monthly*, 282 (6): 51–77.

Schneider, L. (2021) 'Let me take a vacation in prison before the streets kill me! Rough sleepers' longing for prison and the reversal of less eligibility in neo-liberal carceral continuums', *Punishment & Society*, online ahead of print.

Scott, D. (2008) 'Creating ghosts in the penal machine: Prison officer occupational morality and the techniques of denial', in J. Bennett, B. Crewe and A. Wahidin (eds) *Understanding Prison Staff*, Cullompton: Willan.

Scott, D. (2018) *Against Imprisonment: An Anthology of Abolitionist Essays*, Hook: Waterside Press.

Scott, D. and Flynn, N. (2014) *Prisons and Punishment* (2nd edition), London: Sage.

Sellin, J. T. (2016 [1976]) *Slavery and the Penal System*, New Orleans, LA: Quid Pro Books.

Sentencing Project (2016) '6 million lost voters: State-level estimates of felony disenfranchisement', retrieved from www.sentencingproject.org/wp-content/uploads/2016/10/6-Million-Lost-Voters.pdf.

Sexton, L. (2015) 'Penal subjectivities: Developing a theoretical framework for penal consciousness', *Punishment & Society*, 17 (1): 114–136.

Shah, R. (2020.) 'Hidden in plain sight: Architectures of community corrections as public secret', *Probation Journal*, 67 (2): 137–159.

Shalev, S. (2013) *Supermax: Controlling Risk through Solitary Confinement*, Cullompton: Willan.

Shapland, J. and Bottoms, A. (2011) 'Reflections on social values, offending and desistance among young adult recidivists', *Punishment & Society*, 13 (3): 256–282.

Shapland, J. (2016) 'Forgiveness and restorative justice: Is it necessary? Is it helpful?', *Oxford Journal of Law and Religion*, 5 (1): 94–112.

Shapland, J. and Bottoms, A. (2017) 'Desistance from crime and implications for offender rehabilitation', in A. Liebling, S. Maruna and L. McAra (eds) *The Oxford Handbook of Criminology* (6th edition), Oxford: Oxford University Press.

Shapland, J., Robinson, G. and Sorsby, A. (2011) *Restorative Justice in Practice: Evaluating What Works for Victims and Offenders*, Cullompton: Willan.

Sharpe, J. (1990) *Judicial Punishment in England*, London: Faber and Faber.

Sherman, L. (1993) 'Defiance, deterrence, and irrelevance: A theory of the criminal sanction', *Journal of research in Crime and Delinquency*, 30 (4): 445–473.

Sherman, L. and Strang, H. (2011) 'Empathy for the devil: The nature and nurture of revenge', in S. Karstedt, I. Loader and H. Strang (eds) *Emotions, Crime and Justice*, Oxford: Hart.

Simon, J. (2001) 'Governing through crime metaphors', *Brooklyn Law Review*, 67: 1035–1070.

Simon, J. (2007) *Governing through Crime: How the War on Crime Transformed American Democracy and Crated a Culture of Fear*, Oxford: Oxford University Press.

Simon, J. and Sparks, R. (eds) (2013) *The Sage Handbook of Punishment and Society*, London: Sage.

Skarbek, D. (2020) *The Puzzle of Prison Order: Why Life behind Bars Varies around the World*, New York: Oxford University Press.

Skillen, A. (1980) 'How to say things with walls', *Philosophy*, 55 (214): 509–523.

Skinner, Q. (ed.) (1985) *The Return of Grand Theory in the Human Sciences*, Cambridge: Cambridge University Press.

Smith, D. (2005) 'Probation and social work', *British Journal of Social Work*, 35 (5): 621–637.

Smith, D. (2011) *Less than Human: Why We Demean, Enslave, and Exterminate Others*, New York: St Martin's Press.

Smith, P. (2008) *Punishment and Culture*, Chicago, IL: University of Chicago Press.

Snacken, S. (2010) 'Resisting punitiveness in Europe?', *Theoretical Criminology*, 14 (3): 273–292.

Snacken, S. and Dumortier, E. (eds) (2012) *Resisting Punitiveness in Europe: Welfare, Human Rights and Democracy*, Abingdon: Routledge.

Social Exclusion Unit (2002) 'Reducing re-offending by ex-prisoners', retrieved from www.bristol.ac.uk/poverty/downloads/keyofficialdocuments/Reducing%20Reoffending.pdf.

Sparks, R. and Bottoms, A. (1995) 'Legitimacy and order in prisons', *British Journal of Sociology*, 46 (1): 45–62.

Stacey, C. (2019) *Double Discrimination? The Impact of Criminal Records on People from Black, Asian and Minority Ethnic Backgrounds*, London: Unlock, retrieved from www.unlock.org.uk/doublediscrimination.

Stephenson, B. (2015) *Ritual: A Very Short Introduction*, Oxford: Oxford University Press.

Stevenson, B. (2012) 'We need to talk about an injustice', retrieved from www.ted.com/talks/bryan_stevenson_we_need_to_talk_about_an_injustice?language=en.

Stillman, S. (2014) 'Get Out of Jail, Inc.: Does the alternatives-to-incarceration industry profit from injustice?', *New Yorker* (16 June), retrieved from www.newyorker.com/magazine/2014/06/23/get-out-of-jail-inc.

Strawson, P. F. (1962) 'Freedom and resentment', *Proceedings of the British Academy*, 48: 1–25, reprinted in P. F. Strawson (1974), Freedom and Resentment and Other Essays, London: Methuen.

Sumner, C. (ed.) (1990) *Censure, Politics and Criminal Justice*, Buckingham: Open University Press.

Sunstein, C. (2005) *Laws of Fear: Beyond the Precautionary Principle*, Cambridge: Cambridge University Press.

Sykes, G. (1958) *The Society of Captives: A Study of a Maximum Security Prison*, Princeton, NJ: Princeton University Press.

Sykes, G. and Matza, D. (1957) 'Techniques of neutralization: A theory of delinquency', *American Sociological Review*, 22: 664–670.

Tait, S. (2011) 'A typology of prison officer approaches to care', *European Journal of Criminology*, 8 (6): 440–454.

Tankebe, J. and Liebling, A. (eds) (2013) *Legitimacy and Criminal Justice: An International Exploration*, Oxford: Oxford University Press.

Taylor, A. (2019) 'Guilty by design: How architecture influences jury decisions', *Sydney Morning Herald* (29 September), retrieved from https://amp.smh.com.au/national/nsw/guilty-by-design-how-architecture-influences-jury-decisions-20190923-p52u3f.html?

Taylor, I. (1998) 'Crime, market-liberalism and the European idea', in V. Ruggiero, N. South and I. Taylor (eds) *The New European Criminology: Crime and Social Order in Europe*, London: Routledge.

Teague, M. (2016) 'Profiting from the poor: Offender-funded probation in the USA', *British Journal of Community Justice*, 14 (1): 99–111.

Ten, C.L. (1987) *Crime, Guilt and Punishment*, Oxford: Oxford University Press.

Thompson, E.P. (1993) *'Rough Music' in his Customs in Common*, London: Penguin.

Tidmarsh, M. (2020) 'If the cap fits? Probation staff and the changing nature of supervision in a CRC', *Probation Journal*, 67 (2): 98–117.

Tidmarsh, M. (2019) 'Transforming Rehabilitation: Probation practice, architecture and the art of distributions', *Criminology & Criminal Justice*, 21 (1): 72–88.

Todd, M. (2002) *The Culture of Protestantism in Early Modern Scotland*, London: Yale University Press.

Tombs, S. and Whyte, D. (2008) *A Crisis of Enforcement: The Decriminalisation of Death and Injury at Work*, London: Centre for Crime and Justice Studies, retrieved from www.crimeandjustice.org.uk/publications/crisis-enforcement-decriminalisation-death-and-injury-work.

Tombs, S. and Whyte, D. (2015) *The Corporate Criminal: Why Corporations Must Be Abolished*, Abingdon: Routledge.

Tonry, M. (1996) *Sentencing Matters*, New York: Oxford University Press.

Tonry, M. (2004) *Punishment and Politics: Evidence and Emulation in the Making of English Crime Control Policy*, Cullompton: Willan.

Tonry, M. (2007) 'Determinants of penal policies', *Crime and Justice*, 36 (1): 1–48.

Tonry, M. (2010) 'The questionable relevance of previous convictions', in J. Roberts and A. Von Hirsch (eds) *Previous Convictions at Sentencing: Theoretical and Applied Perspectives*, Oxford: Hart.

Tonry, M. (2020) *Doing Justice, Preventing Crime*, New York: Oxford University Press.

Trebilcock, J. (2011) *No Winners: The Reality of Short Term Prison Sentences*, London: Howard League, retrieved from https://howardleague.org/wp-content/uploads/2016/03/No-Winners.pdf (accessed March 2021).

Turner, V. (1995) *The Ritual Process: Structure and Anti-Structure*, New York: Aldine De Gruyter.

Tyler, T. (1990) *Why People Obey the Law*, New Haven, CT: Yale University Press.

Tyler, T. (2003) 'Procedural justice, legitimacy and the effective rules of law', *Crime and Justice*, 30: 431–505.

Tyler, T. (2006) 'Psychological perspectives on legitimacy and legitimation', *Annual Review of Psychology*, 57: 375–400.

Tyler, T. and Boeckmann, R. (1997) 'Three strikes and you are out, but why?', *Law and Society Review*, 31 (2): 237–265.

US Supreme Court (2010) '*Brown, Governor of California, et al. v. Plata et al.*: Appeal from the United States District Courts for the Eastern and Northern Districts of California', retrieved from www.supremecourt.gov/opinions/10pdf/09-1233.pdf.

Uggen, C. and Blahnik, L. (2016) 'The increasing stickiness of public labels', in J. Shapland, S. Farrall and A. Bottoms (eds) *Global Perspectives on Desistance*, London: Routledge.

Ugwudike P., Raynor, P. and Annison, J. (eds) (2018) *Evidence-Based Skills in Criminal Justice*, Bristol: Policy Press.

Ugwudike, P. and Raynor, P. (2013) *What Works in Offender Compliance: International Perspectives and Evidence-Based Practice*, London: Palgrave Macmillan.

van Ginneken, E. (2016a) 'Making sense of imprisonment: Narratives of post-traumatic growth among female prisoners', *International Journal of Offender Therapy and Comparative Criminology*, 60 (2): 208–227.

van Ginneken, E. (2016b) 'The pain and purpose of punishment: A subjective perspective', Howard League Working Papers 22/2016, retrieved from https://howardleague.org/wp-content/uploads/2016/04/HLWP-22-2016.pdf.

van Ginneken, E. and Hayes, D. (2017) '"Just" punishment? Offenders' views on the meaning and severity of punishment', *Criminology & Criminal Justice*, 17 (1): 62–78.

van Kalmthout, A. and Durnescu, I. (eds) (2008) *Probation in Europe*, Oisterwijk, Netherlands: Wolf Legal Publishers.

van Zyl Smit, D. and Appleton, C. (2019) *Life Imprisonment a Global Human Rights Analysis*, Cambridge MA: Harvard University Press.

van Zyl Smit, D. and Dünkel, F. (eds) (2018) *Prison Labour: Salvation or Slavery? International Perspectives*, Abingdon: Routledge.

Vanhaelemeesch, D., Vander Beken, T. and Vandevelde, S. (2014) 'Punishment at home: Offenders' experiences with electronic monitoring', *European Journal of Criminology*, 11 (3): 273–287.

Vanstone, M. (2004) *Supervising Offenders in the Community: A History of Probation Theory and Practice*, Aldershot: Ashgate.

Vanstone, M. (2008) 'The international origins and initial development of probation: An early example of policy transfer', *British Journal of Criminology*, 48 (6): 735–755.

Visher, C. and Travis, J. (2003) 'Transitions from prison to community: Understanding individual pathways', *Annual Review of Sociology*, 29 (1): 89–113.

von Hirsch, A. (1993) *Censure and Sanctions*, Oxford: Clarendon Press.

Wacquant, L. (2000) 'The new "peculiar institution": On the prison as surrogate ghetto', *Theoretical Criminology*, 4 (3): 377–389.

Wacquant, L. (2002) 'Four strategies to curb carceral costs', *Studies in Political Economy*, 69 (1): 19–30.

Wacquant, L. (2002) 'The curious eclipse of prison ethnography in the age of mass incarceration', *Ethnography*, 3 (4): 371–397.

Wacquant, L. (2009) *Punishing the Poor: The Neoliberal Government of Social Insecurity*, Durham, NC: Duke University Press.

Wakefield, S. and Wildeman, C. (2013) *Children of the Prison Boom: Mass Incarceration and the Future of American Inequality*, New York: Oxford University Press.

Walker, N. (1991) *Why Punish?* Oxford: Oxford University Press.

Wallace, G. (1995) 'Wild justice', *Philosophy*, 70 (273): 363–375.

Walmsley, R. (2018) 'World prison population list', retrieved from www.prisonstudies.org/sites/default/files/resources/downloads/wppl_12.pdf.

Ward, T. and Maruna, S. (2007) *Rehabilitation*, Abingdon: Routledge.

Warr, J. (2016) 'The deprivation of certitude, legitimacy and hope: Foreign national prisoners and the pains of imprisonment', *Criminology & Criminal Justice*, 16 (3): 301–318.

Warr, J. (2019) '"Always gotta be two mans": Lifers, risk, rehabilitation, and narrative labour', *Punishment & Society*, 22 (1): 28–47.

Weaver, B. (2009) 'Communicative punishment as a penal approach to supporting desistance', *Theoretical Criminology*, 13 (1): 9–29.

Weaver, B. (2015) *Offending and Desistance: The Importance of Social Relations*, London: Routledge.

Weaver, B. and Armstrong, S. (2011) *User Views of Punishment: The Dynamics of Community-Based Punishment; Insider Views from the Outside*, Research Report no. 03/2011, Glasgow: Scottish Centre for Crime and Justice.

Weaver, B. and Barry, M. (2014) 'Managing high risk offenders in the community: Compliance, cooperation and consent in a climate of concern', *European Journal of Probation*, 6 (3): 278–295.

Weaver, B., Piacentini, L., Moodie, K. and Barry, M. (2021) 'Exploring and explaining non-compliance with community supervision', *British Journal of Criminology*, 61 (2): 434–455.

Weaver, E. (2018) *Time for Policy Redemption: A Review of the Evidence on the Disclosure of Criminal Records*, Glasgow: University of Strathclyde', retrieved from www.sccjr.ac.uk/wp-content/uploads/2019/01/Weaver_SCCJR_2018_Time_for_policy_redemption_a_review_of_the_evidence.pdf.

Weber, M. (2009 [1919]) 'Politics as a vocation', in H. Gerth and C. Wright Mills (eds) *From Max Weber: Essays in Sociology*, London: Routledge.

Western, B. (2007) *Punishment and Inequality in America*, New York: Russell Sage.

Western, B. (2018) *Homeward: Life in the Year After Prison*, New York: Russell Sage.

Whitman, J. (1997) 'What is wrong with inflicting shame sanctions?', *Yale Law Journal*, 107: 1055–1092.

Whitman, J. (2003) *Harsh Justice: Criminal Punishment and the Widening Divide between America and Europe*, New York: Oxford University Press.

Wilde, O. (1999 [1897]) *De Profundis, The Ballad of Reading Gaol and Other Writings*, Ware: Wordsworth.

Wilson, J., Hodgkinson, S., Piché, J. and Walby, K. (eds) (2017) *The Palgrave Handbook of Prison Tourism*, London: Palgrave Macmillan.

Wood, A. (2015) 'Challenging occupational norms: An ethnographic study of female prison officers in a women's prison', PhD thesis, University of Salford.

Wood, V. (2019) 'HMP Bronzefield: Baby dies in private women's prison after inmate "gives birth alone in cell"', *The Independent* (4 October), retrieved from www.independent.co.uk/news/uk/home-news/hmp-bronzefield-baby-death-prison-birth-cell-mother-surrey-sodexo-a9143466.html.

World Prison Brief (2018) 'Highest to lowest: Pre-trial detainees/remand prisoners', retrieved from www.prisonstudies.org/highest-to-lowest/pre-trial-detainees?field_region_taxonomy_tid=All.

Worrall, A. (2020) 'The other prices of privatised justice: Marketing prison alternatives', in P. Carlen and L. Franca (eds) *Justice Alternatives*, Abingdon: Routledge.

Worrall, A. and Hoy, C. (2005) *Punishment in the Community: Managing Offenders, Making Choices* (2nd edition), Cullompton: Willan.

Worrall, A. and Mawby, R. (2014) 'Probation worker cultures and relationships with offenders', *Probation Journal*, 61 (4): 346–357.

Yearwood, L. (2020) 'Pregnant and shackled: why inmates are still giving birth cuffed and bound', *The Guardian* (24 January), retrieved from www.theguardian.com/us-news/2020/jan/24/shackled-pregnant-women-prisoners-birth.

Young, P. (1976) 'A sociological analysis of the early history of probation', *British Journal of Law and Society*, 3 (1): 44–58.

Zedner, L. (2009) *Security*, Abingdon: Routledge.

Zedner, L. (2018) 'What is lost when punishment is privatised?', in T. Daems and T. Vander Beken (eds) *Privatising Punishment in Europe?*, London: Routledge.

Zeleskov Doric, J., Batricevic, A. and Petrovic, B. (2015) 'Experiencing community service in Belgrade: Normative framework and general impressions', *Journal of Criminology and Criminal Law*, 53 (2–3): 185–196.

# INDEX